C000172792

THAILAND

SPIRALGUIDE

AA Publishing

Contents

Written by Jane Egginton
Contributions by David Henley and Andrew Forbes
Revised and updated by Sean Sheehan

Update managed by Lodestone Publishing Limited
Project Designer Lesley Mitchell
Series Editor Karen Rigden
Series Designer Catherine Murray

Published by AA Publishing, a trading name of AA Media Limited,
whose registered office is Fanum House, Basing View, Basingstoke,
Hampshire RG21 4EA. Registered number 06112600.

ISBN: 978-0-7495-6598-5

The contents of this publication are believed correct at the time
of printing. Nevertheless, AA Publishing accept no responsibility
for errors, omissions or changes in the details given, or for the
consequences of readers' reliance on this information. This does
not affect your statutory rights. Assessments of the attractions,
hotels and restaurants are based upon the author's own experience
and contain subjective opinions that may not reflect the publisher's
opinion or a reader's experience. We have tried to ensure accuracy,
but things do change, so please let us know if you have any
comments or corrections.

A CIP catalogue record for this book is available from the
British Library.

Cover design and binding style by permission of AA Publishing
Colour separation by AA Digital Department
Printed and bound in China by Leo Paper Products

Find out more about AA Publishing and the wide range of travel
publications and services the AA provides by visiting our website at
theAA.com/shop

A04026
Maps in this title produced from map data © New Holland
Publishing (South Africa) (PTY) Limited 2009
(except pp175, 182 & 185)
Transport map © Communicarta Ltd, UK

The Magazine

A great holiday is more than just lying on a beach or shopping till you drop — to really get the most from your trip you need to know what makes the place tick. The Magazine provides an entertaining overview to some of the social, cultural and natural elements that make up the unique character of this engaging country.

Spirit
OF A NATION

There is a spiritual element to almost every aspect of life in Thailand. Buses, taxis and boats are draped with garlands of jasmine flowers to appease the spirits and ensure a safe journey. Amulets – maybe a sacred gem or tiger's tooth – adorn the necks of most Thais as protection against everything from infertility to floods and typhoons. Outside almost every building is a miniature wooden house on a pole, built as somewhere for displaced spirits to live.

Mix and Match
For many Thais an acceptance of animism (the belief that inanimate objects have a soul) and a reverence for the panoply of Hindu gods sit happily side by side with their Buddhist faith. The current king, Bhumibol, like those in the Chakri dynasty before him, is known as Rama, to align him with the ideal king in the Hindu epic *The Ramayana*, and he regularly uses Brahmin priests at royal ceremonies.

Shrines to the Spirits
The Erawan Shrine is a Hindu shrine outside the Grand Hyatt Erawan hotel in Bangkok, built to placate the spirits when a series of construction problems blighted the building of the hotel in the 1950s. It receives a

Below: Incense is burned to purify air; above: tattoos have a spiritual significance

constant swarm of worshippers who believe it will bring them good luck. A shrine to phalluses in the grounds of the Hilton Hotel in Bangkok attracts those hoping for fertility who come here to leave phallic offerings.

Everything Should Be Fun

Despite the seriousness of their beliefs, however, Thais believe that whatever we do should be fun, or *sanuk*. This applies equally to work in a field or work in a bank. It is partly this philosophy that makes Thais smile, whatever the situation. They also highly value a "cool heart" or a calm manner. This means being discreet when it comes to displaying affection or emotion in public, using soft speech and avoiding becoming impatient or angry. The more you can achieve this, the more you are respected. On the whole Thais are incredibly tolerant – just so long as you dress modestly and don't show disrespect to their royal family or religion.

SPIRITS AND SUPERSTITIONS

- Spirits are said to live in the doorsills of temples, so it is considered bad luck to step on them.
- Many Thai men, including monks, have tattoos to ward off evil spirits.
- Astrologers are regularly consulted to find an auspicious day for an important occasion, such as starting work on building a house or opening a new business.

What's **WAT**

A TEMPLE TOUR

Thailand's 30,000 *wats* (temple complexes) are more than just places of worship. As well as drawing tourists to their stunning architecture and elaborate decoration many serve an important role in the lives of their local communities.

Historically *wats* were centres of education and some, especially those in rural areas, continue this role. **Wat Po** in Bangkok (➤ 47–48) was the first centre for public education and today houses the national headquarters for traditional Thai medicine and massage. Some, such as Krabi's **Wat Tham Seua** (➤ 160), surrounded by limestone cliffs and tropical forest, are worth visiting for their scenic locations alone.

Symbols and Symbolism

The buildings are rich in symbolism. Roofs with three tiers symbolise the "triple gems" of Buddhism: the Buddha (the teacher), the Dhamma (the act of teaching) and the Sangha (the followers of the teachings). The reclining Buddha is usually shown with his head resting on a lotus, a thing of great beauty, suggesting that Buddha is within us all. The garuda bird that is often seen supporting buildings in a temple complex is a royal Hindu symbol of strength. Rounded Khmer *prangs* (towers) symbolise Mount Meru, home of the Hindu gods, while large towering *chedis* were designed to stand as testament to the enduring stability of Buddhism.

What's in a Temple?

At the heart of each temple complex is a *bot*, an ordination hall open only to monks who meditate and carry out ceremonies. It has eight

---

TEMPLE ETIQUETTE

■ Remove shoes.
■ Dress modestly and avoid wearing shorts and sleeveless T-shirts.
■ Avoid handling, or being photographed in front of, a Buddha image.
■ Do not point your feet towards a person or a Buddha image.
■ Sit on the floor.
■ Women should try to avoid physical contact with a monk.

surrounding stones, looking rather like gravestones. Decorated with carvings of Buddhist scenes, these sacred stones protect the consecrated ground on which the *bot* is built.

Relics and Remains

A *viharn* looks very similar to a *bot*, but is the assembly hall containing the Buddha image. This is where worshippers and visitors tend to head. Large *wats* may have more than one *viharn*. The *wats* are often dominated by cone-shaped towers known as *chedis* or *stupas* (in the north they are called *thats*), containing Buddha relics or the remains of deceased local dignitaries. Additional elements may include a *mondop* to house a Buddha statue, a *ho trai* or library of holy scriptures and a *sala* for lectures or meetings.

Above: Detail of a stone tortoise at Wat Neua in Roi Et, northeast Thailand
Right: Ornately carved ceiling of the *bot* at Wat Na Phra Meru, Ayuthaya
Below: This whiskered statue is among the many sights at Wat Arun

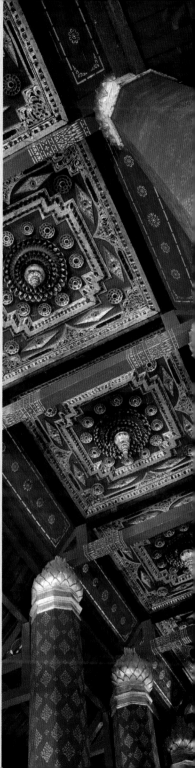

EXCITING
THE senses

On a trip to Thailand the experience of eating authentic Thai food is one that you are unlikely to forget. Although Thai restaurants are now found around the globe, and many visitors have tried Thai cuisine elsewhere, there is still something wonderful about tasting genuine Thai cooking for the first time.

Whether you are picking dishes from street market stalls, or enjoying the sumptuous decor and effortless sophistication of a restaurant, the common factor in Thai cooking is the simple combination of fresh ingredients, cooked in minutes in a wok. The resulting dish excites the taste buds and releases complex but harmonious flavours that caress the senses.

Firm Favourites
Noodles mixed with tiny pieces of meat and an array of colourful vegetables, seasoned with piquant sauces and spices, and garnished with herbs are a popular basis for Thai dishes. *Pad thai* – noodles mixed with stir-fried shrimp, tofu and egg, enhanced by side-dishes of chilli, lime pieces and ground peanuts – is a staple of menus in Thai restaurants back home but will never have tasted so good as it does here, and provides the perfect introduction before before venturing into more esoteric variations.

Thai curries, presented in a myriad of forms and colours, are characterised by the use of coconut milk, chillies, lemon grass and galangal. Thai soups are equally eclectic, the most famous being the seafood-based *tom yam*. If you are not used to the authentically aggressive *tom yam*, don't consume it in large spoonfuls but shift the solid ingredients onto rice to eat, then take small, gentle sips of the broth.

Regional Specialities
Many regional speciality dishes seem recklessly liberal in their use of hot spices but, at their best, are nuanced by sour and salty flavours that harmonise the overall taste. If you really want to challenge your taste buds try *kaeng leuang*, a fiery curry consisting of a mouth-tingling mix of herbs and spices. More humane on the tongue while still displaying attitude are salads from the northeast (the word Issan on menus indicates a dish from this region). Look for the Issan papaya salad, called *som tum thai* when using dried shrimp and peanuts or *som tum pbooh* with salted crab.

A *kaeng matsaman* curry dish made during a cooking course in Chiang Mai

Curries from the south can be as hot as those from Issan but what distinguishes the cuisine of southern Thailand, not surprisingly given its two coastlines, is the abundance of seafood. Ko Samui's microclimate is perfect for growing coconut trees, so coconut is a characteristic flavour.

Northern dishes include glutinous rice and curries that range from mild to hot. Look for *naem*, small, square packages made from minced, fermented pork wrapped and steamed in a banana leaf, hanging from most fresh produce stalls. Central Thailand is famed for its steamed jasmine rice and chilli-based sauces *(nam prik)* made from shrimp paste and served with local, seasonal vegetables like morning glory and *mamok*.

Street Food

Try not to leave Thailand without experiencing some of the delicious food sold by street vendors. What you see being cooked is what you get, from deep-fried banana fritters coated in a mixture of coconut, palm sugar and roasted rice to whatever broth is bubbling away inside a giant stockpot. Try *kway tiaw* (rice noodles) with dumplings and blanched vegetables.

COOKING SCHOOLS

Cooking schools, concentrated in Bangkok, Chiang Mai, Phuket and Ko Samui, offer a variety of courses. The more interesting courses begin with a visit to a local market, where the ingredients are purchased, and focus on dishes characteristic of the region. Spices used in Thai cooking can usually be obtained back home but they will be infinitely cheaper if purchased in Thailand. Look, too, for dried lotus root or sticks of cinnamon which will easily fit into your luggage and last for ages.

ROYALISTS

Thais are utterly devoted to their royal family. Vast illuminated pictures of King Bhumibol and Queen Sirikit appear at the roadside and it would be hard to find a family that doesn't have at least one, if not several, framed photographs of the royal family in pride of place.

Humanitarian Monarchs

King Bhumibol, or **Rama IX**, is the latest in the line of the Chakri dynasty, which began in 1782. His great grandfather, **Rama IV Mongkut** (1851–68), spent 30 years as a monk, yet embraced modernism. **Rama V Chulalongkorn** (1868–1910) ended outdated medieval court rituals and established the first school system, a railway network and the country's first hospital. **Rama VI Vajiravudh** (1910–25) was committed to bringing Thailand in line with the Western world. Thai people were known only by their first names until 1913, when Rama VI introduced surnames. He also made primary education compulsory and founded the first university.

A respected author, **Rama VII Prajadhipok** (1925–35) set up the National Library, the Fine Arts Department and the National Museum.

So great is their devotion that at eight o'clock every morning in Bangkok's central train station, city commuters stop and stand in silence as the national anthem is played out over the loudspeaker system. This performance is repeated again at six o'clock in the evening.

A Revered Leader

King Bhumibol's name means "the strength of the land", and he is regarded by his kingdom in a similar way as the Tibetans see their spiritual leader, the Dalai Lama, rather than any comparable monarch. Most Thais would agree with the Thailand tourist office website that describes him as a "paragon of virtue" and a "literary genius". This is partly due to history and a constitution that states that the king must be "enthroned in a position of revered worship", but it is also possibly because Thailand

King Bhumibol and the future Queen Sirikit in January 1950, the year of their marriage

has never previously had clear and consistent political leadership. The country has, for centuries, been dogged by a combination of government corruption and incompetence.

Thailand had an absolute monarchy until 1932, when a coup established a constitutional monarchy, as in the UK. King Bhumibol was born in the United States, educated in Switzerland and came to the throne in 1946 – the country celebrated his Golden Jubilee in 1996. But unlike British royalty, the Thai royal family does not receive any money from the royal treasury. Their power cannot be ignored by politicians: in 1992 the prime minister and his opponent prostrated themselves at the king's feet on live television while he instructed them on how to deal with a national crisis. Chief executives of international companies have also reported being literally "floored" by his presence. In King Bhumibol's opinion

PUBLIC HOLIDAYS

- **Chakri Day**, 6 April, honours Rama I, the founder of the Chakri dynasty
- **Coronation Day**, 5 May, honours King Bhumibol and Queen Sirikit's joint coronation
- **The Queen's Birthday**, 12 August
- **Chulalongkorn Day**, 23 October, in honour of King Chulalongkorn, Rama V
- **The King's Birthday**, 5 December

"A successful monarch must become the living symbol of the country"

  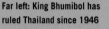

Far left: King Bhumibol has ruled Thailand since 1946

Left: Queen Sirikit is known for her charitable work in Thailand

"a successful monarch must become the living symbol of the country. He must change with the country but at the same time keep the spirit of the country", this is something that he and his family before him, has somehow managed to achieve. King Bhumibol's older brother, Ananda, is credited with being responsible for establishing modern medicine in Thailand, and his mother founded the flying doctors to give medical assistance to remote parts of the country. Between them, King Bhumibol and Queen Sirikit have established more than 4,000 projects to give assistance in rural areas, particularly in the poor northeast.

Royal Etiquette
As a visitor to Thailand the worst thing you can do is criticise the royal family. It is best not to mention them – most Thai people do not think themselves worthy of discussing them in idle conversation or talking about who will succeed the world's longest serving monarch. In 2008 an Australian writer was sentenced to three years in prison for criticising the king. He was granted a royal pardon after five months of incarceration.

THE KING AND I

King Mongkut was unfairly portrayed as bad tempered and naïve in the fictionalised account of his court, which was portrayed in the musical *The King and I*. The film is still banned in Thailand, along with the 1946 film *Anna and the King of Siam* and the more recent film *Anna and the King* starring Jodie Foster.

Buddha **Images**

Representations of the Buddha can be found everywhere in Thailand, but they are intended to be symbols of his teachings, rather than accurate images of the man.

The Buddha appears in one of only four postures, or *asanhas*. By far the most common is the sitting, or meditating, Buddha. The reclining Buddha represents his entering nirvana, and in the standing or walking position he is descending from heaven. The hand gestures *(mudras)* of the Buddha distinguish one activity from another. The following are the most common:

- **Bhumisparca mudra** Seated with the left hand in the lap and the right hand on the right knee with the tips of the fingers pointing to the ground, the Buddha is harnessing the power of the earth to meditate.
- **Abhaya mudra** The Buddha teaching stands with the palm of the right hand and sometimes both hands raised outwards.
- **Vitarka mudra** The thumb and index finger of the right hand in a circle represents the teachings of the Buddha.
- **Dhyana mudra** The meditation position has both hands in the lap with palms pointing upwards.
- **Abhaya mudra** Dispelling fear, the right hand is held up as if to say "stop".

Buddhas in saffron robes display some of the *asanhas* and *mudras*

HINDU GODS

Alongside Buddhist iconography, Thai temples often incorporate the rather fantastical gods of the Hindu religion:

- **Vishnu** with four arms, usually wearing a crown
- **Garuda**, half-man, half-bird
- **Shiva**, a mythical creature like the garuda, with his four arms carrying different objects and showing gestures of peace and sacrifice
- **Ganesh**, with the head of an elephant

Outdoor
ADVENTURES

Thailand offers a superb range of outdoor activities for anyone seeking adventure, excitement or just something a little less ordinary. Trekking in Northern Thailand, cycling through historical Sukhothai, elephant rides through the jungle or diving among the coral reefs to swim with the manta rays are just some of the options. From extreme sports to yoga, in Thailand you can try out something new or enjoy a familiar activity in a unique environment.

Trekking
Trekking is a well-developed activity for visitors to Thailand and, while it is principally based in the north and northwest (➤ 95–97), it is also possible to organize trips around **Kanchanaburi** (➤ 68–69) and in national parks like **Khao Sam Roi Yot** (➤ 132–133). Hundreds of companies offer treks in northern Thailand, some more ecologically conscious than others, so it pays to look around for the best one for you. (For trekking companies ➤ 108.)

Cycling
Bicycles can be hired in most of the popular destinations and sometimes, as when seeing the historical sights of Sukhothai, cycling is the best way to get around. Most of the guest houses

Cycling – a fine way to see sights in Sukhothai

Trekking by elephant through the jungle is an unusual way to get around

in Sukhothai have bicycles for hire. Cycling is also a great way to get around the centre of Chiang Mai and visit temples on its outskirts. Even in Bangkok, where the prospect of taking to two wheels might at first seem suicidal, safe cycling is an option if you join a bicycle tour exploring green areas in and around the sprawling metropolis, visiting floating markets, rice fields, pottery villages and the small island of Ko Kret. Cycle tours last at least half a day but longer trips are possible, like the innovative but not too demanding Wine Trail through Khao Yai National Park, run by Bangkok Bike Rides, covering 60km (37 miles) over two days and one night.

Water Sports

A number of water sports can be enjoyed in Thailand without inflicting damage on the environment. The country is justly famous for its diving holidays but the sea is home to hundreds of species of coral and divers need to be alert to the danger of damaging delicate reefs. Responsible companies are well aware of this: Blue Planet Divers is worth mentioning in this respect because they also offer an experience that will be new to many – free diving (using a single breath of air to explore some of the wonders of the undersea world).

Divers, in particular free divers, need to master breath control. Yoga techniques offer one of the best ways to improve breath-control skills, and courses for those interested in trying free diving begin with preparatory yoga sessions. On Phi Phi island you can combine scuba diving and yoga, under the direction of Keira White and her company Keiritas Yoga. Full PADI instruction is given for those who have never dived before or need a refresher course, and all equipment can be hired.

The islands you are likely to visit have safe opportunities for snorkelling. Equipment is always available for hire, but you might prefer to bring your own mask and snorkel to be sure it is up to the required safety standards.

For those in search of a greater adrenalin rush, windsurfing is well provided for on **Ko Samui** (➤ 134–137) and in **Pattaya** (➤ 120). Kayaking is popular along the Andaman coast where a wealth of lagoons and caves can be safely explored.

Rocks and Rivers

Another adventure sport readily accessible to visitors to Thailand is rock climbing, especially in the **Krabi region** (➤ 159–161) and on Ko Phi Phi. Courses are available for absolute beginners and a harness ensures your safety. Activity-based tours in the north often feature bamboo rafting down a river – **Pai** (➤ 99) is a good base.

Before undertaking the activities described on these pages, it is essential that you use qualified instructors and equipment that conforms to recognised international safety standards.

Rock climbing at East Rai Leh in Krabi

FURTHER INFORMATION

For more information about the activities and holidays mentioned here take a look at the following websites:

- www.responsibletravel.com for holidays
- www.bangkokbikerides.com or www.thailandgreenride.com for cycling tours of the country
- www.blueplanetdivers.net for free diving and scuba diving
- www.hippodivers.com, www.visadiving.com and www.blueviewdivers.com are dive schools for diving around Phi Phi
- www.keiritasyoga.com for Hatha and Ashtanga yoga on Phi Phi, and combining it with scuba diving

Thailand's
HILL TRIBES

Thailand's hill tribes are remarkably adept at preserving their way of life, despite the pressures of the modern world on their semi-nomadic lifestyle and culture. Tucked away in fertile valleys, or perched close to the top of mountains, the hill tribes continue to farm in time-honoured ways and celebrate important occasions with customary practices and traditional forms of dress.

Northern Thailand is home to the seven main hill tribes: Akha, Lahu, Lisu, Karen, Hmong, Mien and Paduang, and each has its distinctive clothing and culture. Several tour companies offer a visit to a hill tribe village, staying at one of the village houses. Displays of weaving, dances or other traditional activities may well be organized principally for the enjoyment of visitors, rather than constituting a genuine display of the culture, but in some ways such events are helping to preserve ancient traditions.

Above: Karen handwoven fabric; below: A highly decorated Lisu sash

Girls of the Lisu hill tribe harvest rice near Pai

The Lisu

The Lisu are thought to have migrated to Thailand from China some time in the early 20th century. Numbering about 25,000 and living in the hills to the north of Chiang Mai, they are one of the smallest tribes but also one of the most successful at conserving their culture.

The day-to-day life of the Lisu revolves around subsistence farming and the crafting of goods – jewellery, domestic tools fashioned from wood, items of clothing – for a retail market that includes tourists, neighbouring non-Lisu villagers and Thai townspeople. Their homes are constructed from the produce of the forests with bamboo walls and thatched roofs, and the forest also provides wild game and birds to supplement the rice and corn that they grow. Opium is still cultivated in the hills but, with government assistance, the Lisu are also farming alternative cash crops such as coffee.

Religion and spiritual beliefs lie at the heart of the village life: Lisu culture is imbued with animist beliefs (the idea that inanimate objects have souls) and a spiritual regard that secures a role for the village's spirit doctor and maintains a small shrine within every home for the honouring of family ancestors. Village celebrations accompany births and weddings, but the most important calendar event, Chinese New Year, occurs in February. Coinciding with the completion of crop planting, the new year celebrations (a legacy of their origins that distinguishes the Lisu from many other hill tribes) lasts several days. During this festive time visits are made to each other's homes and the evenings bring colourful displays by women of long-established dances and costumes. The men discuss affairs with the village elders and drink their potent corn-based whisky. This is also the time of year when partnerships are formed between young men and women with gifts of silver or hard cash determining the bride's "price". Negotiations are carried out and the final agreement is toasted with yet more whisky.

An Enduring Culture

Although there has been some erosion of traditional culture, many village communities have found ways to embrace the benefits of mobile

Lisu women wear vibrantly coloured traditional dress with elaborate headdresses

phones, modern medicines and education without losing their ancient heritage. They are also benefiting from government schooling and are finding ways to earn a living, often related to tourism, without sacrificing their traditions and age-old customs.

HILL-TRIBE DIVERSITY

The seven main hill tribes share similar characteristics in their day-to-day way of life, but each has its own particular cultural variations.

■ The Karen, who came to Thailand from Burma, form the largest tribal group and are noted for their skill in weaving cloth. Unmarried girls wear white while embroidered blouses and shirts distinguish married women.

■ The culture of the Akka, living in poorer areas in the far north, is embodied in their particular village architecture that features a wooded gateway and a village swing. The swing is the focus of a time-honoured swinging ceremony celebrated in August.

■ The Lahu, Lisu and Hmong people live in the higher altitudes of northern Thailand. Subgroups within the Lahu each have their own forms of dress while the Hmong favour plain jackets with red or black baggy trousers. The Lisu wear the most brightly coloured garments of all the tribes: female headdresses ornamented with hundreds of coloured tassels, a multicoloured tunic and black trousers held together with a long sash, and festooned with silver ornaments on important occasions.

■ The Mien share a Chinese origin with the Lisu and also, uniquely, preserve a form of writing based on Chinese characters. They live in extended families and practise polygamy.

■ The most distinguishing feature of the Paduang tribe is the brass coils worn around the necks of females to create their long-necked look (▶ 99).

"He who is AWAKE"
Thai Buddhist Faith

Buddha translates as "he who is awake" but has come to mean one who has gained enlightenment. The Buddha advocated a "Middle Way" between the extremes of indulgence and austerity where everyone is responsible for what happens in the world – as there is no single god to look to, Buddhism requires that you seek enlightenment from within. These principles are interwoven with everyday life but for the visitor there is no stronger evidence of faith than the Buddhist monks.

The symbols of Buddhism are apparent in the golden spires of the thousands of temples and the saffron-robed monks, and its ethos is evident in the Thai people themselves. No fewer than 95 per cent of the country's 60 million inhabitants are Buddhist, and this is obvious in the gentle respect they show

"Most Thai men are ordained at some time in their life"

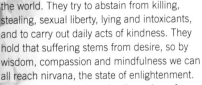

the world. They try to abstain from killing, stealing, sexual liberty, lying and intoxicants, and to carry out daily acts of kindness. They hold that suffering stems from desire, so by wisdom, compassion and mindfulness we can all reach nirvana, the state of enlightenment.

The shaved heads and yellow robes of Buddhist monks seem to be everywhere. Most Thai men are ordained at some time in their life, even if only for a few days. Dan, a young novice monk studying English at university, says: "My father became a monk because it was the only way to learn to read and write. Ex-monks were popular choices for women looking for a husband because they were thought to be clever and calm."

Share and Share Alike

Thai people are very practical in their beliefs. When they give alms it is to gain "merit", so they don't give anything unwanted. Curried chicken, teabags and toilet paper are the typically practical contents of a monk's collection bucket. Thai monks are equally practical and will share with everyone else in the temple. If they get too many gifts, they will sell them on to the next temple.

It's a Monk's Life

In Thai culture, monks are greatly revered. The back seats in buses are reserved for them and they have access to a special orchid-covered area at Bangkok's airport.

Novice monks on their way to lessons

THE BEGINNINGS OF BUDDHISM

According to Buddhist belief the Buddha was born as Prince Gautama Siddhartha in the sixth or seventh century BC. When he escaped the royal household at the age of 29 and encountered real poverty, he came to terms with it through meditation. Concluding that all is impermanent, he eventually achieved nirvana and advocated the "Middle Way".

Festive FUN

Thailand's festivals are always joyous events, whether their origins are in agricultural traditions, the Buddhist faith, the royal family or local gods and goddesses. Both the Thai and Chinese New Year and Loi Krathong celebrations take place all over the country and are an unforgettable experience.

New Year Celebrations

Songkran is the celebration of the Thai New Year, held from 13 to 15 April, and it is difficult to miss if you are in Chiang Mai or Bangkok at the time. The festival takes place at a time when the rice harvest has been completed and, this being the hottest time of the year in Thailand, the fun side of celebrations take the form of throwing water at all and sundry. Tourists are not exempt from the celebrations and you may well find yourself being unexpectedly showered or the target of a water gun or even a garden hose. Be prepared to get wet. On the more serious side, many Thais mark the occasion by cleaning and "bathing" Buddha images with water. In Chiang Mai you may well see a procession of Buddha images being carried through the city.

The Chinese New Year, usually around February but subject to lunar calculations, is also celebrated in Thailand. Traditional lion dances are performed and fireworks let off.

Loi Krathong

The visually most engaging of Thai festivals takes place in November on the night of a full moon. Make your way to the nearest river, canal or lake and you will see countless, hand-sized little rafts *(krathong)* floating around *(loi* means to float) and displaying their floral decorations, candles and incense sticks. Official celebrations take the form of larger rafts, elaborately decked out, with firework displays as a bonus. Paralleling the dispersal by water of what is unwanted during Songkran, the *krathongs* float away into the night and take with them all the bad luck of the past.

Songkran is celebrated by splashing water around

FESTIVAL CALENDAR

There are too many other festivals to list and many of them do not have a fixed date but websites like www.thailandgrandfestival.com and www.thaifestivalblogs.com should have up-to-date information on what is happening around the country at the time of your visit. One festival to look out for is the week-long commemoration at the famous bridge in **Kanchanaburi** (➤ 68–69) in late November/early December.

A welcome
Retreat

Whether you are looking for a sophisticated spa or a monastic-style meditation retreat, you are sure to find a choice of therapeutic treatments, from invigorating to calming, wherever you go in the country.

Thailand has long been a favourite destination for stressed-out Westerners and the Thai people's calm and gentle approach to life, typified by the much-used phrase *"mai pen rat"*, or "never mind", helps you to soak up the serenity.

Traditional Thai Massage

The traditional Thai massage, a practice passed down for centuries, is a vigorous, muscle-melting affair using hand pressure and the masseuse's own body to work on pressure points of your body and relieve built-up stress and tension – or, as the parlance goes, to re-align your energy lines. Practised seriously, this process takes from 90 minutes to two hours and, while at times you may feel that parts of your body are being subjected to undue force, the end result is an exhilarating feeling of relaxation and well-being. An oil massage is a gentler process than the traditional Thai massage and uses oils to treat muscle tissue in a therapeutic way.

The centre for studying traditional massage and learning massage techniques in Thailand is the school of natural medicine at Bangkok's **Wat Po** (► 48). It is a far cry from this to the techniques introduced at stylish luxury spas where two masseuses employ four hands in tandem to produce synchronised waves of gentle massaging.

Body-pampering Spa Treatments

Spas are found in a number of hotels up and down the country and nearly all of them are open to non-residents. It is just a matter of making a reservation and paying the scheduled charge. There are also a number of highly sophisticated spas that operate in their own right, unconnected to any hotel, and they offer a wide range of treatments that include pure body pampering as well as various massages from traditional Thai to Ayuvedic treatments using a variety of oils.

Unashamed body pampering comes in the form of body wraps with alluring names such as "mangosteen peel body wrap" or "blue lotus aloe wrap", with promises to decrease wrinkles and generally make you feel and look years younger. Extracts of seaweed, mineral-rich muds and even, at the shamelessly luxurious end of the scale, flakes of pure gold are applied to the skin to rejuvenate the body and leave you feeling blissfully rebalanced and refreshed.

Right: A bedroom at Ban Sabai Spa in Chiang Mai
Opposite: Tamarind Retreat Spa in Ko Samui

SUPERB SPAS

Many of the better hotels have their own spas that are also open to non-residents at guest rates. The more renowned independent spas include:

■ **Kamalaya** (www.kamalaya.com), a Wellness Sanctuary and Holistic Spa resort (► 143) on Ko Samui, which offers a host of treatments that include Indian Ayurveda therapists, acupuncture, yoga, detox, as well as the more usual spa treatments.

■ **Oasis Spa** (www.bangkokoasis.com) has branches in Bangkok, Chiang Mai, Phuket and Pattaya. Thai and oil massages, scrubs, wraps and facial treatments are available, all in elegantly furnished, Thai-style premises.

■ **Devarana Spa** (www.devarana.com) are to be found in Bangkok, Phuket, Hua Hin and Chiang Mai, all offering a luxury spa experience.

The Best of

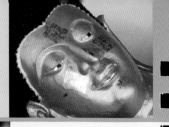

Thailand

Thailand's beaches rival those of the Caribbean; Sukhothai and Ayutthaya are World Heritage Sites; and the diving is some of the best on the planet. Here are a few of the highlights which make Thailand a world-class destination.

National Parks

Thailand has more than 80 national parks. **Khao Sok** (➤ 154–155) offers a real jungle experience with leopards, tigers, treehouses to stay in and the largest known flower in the world, the *Rafflesia kerri meyer* or wild lotus. **Doi Inthanon** (➤ 99) has the highest mountain in the country, and **Thale Ban** (➤ 167) is home to hundreds of species of bird life.

Buddha Statues

The most sacred Buddha statue in the country is the **Emerald Buddha**, in Bangkok's **Wat Phra Kaeo** (➤ 44–46). Wat Traimit, or the Temple of the Golden Buddha in Bangkok, is home to a solid gold Buddha, the largest in the world at 4m (13 feet) high.

Journeys

For many visitors the most memorable journeys are **treks** through jungle to hill-tribe villages in the north (➤ 95–97). Buzzing past **James Bond Island** in a longtail boat in Ao Phang Nga comes a close second (➤ 156–158).

Diving

Thailand's diving mecca is the small turtle-shaped island of **Ko Tao** (➤ 136–137). Those in the know go there for some of the cheapest and best diving in the world. **Pattaya** (➤ 120) is the unchallenged water-sports capital.

Retreats

Riverside retreats are found throughout the country, from the peaceful towns on the northern border of the Mekong River to the floating lodges of **Kanchanaburi** (➤ 68–69). Even Bangkok's **Chao Phraya River** (➤ 49–50) offers relief from the city.

Ancient Sites

The ancient cities of **Sukhothai** (➤ 75–77) and **Ayutthaya** (➤ 72–74) are both World Heritage Sites. Although Ayutthaya is magnificent and within easy reach of Bangkok, Sukhothai wins for its scenic qualities which hark back to a golden age.

Thai Massage

If you have only one Thai massage, make it at **Wat Po** in Bangkok, the national massage training school (➤ 48). Thai massage is a combination of Western massage and foot reflex-zone massage. The highly trained masseurs and masseuses are expert in reducing tension in their clients.

Finding Your Feet

First Two Hours

Most international visitors travelling by air arrive in Bangkok at the city's Suvarnabhumi Airport. Visitors from Malaysia usually travel by train to Padang Besar and it is possible to make the journey overland from Cambodia to Ban Hat Lek, although this route will involve several changes of transport. A network of intercity buses connect Bangkok with outlying areas.

Arriving by Air

Bangkok's Suvarnabhumi Airport serves international airlines and is located 25km (15 miles) east of the city. A small number of non-Thai Airways domestic flights use Bangkok's former international airport, Don Muang (25km/15 miles northeast of Bangkok), so if you have a connecting flight you should check if you need to change airports.

Airport Facilities

Facilities at Suvarnabhumi Airport (www.bangkokairportonline.com) include a currency exchange, a post office, a telephone communications office, car rental agencies and left luggage, all of which are open 24 hours. There is also a tourist office, a Thai Hotel Association reservations service on Level 2, and a multitude of bars, coffee shops and restaurants.

From the Airport to Bangkok by Taxi

- Travelling by **taxi** into town from Suvarnabhumi Airport is probably the best choice after a long flight. The journey should take around one hour into the city centre.
- The **taxi fare** should be around 350 baht, which includes a 50 baht airport surcharge plus expressway tolls.
- Take a **licensed cab** from the booth on Level 1.
- Ignore any **drivers or their touts who approach you directly**. These operators may be unlicensed and will almost certainly try to charge you an extortionate fare.
- The booth will fix the fare for you, though you can also opt for a **meter taxi**. There's little difference in price, although in rush hour a metered ride can soon escalate.
- Confirm that the **expressway tolls** are included in the fare.

From the Airport to Bangkok by Limousine

- Costing about **twice the price of a taxi**, taking a limousine is still a relatively reasonably priced option.
- As well as enjoying a little extra luxury, it means you can **avoid having to queue** for a taxi.
- The **Limousine Counter** is open 24 hours a day and is located in the Arrivals Hall on Level 2.
- Make sure you **establish a price** beforehand.

From the Airport to Bangkok by Airport Express Bus

- This efficient, frequent, air-conditioned service is in operation from **5am to midnight**.
- Much more comfortable, and faster than catching the public bus, the **airport bus** costs 150 baht and leaves from Level 1.
- Although the chances are the airport bus won't take you exactly to your destination, the service does stop at some of the city's **larger hotels** as well as the central railway station.

From the Airport to Bangkok by Train

- The opening of a **train link** from the airport to Bangkok has been delayed more than once – it is currently scheduled for December 2009.
- When the train link is up and running it will enable passengers to access the city's **Skytrain** (▶ 40 and www.bts.co.th) and **subway network** (www.mrta.co.th).

Intercity Buses

- **Free shuttle buses** will take you from Level 2 to the Intercity Bus Counter. Intercity buses travel to towns around Bangkok, including **Pattaya**.The service operates from **6am to 9pm**.

From Suvarnabhumi Airport to Don Muang Airport

- **BMTA public buses** and vans run a 24-hour service between the two airports for about 50 baht.
- **Taxis** are quicker and you can pay a fixed price at the booth on Level 1.

Tourist Information

- The **Tourist Authority of Thailand** is usually known, and referred to throughout this book, as **TAT**. The **airport office** is open 8am–10pm.
- The **central tourist information office** is located at 1600 Thanon Phetchaburi Makkasan, Ratchathewi, Bangkok 10400 (tel: 02 250 5500, www.tourismthailand.org, open Mon–Fri 8:30–4:30)
- TAT has an **English-speaking call centre**. The number is 1672.
- There are TAT offices **throughout the country**.

Getting Around

"Pai nai?" ("Where are you going?") is the regular cry of taxi drivers and boatmen eager to sell you a ticket, but it's also a standard Thai greeting that translates as "How's it going?" or simply "Hello". Travelling around Thailand is surprisingly straightforward. Bus and train services are frequent and very reasonably priced. A little comfort can be had for a small price, in the form of first-class rail travel, air-conditioned buses and internal flights.

Buses

- **Air-conditioning** is essential in order to ensure a comfortable bus journey in Thailand, so it is worth travelling by the slightly more expensive air-conditioned **government or private buses** whenever possible, particularly at night.
- The government service is known as **Bor Kor Sor (BKS)** and they come in several classes, from ordinary non-air-conditioned services for shorter journeys to comfortable air-conditioned superior ones for longer journeys. So-called VIP buses have reclining seats, hostesses who serve drinks or a refreshment station and toilets. They are excellent for overnight journeys as the seats can be reclined to near horizontal.
- **Superior buses** for longer journeys tend to leave in the early morning or early evening, while **ordinary buses** leave throughout the day from the centre of towns at unfixed times.
- The long-distance northern and southern bus terminals can be bewildering due to the number of **ticket counters** attached to different bus companies. If you arrive by taxi ask your driver to drop you at the ticket counter of the company offering a service to your destination. Many taxi drivers will

accompany you to the relevant counter and even help you buy your ticket. Ticket counter staff are also invariably friendly and helpful.

■ Air-conditioned **mini vans**, available at busy tourist hubs like Khao San Road in Bangkok, may seem more convenient, but they rarely run on time, can be cramped and are a lot more expensive. You may be taken to a ferry company or a hotel that is not your choice, but which earns the bus company a commission. Often the services are illegal, with bad-tempered, overworked drivers who may have a poor safety record.

■ *Songthaews* are pickup trucks with two rows of bench seating that operate like buses, although if they are otherwise empty you can often charter the whole vehicle.

Trains

■ Try to use the **well-run** train network wherever possible in Thailand as it's a comfortable way to travel, especially if you book an overnight sleeper (www.seat61.com is a useful source of information).

■ There are **four train lines**, running from Bangkok to Chiang Mai (➤ 92–94) in the north, to Hua Hin, Surat Thani – jumping off point for Ko Samui (➤ 134–137) and the Malaysian border in the south – and into the Isan provinces in the northeast. The northern line from Bangkok to Chiang Mai stops at Ayutthaya (➤ 72–74) and Lampang.

■ **Tickets** should be booked in advance. It is often worth paying a travel agency premium for them to purchase tickets for you to avoid the hassle of having to visit the station and then return to your hotel.

■ There are **three classes** (1, 2 and 3) and **three types** of train (Special Express, Rapid and Ordinary). First-class overnight accommodation is in two-berth sleeping compartments, second-class is in Pullman-style sleeping cars, third class in upright seats. Unless you value the privacy of first class, the second-class compartments are clean, comfortable and exceptional value. Dining cars are on most overnight trains, although a buffet service is provided on all.

Domestic Air Travel

■ **Thai Airways** (tel: 02 356 1111) maintains its dominance of the domestic network, and if you're planning your trip in advance it's advisable to reserve either with them or with one of the smaller airlines: **Bangkok Airways** (www.bangkokair.com), **Air Asia** (www.airasia.com), **NOK** (www.nokair.com) and **One-Two-Go** (www.fly12go.com).

■ A useful flight that can save time is the daily flight with Thai Airways from **Chiang Mai to Phuket**, stopping at Bangkok en route.

■ As flights are often booked up, especially at weekends and during holidays, **reserve ahead** as far as possible.

Taxis

■ Always **agree a price** – you may have to bargain hard – or establish that the meter is used, before getting in.

■ Some taxi drivers, especially at busy transport hubs and popular attractions, try to take advantage of tourists, quoting a price that is several times greater than the price should be. In general **avoid drivers who approach you** or at least try to find out what the price should be before starting to negotiate.

■ Hiring a taxi even for a **trip of several hours** is worth considering, particularly if public transport connections are difficult, you want a bit of comfort, or local transport is inconvenient.

Tuk-tuks and *Saamlaws*

■ Three-wheeled, open-sided motorised vehicles known as *tuk-tuks* or *saamlaws* (non-motorised versions are also to be found) provide a **cheap and fast** means of transport, particularly in Bangkok, but they are very noisy and the journey can be hair-raising.

■ *Tuk-tuks* don't have meters so it is vital to **agree a price** with the driver before getting aboard.

Car Rental

■ Car rental is **relatively inexpensive** and available in most places.

■ Negotiate a **discount** if you want the car for more than a day.

■ If you don't want to drive yourself, a **driver** can normally be engaged for around half the daily car-rental fee.

■ Ask to see **insurance details**. In the event of an accident you may be liable.

■ You will need an **international driving licence**, although more often than not it is not asked for.

■ Generally, arranging car-rental **from your own country** is more expensive than waiting until you arrive in Thailand.

Driving Essentials

■ Drive on the **left**.

■ Be prepared for a certain amount of **chaos**. There are very few rules of the road in practice, except for the one that says the bigger your vehicle the more rights you have.

■ Attitude to wearing **seatbelts**, keeping within the **speed limit** and **parking** tends to be rather relaxed.

■ **Flashing your lights** is a warning, not a signal that the coast is clear.

■ **Beeping the horn** is not aggressive, but an indication to other vehicles that you are about to overtake.

■ **Kilometre markers** are found along bigger highways.

Car-Hire Companies

The following companies cover the main tourist destinations in Thailand:

■ **Avis:** 08445 818181 (in UK), www.avis.com

■ **Budget:** 08701 565656 (in UK), www.budget.com

Crossing International Borders

■ The crossing to **Cambodia** from Ban Hat Lek involves changing modes of transport several times, which often takes a full day. Checking passports, visas and clearing paperwork can necessitate a long wait. As procedures are subject to change, check with the Cambodian Embassy in Bangkok (185 Thanon Ratchadamri Lumphini, tel: 02 254 6630) before travel.

■ The best route across the border to **Malaysia** is by train from Padang Besar (4 hours to Butterworth). Air-conditioned buses also operate from Hat Yai, Phuket, Krabi and Bangkok.

ADMISSION CHARGES
The cost of admission for museums and places of interest featured in the guide is indicated by the following price categories:
Inexpensive = under 50 baht
Moderate = 50–100 baht
Expensive = over 100 baht

Accommodation

Accommodation opportunities in Thailand are many and varied, although you will find the distribution rather uneven. Bangkok, Chiang Mai, Phuket and Ko Samui have a choice of everything, from cheap and cheerful guest houses to luxury hotels that have often been voted the best in the world. In other places, such as Ayutthaya and Sukhothai, the choice is not nearly as good. Thailand's tourist season runs from November to March and bookings are essential at this time for the more expensive hotels and resorts. Bangkok has a vast array of accommodation from budget to luxury.

Guest Houses

- **Quality** varies, but most are clean and well maintained.
- In Bangkok's **Khao San Road** area a very basic room can be found for under 200 baht. Similar prices can be found in Chiang Mai, but standards at this cheap end are higher in Chiang Mai.

Luxury Hotels

- Considering the quality available all over the country, **prices** for accommodation in hotels are **very reasonable** compared to just about everywhere else in the world.
- Many of the luxury hotels are run by well-known **international chains** and offer all the amenities and facilities found in their Western branches, often at half the price.

Resort Hotels

- Many of Thailand's resort hotels double as spas and health centres.
- **Standards** are extremely high.
- Be aware that Thais will sometimes use the word "resort" for any hotel or guest house located **outside a town** or built-up area.

Laundry

- Just about every hotel and guest house offers an efficient, clean and inexpensive laundry service. Clothing is returned washed, dried and ironed within 24 hours, although a faster service is available on request.

Toilets

- **Western-style toilets** and bathroom facilities are increasingly the norm, but anywhere outside Bangkok and at smaller or older hotels you will encounter squat toilets, and water and a jug rather than toilet paper.

Booking

- It is advisable to **book ahead** for the large Bangkok hotels, although Bangkok is overflowing with high-quality rooms.
- It is also a good idea to book hotels in advance in Chiang Mai, on Ko Phuket and in Pattaya **during festivals** (➤ 24–25) and in **December, which is at the height of the tourist season**.

Tax and Tipping

- Luxury hotels generally charge a 10 per cent **service charge** and 7.5 per cent **government tax**.
- **Tipping** is not a requirement but is obviously appreciated.
- **Guest houses** and more reasonably priced hotels do not charge any tax, nor is tipping required.

Food and Drink

Thai cuisine, held by its many enthusiasts to be the best in the world, is incredibly diverse and sophisticated. It is generally very reasonably priced, too. Visitors will be pleasantly surprised how far their money goes in Thai restaurants, of which there are thousands. Bangkok, as well as most Thai cities, also offers a wide range of other cuisines, ranging from regional (Vietnamese, Cantonese, Filipino, Malay and Yunnanese – from Yunnan Province in southwest China) to international (Japanese, Korean, French, German, Italian and even Mexican). Thai cuisine now shares pride of place with French, Italian and Chinese as one of the all-time great schools of cookery.

Traditional Thai

- Thai cuisine, like that of neighbouring Southeast Asian countries, revolves around **rice**, although the national fondness for noodles shows the strength of Chinese influence.
- Thais eat two kinds of rice, the slightly fluffy, long-grain rice familiar in the West, eaten with a spoon and fork; and "sticky rice", usually served in the north and northeast, which is eaten with the fingers.
- **Noodles** are always eaten with chopsticks.

Practical Tips

- Generally Thai restaurants serve all the **main dishes** at the same time.
- **Rice** plays a central role and is served in a large container.
- Diners are served with an individual portion of rice and then **help themselves** to small portions of curry, soup, fish, poultry and meat dishes.
- It is polite to **offer dishes** to guests, older people and women first.
- Thais are generally fastidiously clean and admire good manners. If you adhere to this, you will be considered a *pu-di angkrit*, an "English gentleman" (or lady)!
- Thais always eat rice and accompanying dishes using a **fork and spoon**. Knives are only used for European-style meals, as Thai food is generally served pre-cut into bite-sized pieces.
- There are no **fixed eating hours** in Thailand; Thais will eat at any time of the day or night. **Opening times** vary, but most restaurants are open seven days a week. Unlike many other countries there are no limitations on opening hours. Restaurants have very flexible hours, although they will probably be closed after 1am. Some street food stalls might not open until as late as 10pm and will continue serving until dawn.
- Thais eat when they are hungry, and also tend to eat less than Westerners, but more frequently. That said, **restaurants catering for foreign visitors** recognise the strange international habit of eating three fixed meals a day, and make allowances for it in their schedules. Hua Hin has a fine variety of Thai and international restaurants clustered in quite a small area. Ko Samui caters for just about every taste.

- Many of the top hotels around the country offer a great value **buffet lunch**. Check the local monthly listings magazines in Bangkok, Chiang Mai and Ko Phuket to see who's offering what.
- **Bars and restaurants are banned from serving alcohol on royal birthdays,** on holy days in the Buddhist calendar and during elections. In these cases, special allowances are generally made for foreign visitors.
- **Tipping** is not generally expected in Thailand, although many upmarket restaurants will add a 10 per cent service charge to a bill. Ordinary restaurants will not add any service charge but, like anywhere else in the world, a small tip is usually much appreciated.

Bests...
...**floating restaurant:** Mae Nam (➤ 85)
...**Indian:** Ali Baba (➤ 145)
...**Isaan:** Vientiane Kitchen (➤ 60)
...**ocean view:** Old Siam (➤ 171)
...**seafood:** Captain's Choice (➤ 145)
...**Thai food:** Lemongrass (➤ 60), Spice Market (➤ 60)
...**traditional Thai surroundings:** Sala Thai (➤ 171)
...**unusual:** Cabbages & Condoms (➤ 58)
...**vegetarian:** Whole Earth (➤ 60)
...**view:** Border View (➤ 107)

RESTAURANT PRICES
Expect to pay per person for a meal, excluding drinks and service:

£ under 300 baht   ££ 300–600 baht   £££ over 600 baht

Shopping

Thailand offers some of the best shopping in Asia, also some of the most interesting and beautiful antiques and crafts anywhere in the world. The north, Chiang Mai in particular, is the centre for most local crafts, ranging from exquisite lacquerware plates and vases to colourful hill-tribe embroidered cloth bags, textiles and jewellery. Other crafts and items specific to Thailand include celadon (translucent Chinese porcelain, usually pale green), nielloware (vessels made of a mixture of silver, copper and sometimes lead, decorated with incised patterns), rattan and pewter products.

Markets
- Every village, town and city in Thailand has a **fresh produce** market at least one day a week.
- For Thais the fresh market is the **cornerstone** of their daily food shopping and therefore a fascinating place for the visitor to wander around.
- Many larger markets also incorporate a **dried goods** section, a good example of which is Warorot Market in Chiang Mai (➤ 92–94).
- Bangkok's enormous **Chatuchak Market** (➤ 51) sells everything from pets to opium pipes and pots to herbal remedies. You'll also find musical

instruments, hill-tribe crafts, religious amulets, antiques, flowers, clothes imported from India and Nepal and camping gear.

■ While each of Thailand's regions has its own specialities, crafts and produce from all over the country are available in Bangkok. You'll find the widest selection of goods and the best prices in the markets and malls.

■ **Suan Lum Night Market** (▶ 61) in Bangkok is the place to go for arts and crafts. It was supposed to have closed down in 2007 but is still there and is well worth a visit.

How to Pay
■ Street vendors will only accept **cash**.
■ Many shops will take **credit cards** but some impose a 3–5 per cent surcharge for their use.
■ Craft and antiques shops can usually arrange packing, shipping and documentation at reasonable prices.

Antiquities and Buddha Images
■ It is **illegal** to export valuable antiquities without a licence. Having said that, Thai artisans produce a good range of authentic-looking reproduction antiquities.

How to Bargain
■ Thais generally like to bargain, so **expect to haggle** over prices, especially in small shops and from individual stalls, and particularly in Bangkok, Chiang Mai and Phuket.
■ Bargaining doesn't apply in **fixed-price** establishments like supermarkets and department stores, but it *does* apply in markets and souvenir shops.
■ The **general rule** is to offer half the price quoted and then slowly move towards a middle price that means you end up with a discount of between 25 and 30 per cent.
■ The trick is to appear **friendly**, even jovial – but to bargain hard and to be prepared to walk away, still smiling. The chances are you'll be called back – probably also with a smile!

Opening Hours
■ Most **shops** open seven days a week from about 9am to 5:30pm.
■ Many **convenience shops** stay open until 9pm. In Bangkok, Chiang Mai and many resorts, 7-Eleven chain stores are open 24 hours.
■ **Department stores** open from 10am and close at either 9 or 10pm.
■ In the larger cities some **pharmacies** stay open 24 hours.
■ **Markets** open as early as 3am and many are finished by 8am, others stay open until the early afternoon.

Bests...
...**crafts:** Baw Sang Village (▶ 108)
...**department store:** Central, Thanon Ploenchit (▶ 61)
...**fabrics:** Ban Boran Textiles (▶ 172)
...**hill-tribe crafts:** Hill Tribe Products Promotion Centre (▶ 108)
...**markets:** Chatuchak (▶ 51), Warorot (▶ 108), Night Bazaar (▶ 108), Suan Lum Night Bazaar (▶ 61)
...**sarongs:** Sathorn Gold and Textile Museum (▶ 86)
...**silk:** Jim Thompson Silk Shop (▶ 61)
...**silver:** Lumchad Ancient Silver (▶ 86)

Entertainment

If you want a break from sightseeing or the beach, there are plenty of things to do in Thailand, both during the day and at night. All major tourist destinations in Thailand have one or more free listings magazines readily available in bars, restaurants, cafés and travel agents. In Bangkok, *BK magazine* (www.bkmagazine.com) and *Bangkok 101* both provide good listings and news of current entertainment events. Nearly every provincial capital has a Tourist Authority of Thailand office with a wide range of information.

Festivals and Events

■ Thailand offers a huge number of **festivals** and **temple fairs** during the year. Across the country there is always something going on, especially between late October and April (➤ 24–25). **Dates** can vary from year to year – check with the tourist office or what's on magazines.

■ Among the most important nationwide festivals are **Songkran** (traditional Thai New Year, ➤ 24) and **Loi Krathong**, at November full moon (➤ 25).

Nightlife

■ Thailand's nightlife is legendary – and contrary to some Western opinion it does not just revolve around the sex trade. Thais take their free time seriously, and love nothing better than eating, drinking and dancing.

■ Most **bars** open late afternoon or early evening. Under current legislation, bars and discos have to close at 1 or 2am, depending on their location.

■ Bangkok is Thailand's main nightlife venue, but good **nightclubs** and **bars** can be found in Pattaya (➤ 124), on Ko Phuket (➤ 172), Ko Samui (➤ 148) and to a lesser extent in Chiang Mai (➤ 108).

■ **Live music** is popular everywhere, although it will generally be Thai music or Thai versions of well-known Western hits.

Outdoor Activities

■ Northern Thailand is popular for **trekking** (➤ 16, 95–97 and 108), with the added attraction of visiting various hill tribes.

■ **Mountain biking, white-water rafting and rock climbing** (➤ 18, 160) opportunities are also excellent throughout the country.

■ Southern Thailand, especially the Andaman Coast, offers some of the best locations for **diving and snorkelling**. The area around the **Similan Islands** (➤ 164) is considered one of the greatest dive sites in the world.

■ The coastal destinations, Ko Phuket (➤ 164), Ko Samui (➤ 134–137), Hua Hin (➤ 130–131) and Pattaya (➤ 120), provide all kinds of **water sports**, including windsurfing, parasailing and yachting.

Sport

■ *Muay thai*, Thai kick-boxing, is Thailand's national sport. It's a tough activity where, in addition to gloved fists, elbows, knees, feet and indeed any part of the body (except the head) can be used to strike the opponent. It's skilled, fast-moving and can be very entertaining. The most popular venues are **Lumpini Boxing Stadium** (Thanon Rama IV, near Lumpini Park, Bangkok, tel: 02 251 4303), and **Ratchadamnoen Boxing Stadium** (1 Thanon Ratchadamnoen Nok, Bangkok, tel: 02 281 4205).

■ Although *muay thai* is the national sport, **football** is the most popular spectator sport. There's big local support for the English teams Manchester United and Liverpool, while Everton's deal to carry a Thai brewery's logo on its team shirts has won that club a large following, too.

Bangkok

Getting Your Bearings

Most visitors to Thailand arrive in Bangkok, the country's exciting metropolis. Thoroughly modern, and with a vibrant financial centre and shining skyscrapers, it is also an historic capital steeped in the traditions of its beloved royal family and the Buddhist religion. Bangkok is known the world over for the infamous red-light district of Patpong and the budget travellers who swarm to Khao San Road, but it is also the place Thais know as the "City of Angels", with glittering palaces, magnificent temples and giant golden Buddhas.

Crazy little three-wheeled *tuk-tuks* buzz around streets crammed with stalls tossing together exquisite dishes. You can find a serenity of sorts on the mighty Chao Phraya River with a ride on a traditional longtail boat or a luxurious teak barge that is the naval equivalent of the *Orient Express*. Or take the air-conditioned Skytrain railway system that whizzes high above the crowded streets. A single-line underground metropolitan railway system, the MRT, runs from Bangkok's main railway station, Hua Lamphong, to Bang Sue, near the northern bus terminal. There are stops in all the main tourist and hotel zones: Rama IV Road, Silom, Sukhumvit and Asok Road, and also at the Chatuchak Market.

Explore the canal network that gave Bangkok its nickname "Venice of the East" and the tiny alleyways of colourful Chinatown packed with gold shops and exotic produce. Follow in the footsteps of authors from Joseph Conrad to Graham Greene and take tea in one of the best hotels in the world, the Mandarin Oriental. Then enjoy endless shopping opportunities, from the mammoth weekend Chatuchak Market to the air-conditioned shopping malls, and visit the enormous treasure house of the National Museum, telling the story of Thailand's history and royal family.

An ornately decorated statue guards the temple of Wat Phra Kaeo in Bangkok

THANON SOMDET PHRA PIN KHAO

BANGLAMPHU

THONBURI

THANON CHAKRABONGSE

Soi Samsen 5

Soi

National Museum 5

Khao San Road 6

PHRA NAKHON

Sanam Luang

THANON ATSADANG

THANON RACHINI

Thanon Ti Thong

Wat Phra Kaeo 1

Grand Palace 1

Thanon Ratchadamnoen Nai

THANON CHAROEN

Wat Po 2

Thanon Sanam Chai

Thanon Phahurat

PHAHURAT

Thanon Maharat

MEMORIAL BRIDGE

PHRA BUDDHA YODFHA BRIDGE

PHRA POKKLAO BRIDGE

★ Don't Miss

At Your Leisure

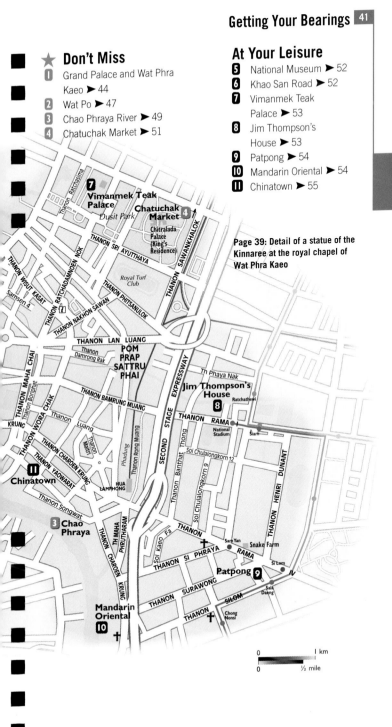

Page 39: Detail of a statue of the
Kinnaree at the royal chapel of
Wat Phra Kaeo

In Three Days

If you're not quite sure where to begin your travels, this itinerary recommends three practical and enjoyable days out in Bangkok, taking in some of the best places to see using the Getting Your Bearings map on the previous page. For more information see the main entries.

Day 1

Morning
Get up early to beat the crowds at the ❶ **Grand Palace** (below, ➤ 44–46), which opens at 8:30am. Have lunch at one of the cafés near the Grand Palace. Turn left at the palace entrance on to Thanon Na Phralan and walk past Silpakorn University for Fine Arts and over Thanon Mahathat to the Tha Chang Pier on the ❸ **Chao Phraya River** (➤ 49–50).

Afternoon
Take the Chao Phraya Express Boat to Tha Tien for ❷ **Wat Po** (➤ 47–48). Spend an hour exploring and end with an hour-long traditional Thai massage at the highly acclaimed massage school.

Evening
Jump in a *tuk-tuk* to **9 Patpong**
(➤ 54), the legendary red-light
district, which also has a vibrant night
market and bar scene.

Day 2

Morning
Start the day at the **5 National Museum**
(right, ➤ 52) where you will need
several hours to take it all in. Its
simple but pleasant café is a good
spot for a coffee. Afterwards, you can
walk (or take a taxi) to the river by
turning right out of the entrance on
Thanon Na Phra That and taking the
first right on to Thanon Phra Chan.
The Chao Phraya Express Boat stop of
the same name is at the end of this
road, but if you continue the short
distance to the Tha Maharat stop there
are riverside restaurants that make a
pleasant stop for lunch.

Afternoon
Take the Chao Phraya Express Boat to
11 Chinatown (below, ➤ 55), getting
off at the Tha Rachawong stop, less than 10 minutes away. Wander around
the absorbing alleyways or follow the **walk** (➤ 174–176), which guides
you through the maze to hidden temples.

Day 3

If you are here on a Saturday or Sunday spend a day at the weekend-only
4 Chatuchak Market (➤ 51), either to shop or just marvel at the weird and
wonderful goods on sale, from traditional musical instruments to Siamese
fighting fish. Have lunch in one of the air-conditioned restaurants in the
"Dream Section". If a weekend isn't included in your trip, try **6 Khao San
Road** instead for the street circus and lively atmosphere (➤ 52).

❶ Grand Palace and Wat Phra Kaeo

A combination of beautiful serenity and dazzling over-the-top royal splendour, the magnificent Grand Palace is the perfect first stop for any visitor to Bangkok. It offers a spectacular introduction to the twin themes that weave through almost every aspect of Thai life: Buddhism and royalty. Undoubtedly at the heart of the capital, this city within a city also contains the most sacred of all the country's many Buddha images.

Allow at least a couple of hours to see the highlights of this 24ha (59-acre) walled complex. A fair amount of walking is involved, queues can eat into your time and this is not a place to rush. Admission includes a brochure, which is hard to read and sadly lacking in detail, although the map covering the main buildings is useful for finding your way around.

More than 100 mansions, halls, pavilions and temples with **exquisite mosaic-encrusted spires** and pillars make up a fascinating combination of Victorian, Italian Renaissance and other styles, the oldest of which dates back 200 years.

Beautiful **murals** found inside the compound walls show the *Ramakien*, the Thai version of the Hindu epic, the *Ramayana*. Lovingly restored, they date from King Rama I (1782–1809).

Head first to the main attraction, the **Emerald Buddha**, housed in **Wat Phra Kaeo**, a glitteringly decorative royal

A mural decorating the royal chapel of Wat Phra Kaeo

Grand Palace is only sometimes used for royal occasions

chapel. The Buddha is in fact made of jade, not emerald, and at only 60cm (1.5-feet) high is an almost invisible figure, perched high on a mountain of gold. It is the holiest Buddhist site in Thailand. It's unclear when the figure – Thailand's most revered Buddha image – was made, but historical records trace its origins back at least to the 15th century. It reached Bangkok at the end of an eventful journey from the north, and was once in its colourful history stolen by Laotian forces and then recovered in battle by the outraged Siamese.

Around the Temple

In a row on the northern side of the temple are the Phra Si Ratana, a golden *chedi* (► 8–9 and 194), Phra Mondop, containing a Buddhist library not open to the public, and Prasad Phra Thep Bidom, the royal pantheon.

Outside the *wat* complex, to the south, is the surprisingly low-key **Amarindra Winichai Hall** (Audience Hall), where at one time the people petitioned the king. Every new king spends the first night after his coronation here, where coronation ceremonies still take place. King Bhumibol makes his birthday speech at the Winichai Hall.

Royal Resting Places

The next structure along to the west is **Chakri-Mahasprasad Hall**, once the royal harem. Although British-designed, Siamese towers were added at the request of concerned court elders, who wanted the building to look traditional, and not too European. The tallest, central spire holds the ashes of the Chakri kings, the shorter spires on either side contain those of the princes.

West again is the serene **Dusit Hall**. This funerary hall, modelled on the one at Ayutthaya (► 72–74), is still used for members of the royal family when they are lying in state.

At the end of your visit, make the **Wat Phra Kaeo Museum**, which houses a collection of gifts left for the Emerald Buddha, your final stop (► 46).

TAKING A BREAK

Sip a chilled coconut water on the usually uncrowded wooden veranda of the **café** next to the Wat Phra Kaeo Museum.

✚ 200 A3 ✉ Naphralan Road ☎ 02 623 500 and 02 222 0034; www.palaces.thai.net ⊘ Daily 8:30–3:30 💷 Expensive 🚌 8, 12

A detail of a golden Buddha set before the temple of Wat Phra Kaeo

GRAND PALACE AND WAT PHRA KAEO: INSIDE INFO

Top tips The best time to visit is the **early morning**, when the heat and crowds are at their most bearable.

■ Do not wear **clothes** that reveal arms or legs, or even casual clothes or footwear like vests, shorts, sarongs, mini-skirts, slip-on sandals or flip-flops. It is considered disrespectful and you will be refused admittance. You may, however, be able to borrow suitable attire from the office at the entrance.

■ Consider taking one of the **English-language guided tours** (four times a day between 10am and 2pm; 100 baht) to learn about the history of the many buildings. A credit card or passport is required as deposit for the tape recorder and headphones.

■ The **entrance fee** includes entry to the Vimanmek Teak Palace (➤ 53), the Royal Thai Decorations and Coins Pavilion in the palace grounds, and a brochure which covers the main buildings.

Hidden gem Most visitors miss the **Wat Phra Kaeo Museum**, tucked away at the opposite end of the complex. Although the exhibits are not of major interest, it offers an oasis of cool away from the Grand Palace crowds and is the perfect antidote to all the glitz. Pad barefoot on polished wooden floors among paraphernalia dedicated as offerings to the Emerald Buddha. This endearing collection of gifts includes porcelain from Europe, an inlaid mother-of-pearl royal couch and cabinets of brightly coloured Buddha images, as well as tools and tweezers used in repairs.

2 Wat Po

This superlative royal monastery is not only the city's largest and oldest but also contains the country's longest reclining Buddha. Dotted with *chedis*, pagodas and *stupas* (▶ 8–9 and 194), this walled complex was built during the reigns of King Rama I and King Rama III by the best craftsmen in the land.

Established as the country's first centre of education and Thai arts, it continues the role to this day as a living complex peopled with masseuses, astrologers and schoolchildren. At the same time, it is a peaceful oasis of beautifully landscaped areas with waterfalls, rock gardens, stone animals and tree-filled courtyards.

The most interesting sights are clustered around the northern section of the monastery. From the Thai Wang Road entrance, make the **Reclining Buddha** your first stop. The massive 46m-long (150 foot) Buddha looks as if it has been squeezed into the *viharn* (▶ 9 and 194). Gleaming gold leaf covers the stuccoed brick statue of the dying Buddha who is just about to enter Nirvana, and exquisite murals cover the walls. Make sure you walk all the way around the figure to see its feet, which are inlaid with mother-of-pearl, showing the 108 symbols of enlightenment.

The Reclining Buddha gleams with gold leaf

Leaving through the same door that you entered, walk past the waterfall on your right and between the two guarding "**rock giants**". There are fortune-tellers and a souvenir kiosk/snack bar on the left.

Turn right where **four towering pagodas** decorated with glazed tiling and mosaics commemorate the first kings of the Chakri dynasty, founded in 1782.

On the left is the main **chapel of Phra Uposatha**, at the heart of the monastery, surrounded by a marble wall with eight sheltered gates and stone carvings of natural scenes. Balustrades with 152 reliefs of the Hindu epic the *Ramayana* (a Sanskrit poem regarded as sacred by the Hindus) were taken from the ruins at Ayutthaya; rubbings from the panels are sold at the temple and throughout Thailand. Walk a quarter of the way around the cloisters to the **Contorted Hermit Mount** to enter. It is covered with stone statues of exercising hermits, which were used to teach illiterate people about illnesses and massage methods. Inside is a seated Buddha in the position of meditation (► 15). Cloisters all the way around display hundreds of gold-leaf Buddha images in glass frames as well as Buddhist poems.

At the southern end of the monastery, a **massage school** functions as the national headquarters for Thai massage and medicine. If you only have one massage in Thailand, this is the place to have it. Traditional Thai massage is always applied with the recipient fully clothed, no appointment is necessary.

With saffron-coloured umbrella to match his robes, a Buddhist monk crosses the sunny courtyard at Wat Po

TAKING A BREAK

There is a small **snack bar** in the temple compound, which is fine for a cold drink.

✚ 200 B3 ✉ Sanam Chai Road and Maharaj Road ☎ 02 222 0933 🕑 Daily 9–5 💰 Inexpensive 🚌 6, 8, 12

WAT PO: INSIDE INFO

Top tips Dress **respectfully** and cover up, although you can borrow a wrap to see the Reclining Buddha.
- Visitors are also requested to act **calmly and politely**.
- The **guidebook** for sale inside the Reclining Buddha chapel and at the entrance is beautifully produced, has a good map and unusually lively text.
- **No entrance** is permitted between noon and 1pm.

Ones to miss The crocodile pond and the belfry are not worth seeking out.

3 Chao Phraya River

The majestic waters of the "River of Kings" that snake their way through the city, provide both a fascinating perspective on the city and a peaceful thoroughfare. The river, as well as many smaller canals, or *khlongs*, gave Bangkok the title "Venice of the East". Colourful floating markets cruise the waterway and luxury hotels and ancient temples line its banks. A concentration of major attractions from the National Museum and the Grand Palace down to Wat Po and Wat Arun form a "royal mile", all serviced by convenient pier stops.

Longtail boats on the Chao Phraya sail past Wat Arun

Two river boat services ply up and down the Chao Phraya: the public commuter service, crowded but very cheap, and the Chao Phraya Express Boat company's tourist line (► 50), which offers a day's 75 baht ticket allowing you to jump off or jump on at any point. A guide aboard every boat explains the sights en route. Industrial tugs, rice barges and longtail boats (narrow boats with high-powered engines attached by a pole or "tail") buzz along the waters, while slow river ferries zigzag from bank to bank.

An hour loop on a chartered longtail boat from **Tha Chang**, the pier near to the Grand Palace, costs around 400 baht. It passes the Royal Barge Museum and Wat Arun, but you will need to arrange in advance if you want to visit either of these attractions. Your boat driver may stop to buy a kebab from another vessel or even point out a stalking iguana, but these tours are not officially guided. Relax and catch a glimpse of waterside life, basic canalside homes and upmarket compounds, cruise past tree-lined banks and brightly coloured boats festooned with flowers, and catch glimpses into back gardens dotted with spirit houses (➤ 6–7).

When darkness falls, the river sparkles with the reflections of the many bankside illuminations. An **evening cruise** is the best way to see the lights of **Wat Arun** (open 7:30–5:30), and **Rama IX Bridge**, the longest single-span suspension bridge in the world.

TAKING A BREAK

Both dinner and sunset cocktail cruises are offered by riverside hotels like the **Mandarin Oriental** (tel: 02 659 9000, ➤ 54) and the **Marriott Resort and Spa** (tel: 02 476 0022).

Below: Ferry boats operate a regular service on the river

✚ 200 C2

CHAO PHRAYA RIVER: INSIDE INFO

Top tips Two river-boat lines operate on the Chao Praya River. The cheaper of them is the regular public service.

■ Boats are frequent (about every 15 minutes) but crowded.

■ For a little more money (100 baht) you can buy a ticket that allows you to use the Chao Praya Express Boat company service (tel: 02 623 6001/2/3) from 9:30am to 3pm, jumping on and off at any of the stops en route. The boats have a guide aboard and the ticket includes a useful map of the river and its attractions.

■ Longtail boat operators also ply for business, particularly at the Pra Athit pier, next to the Saphan Taksin Skytrain station. They demand sometimes ridiculously inflated prices, so be sure to bargain keenly.

❹ Chatuchak Market

This mammoth market, with more than 6,000 stalls, is a fascinating collection of everything from fighting cocks and poodle-grooming to towering plants and fake flowers. Thailand's best venue for a shopping spree makes for a weekend outing (it's only open on Saturday and Sunday) where you can wander among octagenarian violinists, young buskers and locals looking for the latest in interior decor.

Bright young things hunt for the latest fashions

Arrive at around 9am to beat the crowds. If you are a serious shopper, **Nancy Chandler's Map of Bangkok** (available from souvenir shops in tourist areas) shows all the stalls in detail. The clock tower in the centre is a good landmark and serves as a popular meeting point.

Types of goods for sale are grouped together in sections, each with their own distinct personality.

The "**Dream Section**" (indicated by a large sign) has toilets, restaurants, upmarket household goods, clothes stalls and cash dispensers. This is a good place to go if the noisy local flavour gets too much. Otherwise there are stalls selling cheaper household goods, second-hand trainers, traditional lacquerware, antiques and yoghurt fruitshakes. You will probably find an area you feel particularly at home in, whether you immerse yourself in the rattan goods and floating candles or gawp at the bizarre selection of pets which includes everything from beetles to iguanas (many imported illegally). Bargain, but politely.

TAKING A BREAK
The best area of the market to get something to eat is in the **Dream Section**, which has plenty of air-conditioned places.

🚩 201 off F5 ✉ Thanon Phahonyothin 🕐 Weekends 8–6 💷 Free 🚍 2, 3, 9, 10, 13; Skytrain and MRT: Mo Chit, Chatuchak Park

At Your Leisure

Buddhaisawan Chapel at the National Museum, Bangkok

5 National Museum

This delightful national institution, with its spacious lawns and separate buildings, was originally a palace. A good map with a brief guide is given free with the entrance fee. The first room near the entrance to the museum contains grand funeral chariots that knock spots off the average carriage of European royalty. The most ornate dates back to the late 18th century and was last used in 1985 for the queen of King Rama VII. The museum's café is situated next door to this room and, although the fare is unsophisticated, it can be more relaxing than the hectic food scene found outside the museum on the way to the pier.

Don't miss the Red House, once the private living quarters of Queen Sri Suriye, sister of King Rama I. Other highlights of the museum are the Elephant Armoury, a selection of articles from the Grand Palace theatre and the games room. Be sure, also, to visit the Buddhaisawan Chapel, home to the revered Phra Sihing Buddha and an outstanding set of 200-year-old murals.

A visit could be combined with the National Gallery near by (4 Chao-Fa Road), which has an interesting collection of Thai art. Guided tours in English on Wednesday and Thursday at 9:30am focus on specific aspects of the museum and are very worthwhile.

🚻 200 A4 ✉ Thanon Naphrathat ☎ 02 224 1333; www.thailandmuseum.com ⏰ Wed–Sun 9–4 💷 Inexpensive 🚌 3, 6, 38; River Express: Tha Chang

6 Khao San Road

The street circus that is Khao San Road attracts tourists from around the world. Squeezed into a strip of under a kilometre are stalls three-deep selling clothes, food and souvenirs, as well as a maze of streets with cramped, basic travellers' accommodation. Although it is very much youth and budget orientated and crawling with backpackers, Khao San Road is always lively and friendly and offers a place to relax when frantic Bangkok gets a bit too much.

This is where to come for an English breakfast, restaurants showing American films and English and other language books. The city's cheapest internet connections are found here and travel agents fight for attention. Towards the beginning of the evening the music cranks up and the street becomes a riot of neon. Tourists eat banana pancakes in the street pursued by a constant parade of *tuk-tuks* and vendors.

🕂 200 B4

7 Vimanmek Teak Palace

This sumptuous royal mansion is the largest golden teak building in the world, with more than 80 separate rooms. It was built by Rama V, King Chulalongkorn in 1868 as a summer retreat on Ko Si Chang island and then was moved here piece by piece in 1910. A guided tour (included in the entrance fee) takes you around the interior, with its European influences.

Also in the compound of this Dusit palace is a building housing a collection of crafts donated by Queen Sirikit, the present queen, and another displaying King Bhumibol's photography. Traditional Thai dancing is performed in the grounds daily at 10:30am and 2pm. The same dress rules apply here as at the Grand Palace (➤ 46).

🕂 200 C5 ✉ Thanon Ratchawithi ☎ 02 628 6300/9; www.vimanmek.com 🕓 Daily 9:30–4 (guided tour only every 30 minutes, last tour 3:15) 💷 Moderate (free with a Grand Palace ticket) 🚊 3 or 10

8 Jim Thompson's House

Jim Thompson, an American architect, adventurer and entrepreneur, and Thailand's most famous expatriate, is credited with single-handedly reviving the country's ancient tradition of silk-weaving. His home is actually six teak houses (most over 200 years old), which he reconstructed on this canalside site around a tropical garden and flower-filled courtyard, and then crammed with antiques. The highly informative compulsory tour tells how he loyally followed traditional Thai building practices, even consulting an

The house of adventurer Jim Thompson is made from six traditional teak houses

The Mandarin Oriental hotel is set in lush, tropical gardens

CITY SANCTUARIES
The secret to surviving hot and hectic Bangkok is to make regular escapes to oases of cool and calm.
■ **Chao Phraya River** (➤ 49–50).
■ High tea at the luxurious **Mandarin Oriental** hotel (➤ 54).
■ **Lumphini Park's** lake and lawns, the city's lung and very popular with the locals. Go early at around 7am to see Chinese practising t'ai chi, or take a boat or a picnic.
■ The **Ice Skating Rink**, eigth floor of the CentralWorld, where you can watch professionals and enjoy the cooling temperatures, or take to the ice yourself on rented skates.

---

astrologer for an auspicious date to move in.

Jim Thompson disappeared in Malaysia's Cameron Highlands in 1967 under mysterious circumstances; several conspiracy theories are still alive today. One says he was eaten by a tiger, another that American intelligence agents killed him. The latest theory is that he was run over by a truck and then buried by the frightened driver.

🔢 201 D3 ✉ 6 Soi Kasemsan 2, Thanon Rama I ☎ 02 216 7368; www.jimthompsonhouse.com ⏰ Daily 9–5 (tours every 45 minutes, last tour 4:30) 🎟 Moderate 🚆 Skytrain: Siam Square

❾ Patpong

Crammed into four tiny streets, or *sois*, Patpong is Bangkok's notorious red-light district – a hotbed of go-go bars and sex shows that are sadly pathetic rather than erotic. If you are tempted to go into a bar, check the prices of drinks first – you may be charged an extortionate rate.

Patpong, however, is also a lively area where locals socialise and there's a popular night market frequented by tourists who are thrust menu cards detailing a variety of sex acts on offer. There are a handful of good restaurants (Barbican and Roma) and international designer stores. Food outlets such as KFC and Starbucks are here if you need to seek refuge in anonymous chains.

🔢 201 E2 ✉ Between Thanon Silom and Suriwong

❿ Mandarin Oriental

This riverside hotel was set up by the founders of the Singapore Raffles Hotel in 1876. It is still considered one of the best hotels in the world, offering colonial-style luxury at a high price. It's a great place to go for tea or a drink. The Authors' Lounge is named after world-famous authors such as Somerset Maugham, Joseph Conrad and even Barbara Cartland, who made the hotel their temporary home. Traditional English high tea (sandwiches, cakes, biscuits and tea) is served in the lounge among potted palms and wicker furniture.

Much more than just a hotel, it has a regular cultural programme, a Thai cookery course and its own floating restaurant.

➕ 200 C1 ✉ 48 Oriental Avenue, off Thanon Charoen Krung ☎ 02 659 9000; www.mandarinoriental.com 💰 Expensive 🚇 Skytrain: Saphan Taksin; River Express: Oriental

🔟 Chinatown

This 200-year-old trading site with tiny, characterful streets crammed with exotic goods and dotted with temples is an atmospheric place for wandering (➤ 174–176). Pedestrianised, stall-filled Sampeng Lane (Soi Wanit) is its focus, with the Indian Market, selling mostly fabrics, at the northern end. Wat Leng Noi Yi is the most interesting of the area's several temples, full of Chinese deities as well as a workshop making paper cars, fridges and other household representations for funerals – the Chinese burn these symbols of material wealth to ensure prosperity for their dead loved ones.

➕ 200 C2 🚇 River Express: Tha Ratchawong

BANGKOK FOR KIDS

- Take a ride on a *tuk-tuk*, river boat or the Skytrain.
- Visit **Dusit Zoo** (Thanon Rama V, open daily 8–6, inexpensive), with its playground and boats on a lake – avoid going on Sunday when it can get crowded.
- If you are going to the **Vimanmek Teak Palace** (➤ 53) call in at the small **Elephant Museum** in the palace grounds.
- Watch cobras being milked at the **Snake Farm** (Thanon Rama IV and Henri Dunant, tel: 02 252 0161; open Mon–Fri 8:30–4, Sat–Sun 8:30–noon, moderate).
- Go on a treasure hunt through **Chinatown** (➤ 174–176).

Bustling Chinatown is full of atmosphere, exotic smells and colourful streets

Where to...
Stay

Prices
Expect to pay per double room per night:
£ under 2,000 baht   ££ 2,000–5,000 baht   £££ over 5,000 baht

A-One Inn £

You've got the best of both worlds with this upmarket guest house. It's situated in a quiet lane, but in the heart of Bangkok's busiest shopping district. The rooms are comfortable, with air-conditioning and satellite TV. The café here is a good place to relax after a hot day on the busy streets. The friendly staff create a family atmosphere. A-One is within walking distance of Siam Square, the CentralWorld complex and Jim Thompson's House (▶ 53–54).

➕ 201 E3 ⊠ 25/13 Soi Kasem San 1, Thanon Rama I, 30 ☎ 02 215 3029; www.aoneinn.com 🚇 Siam

Asia Bangkok ££

This hotel is near the Siam Discovery Centre, Siam Square and the CentralWorld. Facilities include a sauna, health club and two swimming pools. Rooms are tastefully decorated, with marble bathrooms. What sets the Asia apart from other moderately priced hotels are its Vietnamese, Chinese and Brazilian restaurants. The Brazilian Rio Grill, a typical *churrascaria*, offering red and white meat grilled on skewers, is unique in Bangkok.

➕ 201 E3 ⊠ 296 Thanon Phayathai ☎ 02 215 0808; www.asiahotel.co.th 🚇 Ratchathewi

Beaufort Sukhothai £££

The Beaufort Sukhothai is an exquisite luxury hotel, with much of its decor inspired by the arts and crafts of Thailand's one-time capital, Sukhothai (▶ 75–77). Although on one of Bangkok's busiest roads, the hotel is set well back and provides a quiet oasis. All rooms and suites are decorated with beautiful Thai silks, teak furniture and artefacts you'd usually expect to find only in museums. The teak-floored bathrooms are enormous. Internet access is available from all rooms. The hotel's shopping arcade features outlets specialising in Thai paintings, sculptures and wood-carving. The Sukhothai also has the benefit of housing two of Bangkok's top restaurants, the sumptuous Celadon (▶ 58–59), and the Italian La Scala.

➕ 201 E1 ⊠ 13/3 Thanon Sathorn Tai ☎ 02 287 0222; www.sukhothai.com 🚇 Sala Daeng (the subway and Skytrain stations are some distance; a taxi is the best option)

Dusit Thani £££

The flagship of the Dusit hotel group, this was Bangkok's first high-rise hotel. It is in the heart of the Silom Road business district and close to the main nightlife area, Patpong (▶ 54). The rooms are sumptuous, with much use made of silk and other Thai fabrics, as well as teak furniture. The Dusit is famous for its restaurants, of which there are seven in all, and two bars. The rooftop D'Sens (French) restaurant has panoramic views of the Bangkok skyline and overlooks the city's premier park, Lumphini. Other unusual facilities include an outdoor driving range, so don't forget your golf clubs.

➕ 201 E2 ⊠ 946 Thanon Rama IV ☎ 02 236 9999; www.dusit.com 🚇 Sala Daeng

The Eugenia £££

Close to the heart of the Sukhumvit, but offering tranquillity and elegance, this truly boutique hotel has only 12 bedrooms (with four-poster beds). The Eugenia is built in the style of a late 19th-century colonial house, complete with swaying palms and period furnishings that include copper baths and vintage light switches. There is also a pool, a restaurant for fine dining, afternoon tea service and a comfortable lounge for drinks. Airport transfers are by one of the hotel's old Jaguars or Mercedes Benzes.

🏠 201 off F3 🖂 267 Soi Sukhumvit 31
📞 02 259 9017; www.theeugenia.com
🚇 Sukhumvit

Four Seasons £££

From the fabulous foyer to the picture-perfect rooms, the Four Seasons oozes class and an old-fashioned oriental charm.
Afternoon tea is an experience not to be missed. Three of Bangkok's finest restaurants are within the hotel confines, the Spice Market (Thai, ▲ 60), Biscotti (Italian) and Shintaro (Japanese). Amenities include aerobics, ballroom dancing,

yoga and an excellent spa. Its central location, facing the Royal Bangkok Sports Club, is perfect for shopping trips to the CentralWorld and a visit to the Erawan Shrine, one of Bangkok's best-known religious symbols (▲ 6).

🏠 201 E2 🖂 155 Thanon Ratchadamri
📞 02 250 1000; www.fourseasons.com
🚇 Ratchadamri

Royal ££

The Royal, one of Bangkok's oldest, most venerable hotels, is a bargain. It is situated on Ratanakosin Island, Bangkok's historical heart, close to the Grand Palace (▲ 44–46) and the National Museum (▲ 52) and Wat Po (▲ 47–48). The rooms are comfortable. Restaurants are of standard quality for a hotel of this rating and there is a good swimming pool. What sets the place apart is its great location.

🏠 200 B3 🖂 2 Thanon Ratchadamnoen Klang 📞 02 222 9111 🚇 No subway or Skytrain station near by; it is best to take a taxi

Shangri-La £££

A huge, luxury, riverside property, and one of Bangkok's three best hotels, the Shangri-La is regularly voted on to the list of the world's finest hotels. High tea (sandwiches, cakes, biscuits and tea) is served every afternoon in the foyer-lounge. Rooms are large, with great views of the busy river below. The beautifully landscaped gardens are a breath of fresh air after Bangkok's crowded streets.

🏠 200 C1 🖂 89 Soi Wat Suan Plu, Thanon Charoen Krung 📞 02 236 7777; www.shangri-la.com 🚇 Saphan Taksin

Sukhumvit 11 £

When it comes to budget-priced accommodation, it is hard to beat this delightful retreat close to Sukhumvit Road. It is tucked away down Soi 11 (enter the soi just opposite the Ambassador Hotel) and offers a range of rooms with either shared bathroom and shower or private facilities. There are four levels to the building and no lift.

It is advisable to book well in advance because this guest house is deservedly popular.

🏠 201 off F3 🖂 1/33 Soi Sukhumvit 11
📞 02 253 5927; www.suk11.com 🚇 Nana

Swissotel Nai Lert Park £££

This luxury hotel is set in extensive and beautiful gardens. It has its own fertility shrine constructed to honour the female spirit that supposedly resides in the old banyan tree in the hotel grounds. Today people, mostly women, come to make offerings of carved wooden and stone phalluses to aid fertility. The grounds contain a large swimming pool, attractive Thai pavilions, or *sala*, and pretty ornamental bridges. All rooms have their own private balcony either overlooking the gardens or the Bangkok skyline. Other facilities include the excellent Amrita Fitness Club and Spa.

🏠 201 F2 🖂 2 Wireless Road (Thanon Witthayu) 📞 02 253 0123; www.swissotel.com 🚇 Ploenchit

Where to...
Eat and Drink

Prices
Expect to pay per person for a three-course meal, excluding drinks and service:
£ under 300 baht   **££** 300–600 baht   **£££** over 600 baht

Baan Khanitha ££–£££

Spicy but exquisite Thai cuisine with a terrific choice of salads is on the menu here. Try the spiky pomelo salad with shrimps and chicken. Seafood dishes are specialities of the restaurant, and the curries are delicious. Vegetarians will not be disappointed, though, as there are also plenty of meat-free choices. There is a small garden for alfresco dining on cool evenings but the interior is comfortable and agreeably furnished.

➕ 201 off F3 ✉ 36/1 Sukhumvit Soi 23 ☎ 02 258 4128 🕐 Daily 11–2, 6–11 🚇 Sukhumvit

Bei Otto £££

Established in 1984, this German restaurant with a *bierhaus*, a delicatessen and its own bakery, is one of Bangkok's oldest international restaurants. Popular dishes include Bavarian grilled pork knuckle with potato dumplings and *sauerkraut*, the meat platter *wiener schnitzel* and a selection of cakes. Part of the pleasure of eating here is the knowledge that much of the food is home-made. As you would expect, Bei Otto carries a fine selection of German wines and beers.

Apart from the German restaurant, the premises also houses a good European restaurant serving many international dishes such as pasta, steak and chips, roast beef and similar dishes.

➕ 201 off F3 ✉ 1 Sukhumvit Soi 20 ☎ 02 260 0892; www.beiotto.com 🕐 Daily 11am–1am, delicatessen 7am–midnight 🚇 Asoke

Bourbon Street ££

Bangkok ought to be one of the last cities in the world that you'd expect to find Cajun-Creole cooking, but Bourbon Street has been turning out great dishes for more than 15 years. There's gumbo, blackened red fish, three different choices of jambalaya, barbecued baby back pork ribs and Cajun boiled crawfish, to name just a few. Split into two sections, the bar offers sports on TV, the restaurant a more relaxed atmosphere. On Tuesday nights there's a Mexican buffet.

➕ 201 off F3 ✉ 29 Sukhumvit Soi 22, Washington Square ☎ 02 259 0328; www.bourbonstbkk.com 🕐 Daily 7am–1am 🚇 Phrom Phong

Cabbages and Condoms ££

A great value-for-money place with a serious underlying theme, this particular branch of the chain of Thai restaurants, owned by family-planning campaigner Mechai Viravaidya, was set up in 1986. Furnishings include flower arrangements made from condoms and a carpet embellished with a condom design. The food is generally excellent, with the family-planning theme extending to some of the names of dishes. Why not try the spicy condom salad? The beer garden outside is a great place to sit and drink *bier sot* (draught beer). On leaving, instead of an after-dinner mint, you get a condom.

➕ 201 off F3 ✉ 6 Sukhumvit Soi 12 ☎ 02 229 4611; www.cabbagesandcondoms.co.th 🕐 Daily 11–10 🚇 Asoke

Celadon £££

Set amid a lotus-filled pond, Celadon is another classic Thai restaurant. Dine either in the *sala*, where the decor has a very contemporary Thai feel, or the beautiful garden. The surroundings are calm, quiet and elegant for busy downtown Sathorn. Specialities such as chicken in coconut and *galingal* (ginger) soup, deep-fried *garoupa* (a white fish popular in Southeast Asia) with dry curry, and chicken grilled in screwpine leaves (from the pandanus tree) prove the sophistication of Thai cuisine. Excellent Thai-style salads include banana blossom salad with shredded chicken and prawn.

➕ 201 E1 ⊠ Sukhothai Hotel, 13/3 Thanon Sathorn Tai ☎ 02 287 0222 ⓦ Daily 11:30–2:30, 6:30–10:30

D'Sens £££

Although D'Sens cannot boast an open-air setting like its competitors, the huge advantage of this restaurant is the quality of the food. The snails are from Burgundy, lobster is from Maine, scallops are from Japan, and there is New Zealand lamb – whatever you eat, excellence is assured. The service is

impeccable. This is the best French restaurant in Thailand.

➕ 201 E2 ⊠ Dusit Thani Hotel, Thanon Rama IV ☎ 02 200 9000 ⓦ Mon–Fri 11:30–2:30, 6:30–10, Sat 6:30pm–10pm ⓡ Sala Daeng

Le Dalat ££

A Bangkok fixture, much copied, but never outdone, this is still the place for the best Vietnamese food in Thailand. Approached by a pretty tree-lined pathway, the restaurant is on two levels. The interior has a relaxed feel with some lovely bamboo touches. *Cha ca* (barbecued fish) is a favourite, and if you've never eaten Vietnamese food before, try the house dish, grilled meatballs with slivers of garlic, mango, chilli, ginger and star fruit. The staff are extremely friendly and they'll always go out of their way to help you understand and find your way around the menu.

➕ 201 off F3 ⊠ 14 Sukhumvit Soi 23 ☎ 02 261 7967 ⓦ Daily 11:30–2:30, 6–10 ⓡ Asoke

lobster, goose liver salad and *osso bucco d'agnello* (braised lamb shank). Desserts are wonderful and include a delicious yoghurt and honey mousse, and a tempting *tiramisu* of outstanding quality. The wine list features Italian wines.

➕ 201 F3 ⊠ 34/1 Soi Tonson, Thanon Ploenchit ☎ 02 252 1619; www.giannibkk.com ⓦ Daily noon–2:30, 6–11 ⓡ Ploenchit

Himali Cha Cha and Son ££

There are a number of good-quality Indian restaurants in Bangkok, but few with such an interesting background as this establishment. The original chef and proprietor, the late Cha Cha, worked for Lord Louis Mountbatten in the dog days of the British Raj and then for various Indian ambassadors around the world. His son has now assumed his mantle and Cha Cha's original restaurant can still be found just off Thanon Charoen Krung. All dishes are based on Cha Cha's recipes and are north Indian or

Food Loft £

This is a terrific place to sit down for a meal or a drink after a heavy shopping stint in the Central Childom department store. Customers collect a bar-coded card at the entrance and this is used to record the dishes and drinks you consume; pay on departure at the checkout desk. There is an amazing range of food on offer, both European and Asian, and a decidedly stylish lounge area for relaxing with a drink before or after your meal.

➕ 201 F3 ⊠ 7 Central Childom, Thanon Ploenchit ☎ 02 655 7777 ⓦ Daily 10–9 ⓡ Chit Lom

Gianni's £££

At Gianni's you can enjoy some of the finest Italian food in Bangkok, served in a quiet, modern environment. Proprietor Gianni Favri has managed to re-create a perfect little bit of Italy. The food is simple but excellent, with such delicacies as angel-hair pasta with

Moghul in style. Traditional Indian drinks are served here, including Kingfisher Indian lager.

🚏 201 off F3 ⊠ 2 Sukhumvit Soi 31, Thanon Sukhumvit ☎ 02 259 6677; www.himalichacha.com ⏰ Daily 11–3.30, 6–10.30 🚇 Phrom Phong

Lemongrass ££

This long-established and popular restaurant serves an excellent mix of well-known authentic Thai regional dishes in an elegant old wooden house. The house itself is filled with antique furniture and various interesting knick-knacks, all creating a rather eccentric mix. Look on the menu for *kai yang phak panaeng* (sweet and spicy southern-style grilled chicken) and sun-dried salted fish, both dishes well worth trying. The wine list is a little limited, but Lemongrass does have rather a good selection of drinkable French wines.

🚏 201 off F3 ⊠ 5/1 Sukhumvit Soi 24, Thanon Sukhumvit ☎ 02 258 8637 ⏰ Daily 11–2, 6–11 🚇 Phrom Phong

Spice Market £££

This superb Thai restaurant, decorated in the style of an old Thai spice shop, is one of Bangkok's finest. Rattan furniture and marble-topped tables add to the old-time ambience. Favourite dishes include a magnificent crispy catfish and green mango salad and crispy soft-shell crab in peppercorn.

🚏 201 E2 ⊠ Four Seasons Hotel, 155 Thanon Ratchadamri ☎ 02 126 8866 ⏰ Daily 11:30–2:30, 6–10:30 🚇 Ratchadamri

Supatra River House ££

This was originally the home of Khunying Supatra Singholaga, the founder of the Bangkok River Express boat service, which continues to ferry thousands of people up and down the Chao Phraya River every day (▶ 49–50). It is built in a classical Thai style and has a fabulous view of the Grand Palace (▶ 44–46). Upstairs is an interesting family museum. The menu is authentic Thai, with dishes such as fried scallops with chilli, sun-dried freshwater fish and green mango salad.

🚏 200 A3 ⊠ 266 Soi Wat Rakhang, Thanon Arun Amarin ☎ 02 411 0305; www.supatrariverhouse.net ⏰ Daily 11:30–2; 5:30–11 🚇 River Express: Wang Lang

Vientiane Kitchen £

If you want to try Isaan (northeastern Thai) and Lao food, it's hard to beat this place. Isaan food is generally simple and spicy. The most famous dishes on the menu include *somtam* (papaya salad with fish sauce, garlic, chilli peppers and peanuts) and *larb* (spiced minced meat) served with salad and a side plate of raw vegetables. This is often eaten with *kai yang* (grilled chicken). Another delicacy unlikely to appeal to any but the most adventurous visitor is *nam phrik mot som* (red ant egg dip). All these dishes are traditionally eaten with *khao niaw* (sticky rice), which is served in small woven bamboo baskets and eaten by hand.

Tables surround a large tree and a traditional Isaan musical group does the entertaining.

🚏 201 off F3 ⊠ 8 Soi 36 Thanon Sukhumvit ☎ 02 258 6171; www.vientiane-kitchen.com ⏰ Daily noon–midnight 🚇 Thong Lo

Whole Earth ££

Open for more than 20 years, the Whole Earth regards itself as Bangkok's finest and oldest vegetarian restaurant. In the upstairs section you eat sitting cross-legged on comfortable cushions at low tables. There are a few dishes for non-vegetarians, although the real treats are the mix of Indian and Thai vegetarian dishes. Specialities include Chinese soup with seaweed and black mushrooms, and roasted aubergine and vegetarian *satay*. Wine is available, but it's worth trying the fragrant vegetable and herbal drinks on offer.

🚏 201 F3 ⊠ 93/3 Soi Lang Suan, Thanon Ploenchit ☎ 02 252 5574 ⏰ Daily 11:30–2, 5:30–10:30 🚇 Chitlom

Where to...
Shop

TRADITIONAL CRAFTS

Although Bangkok is the main outlet for antiques and crafts, few are actually produced in the city.

For Burmese wall hangings, Indian and Nepalese jewellery, Balinese woodcarvings and many local products try **Krishna's Asian Treasures** (corner Soi 11 Thanon Sukhumvit, tel: 02 253 7693). **Erawan Antiques** (148/9 Thanon Surawong) sells Buddhist and Hindu religious artefacts, and also some very beautiful antique furniture. The government-run craft store, **Narayana Phand** (127 Thanon Ratchadamri, near CentralWorld), sells a vast range.

A number of antiques and craft outlets are at **River City Shopping Complex** (23 Trok Rongnamkaeng,

Thanon Yotha, near the Royal Orchid Sheraton Hotel), a huge Aladdin's Cave of treasures.

More affordable than glitzy River City, **Silom Village Trade Centre** is a complex of shops at the bottom end of Silom Road, within walking distance of Surasak station and Central Pier, selling silk, jewellery, souvenirs and gifts.

SILK

The **Jim Thompson Silk Shop** (9 Thanon Surawong, tel: 02 632 8100) is perhaps the best place for silk in town, with high-quality clothing and household accessories. **Shinawatra** (Sukhumvit Soi 23, tel: 02 258 0295) offers silk and other textile products. It also has two shops in Chiang Mai.

Traditional silk-weaving methods are in evidence at the classy **Patrizia Thai Silk Design Co** (119/3 Suriwong Road, tel: 02 238 3733). Suits and dresses can be made to measure.

MARKETS

In the north of the city, **Chatuchak Market** (▶ 51, also known as the Weekend Market) at the southern end of Chatuchak Park, off Phahonyothin Road, is a delight to stroll around. It sells everything from exotic fresh vegetables to Thai musical instruments.

Suan Lum Night Market (Thanon Witthayu) is a vast tourist bazaar retailing crafts, textiles and souvenirs, and makes for an enjoyable evening's stroll.

If you're looking for clothes, including designer items, try **Pratunam Market** (at the junction of Phetburi Road and Ratchaprarop Road). For the archetypal Southeast Asian market head for **Pak Khlong Talaat** (Maharat Road, near the Memorial Bridge), where fresh flowers and vegetables are on sale 24 hours a day.

MALLS/DEPARTMENT STORES

Thailand's leading department store chain, **Central**, has six outlets in Bangkok, the largest of which are in the main tourist areas of Silom and Thanon Ploenchit. The stores have stylish bars, cafes and cinemas, as well as a vast range of goods.

The **Siam Discovery Centre** (Thanon Rama 1) offers floor upon floor of designer shops. Further along Thanon Ratchadamri stands the huge **CentralWorld** (Thanon Ratchadamri). There's a duty free shop on its seventh floor, open from 10am–9pm. Opposite CentralWorld, **Gaysorn Plaza** (corner of Thanon Ratchadamri and Ploenchit) has excellent household accessories shops, with unique contemporary Thai-style items.

Where to...
Be Entertained

INFORMATION

There are several free **listings magazines**, available at most bookshops in the city every month. Also try online: www.bangkoktonight.com.

CINEMA

Many of the large shopping malls have multiplex screens, all air-conditioned and very comfortable. Seats are around 100–180 baht and the best place to check what is on, where and when is www.movieseer.com. Most movies are shown in their original language with Thai subtitles. The **Major Cineplex CentralWorld** (Floor 7, Thanon Ratchadamri, tel: 02 255 6565) is centrally located and shows a wide variety of films. For art-house European films, usually shown with English subtitles, see what is on at **Alliance Française** (29 Thanon Sathorn Tai Tai, tel: 02 670 4200; www.alliance-francaise.or.th) and the **Goethe Institut** (18/1 Soi Goethe, tel: 02 287 0942).

THEATRE

The **National Theatre** (2 Thanon Rachini Phra Nakhon, tel: 02 224 1342) has regular traditional performances of *khŏn*, a formal masked dance drama, and *lákhon*, a more general form of dance.

MUSIC

The **Saxophone Pub** (3/8 Victory Monument, Thanon Phayathai, tel: 02 246 5472), offering mainly jazz, is one of the oldest and most popular places, with different bands each night.

A fun night out featuring rock 'n' roll bands can be had at the **Titanium Ice Bar** (Sukhumvit Soi 22, tel: 02 258 3758; www.titaniumbangkok.com) while the **Raintree Bar** (Soi Ruamjit, Rang Nam Road, tel: 02 245 7230; www.raintreepub.com) is an old favourite that has been around for close to 20 years. **Brick Bar** (265 Khao San Road, tel: 02 629 4477), at the rear of the Buddy Lodge shopping arcade, is popular with young revellers. The drinks are not expensive; there is an entrance charge at weekends. The **Common Ground** (59 Samsen Road, tel: 08 9221 7835) has some interesting bands, and there are also plenty of other places with music in the vicinity. Another road with bars with live music is Sarasin Road near Lumphini Park. Here you will find **Brown Sugar** (tel: 02 250 1826), packed every night and especially good fun on Sunday nights.

NIGHTLIFE

Currently the hottest spots in town are the upmarket and trendy **Bed Supper Club** (26 Sukhumvit Soi 11, tel: 02 651 3537) and **Q-Bar** (34 Sukhumvit Soi 11, tel: 02 252 3274). Young Thais and backpackers love the castle-like **The Club** (123 Khao San Road, tel: 02 629 1010). Also worth checking is **P35** (109 Phetchaburi Soi 35, tel: 02 651 6615; www.petburi35.com; daily from 10pm); the main dance floor is at ground level.

CABARET

Calypso Cabaret (Asia Hotel, 296 Thanon Phayathai, tel: 02 653 3960) plays host to a glittering array of Las Vegas-style starlets and is probably the best show in town. You can bring children here without any concerns.

Central Plains

Getting Your Bearings

This landlocked area north and west of Bangkok is a fertile zone irrigated by rivers and waterfalls. Thailand's "rice bowl" and its wealthiest region is literally in the heart of the country. The pace of life here is generally slow.

The extraordinary ancient cities of Ayutthaya and Sukhothai are two historical jewels studding the flat plains at either end of the zone, with the historical towns of Kamphaeng Phet and Lop Buri in between. The landscape becomes more hilly in the west, with forests and wildlife protected in scenic national parks which offer walking and rafting.

At the riverside town of Kanchanaburi is the iconic "Bridge over the River Kwai", along with many other powerful reminders of the thousands of prisoners of war who worked on the Death Railway.

Burma (Myanmar) flanks the western side with a border (Three Pagodas Pass) open only for locally resident Thais and Burmese.

Most people travel around this part of the country, seeing the major sights, which include traditional floating markets, on organized day trips from Bangkok, before heading north to the serene ancient kingdom capital of Sukhothai. If you want a more leisurely pace, you can visit them independently, with the freedom to linger.

Page 63: A Buddha at Wat Phra Mahathat, Ayutthaya

Below: The iconic bridge spans the River Kwai at Kanchanaburi

Mae Sot

Phop Phra

9
Umphang ▲ 1960m

Nam Chon

Phra Chedi Sam Ong
10 ▲1980m
11 Sangkhla Buri

Wachiralongkon

Si Nakarindra
Thong Pha Phum
Si Sawat
323

Kanchanaburi
5

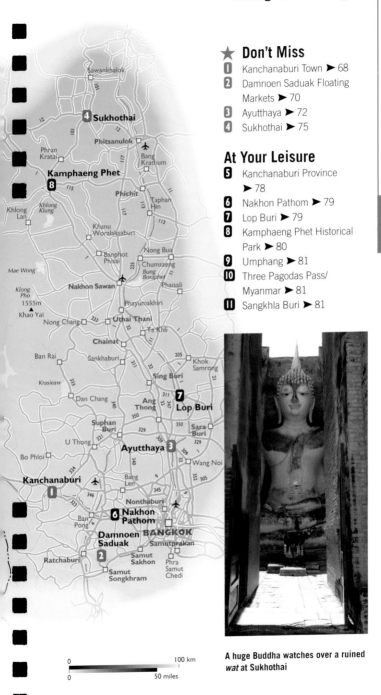

A huge Buddha watches over a ruined *wat* at Sukhothai

In Three Days

If you're not quite sure where to begin your travels, this itinerary recommends three practical and enjoyable days out exploring the Central Plains, taking in some of the best places to see using the Getting Your Bearings map on the previous page. For more information see the main entries.

Day 1

Morning

Day trips make an early start from Bangkok to combine visits to the town of **1 Kanchanaburi** (➤ 68–69), **2 Damnoen Saduak Floating Markets** (below, ➤ 70–71), and a quick tour of **6 Nakhon Pathom's** soaring *chedi* (➤ 79). Other organised tours visit the waterfalls and Hellfire Pass in **5 Kanchanaburi Province** (➤ 78–79) and miss out the floating markets. Tour buses usually stop at an unatmospheric roadside restaurant for lunch, despite the fact that it will probably be called Jungle View.

Afternoon

You will have an hour or so to take in the cemetery in **Kanchanaburi** (➤ 69), the **JEATH War Museum** (➤ 69) and the **Bridge over the River Kwai** (➤ 68) before leaving to go back to Bangkok via Nakhon Pathom.

Evening

A good way of having more time at the Kanchanaburi sights is to take a shared taxi back to Bangkok, for about 200 baht, rather than returning by tour bus. That way you can digest the day and get to sample seafood at the floating restaurants that have a real jungle view. Try those on Song Kwai Road where the ambience may take precedence over the food.

Day 2

Morning

Take an early morning train from Bangkok's Hualamphong station to **3 Ayutthaya** (below, ➤ 72–74) and rent a bicycle on arrival (or go for an organized tour). Enjoy an early, leisurely lunch to avoid the hottest part of the day, at one of the floating restaurants on Mae Nam Pa Sak's west bank near the bridge of Saphan Pridi Damrong.

Afternoon

Continue the tour of Ayutthaya's temples and, if you have time, venture out to the scenic western zone.

Evening

Fill up at the Hua Raw night market next to the river near Chan Kasem Palace. From here you can follow the river back to the ferry point and train station to return to Bangkok on an early evening train.

Day 3

Take a very reasonably priced flight to **4 Sukhothai** (➤ 75–77). If the flights are full (it is best to reserve as far ahead as possible), consider taking the bus. The overnight train from Bangkok arrives inconveniently in the early hours of the morning at Phitsanulok. Rent a bicycle to explore the ruins and stay the night in Sukhothai.

❶Kanchanaburi Town

Kanchanaburi town is a relaxing destination, with riverside raft houses and guest houses in lush green surroundings. It is more famous, however, as the setting for a World War II POW camp, which was the base for workers on the Thailand–Burma Railway. Known as the "Death Railway", its construction cost thousands of lives. Most visitors fix their attention on the River Kwai bridge, which featured in Pierre Boulle's book and, later, the 1957 Oscar-winning film, *Bridge on the River Kwai*.

Bridge Over the River Kwai

There were actually two bridges over the River Kwai, the infamous wooden structure which was the source of inspiration for the film, and a steel and concrete structure built by the Japanese forces when they realised the first bridge was too unstable. Both were destroyed by Allied bombing, but the second bridge was rebuilt and now carries the original Death Railway line.

Allied prisoners of war and conscripted Asian labourers worked on both bridges under brutal conditions. Some 12,000 of the 60,000 POWs building the bridges and the railway line to the Burmese border died. At least 80,000 Asian labourers also perished – a much less well-known figure. It's been estimated that a man died for every sleeper laid.

The story of the Death Railway is related in two museums, both located near the bridge on the banks of the river.

The World War II Museum

This museum contains one end of the original wooden bridge in an eclectic exhibition. It is worth visiting for its war-time

mementoes and Japanese and allied vehicles.

JEATH War Museum
The JEATH War Museum has moving displays with personal accounts and paintings by POWs, and replicas of the bamboo huts in which they lived. JEATH stands for Japan, England, Australia, America, Thailand and Holland – the nationals of which built the railway.

The JEATH War Museum is housed in a replica POW hut

Opposite: The Death Railway tracks and a World War II bomb are chilling reminders of the suffering of thousands

The Cemeteries
Nearly 7,000 POWs are buried in the **Kanchanaburi War Cemetery**. The plaques and epitaphs are poignant reminders of how young these men were. It is immaculately kept, with lawns and plants.

The **Chung Kai Allied War Cemetery**, on the western bank of the river, receives far fewer tourists. Although it's a fair walk, you can cycle there.

TAKING A BREAK
Mae Nam floating restaurant on the river opposite Thanon Song Khwae is a good place for a break. The atmosphere and setting are fantastic and the food is traditional Thai.

198 B4 TAT, Saeng Chuto Road 03 457 7200

JEATH War Museum
Pak Phreak Road Daily 8:30–6 Inexpensive

Kanchanaburi War Cemetery
Saeng Chuto Road Daily 6–6 Free

World War II Museum
Daily 8:30–6 Inexpensive

KANCHANABURI TOWN: INSIDE INFO

Top tips A **tourist train** goes from Bangkok to Kanchanaburi at weekends, leaving at 6:30am and returning to Bangkok at 7:30pm. A return ticket is 200 baht.
- **Read up** before you go if you don't know any of the history of the area, as the tours are perfunctory and, while the information in the JEATH War Museum is fascinating, there is rather too much to take in on one visit.
- If you are not on a tour, consider **renting a bicycle** as the town's sights are spread out over 5km (3 miles) along the river.
- Locals smile when visitors call their river the Kwai, as in "cry". The real pronunciation is "Kway", as in "sway". Pronounced the wrong way, Kwai can have a distinctly sexual meaning!

② Damnoen Saduak Floating Markets

The boats that paddle along the narrow canals (*khlongs*), are packed with produce grown in the agricultural surrounds of the region. One boat may be piled high with fresh coconuts, another packed with garlic; others sell a mix of vegetables and fruit. Mini floating restaurants dole out noodle soup to market workers. Women dressed in traditional, bucket-like straw hats and navy blue outfits typically worn by Thai farmers, skilfully manoeuvre their boats, steering their produce along the canals.

People have been hawking their wares here for more than 100 years. These markets, about 60km (37 miles) southwest of Bangkok, are the traditional way to shop, dating from when the canals were the major thoroughfares. Floating markets have all but died out in Bangkok – the ones that do exist are straggly, touristy affairs. Damnoen Saduak's distance from Bangkok and the fact that it is not accessible by train has in some ways saved it from over-commercialisation, although it is one of the most popular tours from the capital.

Colourful hats make popular souvenirs

Opposite: Fresh produce for sale at Damnoen Saduak market

The main, and oldest, market is at **Ton Khem**, while the more touristy **Hia Kui canal** runs parallel to this. Lined with warehouses, it offers bird's-eye views from its bridges. The colourful scene is a frenzy of activity, with market traders peddling their wares. On shore, the stalls are lined with mostly souvenir-style goods, such as fans, hats and spices – but you will probably be over-charged.

Organized tours are convenient and a good way of combining the floating markets with Kanchanaburi Town or **Phetchaburi** (➤ 138–139). Be prepared to be herded and rushed. These trips can easily turn into a high-pressured shopping tour, with a "sugar factory" (just another market), the floating markets and a crafts centre all crammed into the busy itinerary.

To go it alone, you can take a bus from Bangkok's southern bus terminal. The first air-conditioned bus leaves at 6am and takes two hours, then you need to walk or take a *songthaew* (➤ 32) for 2km (1.2 miles) to the centre of the markets, **Talat Khlong Ton Khem**.

TAKING A BREAK

Buy a **fresh coconut** full of juice from one of the boats on the river.

🏛 198 C4 ℹ TAT, 500/51 Phetkasem Road, Cha-am, Phetchaburi
☎ 03 247 1005

DAMNOEN SADUAK FLOATING MARKETS: INSIDE INFO

Top tips There is a **set price** for a boat (at least 400 baht), irrespective of how many people are on board, so it makes sense to get a group together.
■ The markets are **open** daily 6 to 11am.
■ If you want to **avoid the crowds**, one way is to stay overnight in Damnoen and visit the markets before the tour groups arrive at around 9am.

Hidden gem Talat Khun Phitak canal is the quietest market. Take a water taxi from Khlong Thong Lang to get there, and maybe combine it with a trip to see the surrounding **coconut plantations**.

3 Ayutthaya

This World Heritage Site was once the greatest city in Asia, and Thailand's capital for more than 400 years. Founded in 1350, Ayutthaya was an incredibly advanced civilization – in fact, it was so powerful that it conquered mighty Angkor, in present-day Cambodia, and took on Khmer traditions. It had one million inhabitants in the 17th century – twice that of London during the same period. Visiting merchants from China, Japan, Holland, England and France are said to have declared it the most beautiful city they had ever seen.

Although the glories of its golden age were mostly destroyed by the Burmese in the 1760s, a staggering number of red-brick ruined royal palaces and chapels, monastic temples, halls of worship and pagodas still stand throughout the town.

The vast array of buildings are not consistently interesting and, unless you want to stay overnight, are too much to take in during one day. The best option is to come up by train, rent a bicycle (rental normally includes a free map) and follow the mapped route to the most interesting sites, which can be seen in around three hours. Although you will pass many monuments on the way, most are only interesting from the outside, and so are easily admired. You could also combine this tour with a restful longtail boat ride, taking in some of the riverside temples.

Around Ayutthaya
The site is effectively an island, encircled by three rivers, only partly absorbed by a modern working town. On arrival at the train station, walk straight ahead and over the crossroads. Take the ferry for the short river crossing, and then the second

Above: A Buddha head is caught in the roots of a banyan tree at Wat Phra Mahathat

Towering brick spires at Wat Phra Mahathat

left along Thanon Naresuan to the 14th-century **Wat Phra Mahathat**. This is the biggest and most significant temple complex, which includes the royal monastery. Buddha images found in the ruins here as recently as 1956 are now in the Chao Sam Phraya National Museum (▶ below). Make sure you find the much-photographed Buddha head entangled in a frame of vines. Opposite, **Wat Ratchaburana** was built on the site of a cremation of two kings, and their ashes are contained here in *chedis*. Follow the stairs down to the crypt to see its faded murals.

About 1km (0.6 miles) along this road, **Phra Mongkonbophit** contains a huge, gilded Buddha almost 13m (43 feet) high. The gleaming statue was re-covered in gold leaf in 1992. As a present-day centre of worship, the temple bustles with Thais making offerings of lotus flowers, incense candles and gold plate.

Opposite is **Wat Phra Si San Phet**, built as a royal palace when Ayutthaya was established. Although partly restored, it is still essentially in ruins. A royal temple was built here in 1448, with later additions, such as *chedis*, to contain royal remains and royal halls of worship.

The **Chao Sam Phraya National Museum** (Si Sanphet Road, open Wed–Sun 9–4, inexpensive) is two blocks south of here, crammed full of gold treasures, including an elephant weighed down with jewels, and the original relic casket from Wat Mahathat.

At the end of the road to the right, **Wat Lokayasutharam** has a huge Buddha (37m/ 121-feet long) reclining in the open air, his head cushioned by a lotus.

TAKING A BREAK

Try one of the several floating restaurants on the river either side of Pridi Damrong Bridge, such as **Phae Krung Kao** (▶ 85), south of the bridge, for some excellent seafood. Alternatively there's **Chainam** (▶ 85), for Thai and Western breakfast, plus coffee and inexpensive Thai specialities served throughout the day.

✚ 196 C2   ℹ TAT, Si Sanphet Road, Ayutthaya   ☎ 03 524 6076

Left: Giant
gilded Buddha
at Wat Phra
Mongkon-
bophit

Opposite:
The Buddha
image at Wat
Si Chum in
Sukhothai has
eyes inlaid
with mother
of pearl

AYUTTHAYA: INSIDE INFO

Top tips The booklet *Interesting Temples and Ruins in Ayutthaya* is worth buying
for background information, but the map is almost illegible. It is available all
over the town and at the Chao Sam Phraya National Museum.

■ Tours from Bangkok to the **Bang-Pa-In Palace** (open daily 8:30–noon, 1–4,
moderate) in a longtail boat include two hours in Ayutthaya. Although it's
an interesting way to travel, you won't have too much time to look around
the historical city itself.

■ Whether bicycling or walking, **avoid the heat of the day** (11–3) by starting early
and taking a long break for lunch. Temperatures in Ayutthaya tend to be
even higher than in Bangkok.

■ Wait to **rent a bicycle** until you reach the other side of the ferry crossing,
where prices are lower.

Hidden gem Visit the impressive **Wat Chaiwatthanaram**. In a peaceful grassy
riverside spot on the edge of town, it tends to receive few visitors. From Wat
Lokayasutharam, turn left down Thanon Khlong Thaw, then first right, over the
river and then turn left. This monastery, where royal cremations took place,
was built by King Prasatthon in 1630 on the site of his old home to honour
his mother. It was built in the Cambodian Khmer style, with similarities to
Angkor Wat in Cambodia, and one theory suggests it was constructed to
celebrate the king's victory over Cambodia. Its large, central *prang* stands in
the middle of four smaller ones and eight smaller still, symbolising the centre
of the universe.

One to miss Chan Kasem Palace, on Uthong Road, is a museum with a
rather jumbled selection of exhibits. The palace, once home to the heir to
the throne, was razed by the Burmese. It was rebuilt and now contains a
collection of minor royal objects.

4 Sukhothai

The name of Thailand's original capital (1238–1376) means "rising of happiness" and it is still seen as a symbol of a golden age. Founded in 1238 when two Thai generals took control from the Khmer Empire, Sukhothai became a centre of artistic greatness, where harmony reigned and justice prevailed. Its lawns, lily ponds and buildings, restored with assistance by UNESCO and surrounded by orchards and rice fields, now form one of Thailand's most visited spots.

Sukhothai's decline came in the 15th century when Ayutthaya (➤ 72–74) gained political dominance. Houses at that time were mostly built of wood and haven't survived, so what remains are the crumbling brick religious buildings. However,

unlike Ayutthaya, the old and new cities are separate, which makes a visit here much more enjoyable. Most people stay in the new city, with its better range of accommodation and long-distance bus connections, and travel the 12km (7.5 miles) to the old city by *songthaew* (similar to a *tuk-tuk*: noisy, with two benches facing one another in the back; ➤ 32). The best way for visitors to get round Sukhothai is by bicycle which can be rented at the main entrance. Each of the sights mentioned here takes about 20 minutes to visit, with about 5–10 minutes travelling time in between.

Sukhothai Historical Park
The original walled city is now covered by **Sukhothai Historical Park** (Muang Kao Sukhothai), which is divided into five zones, each charging a separate entrance fee. Most of the interesting temples are in the central zone, although even here you need to be selective. Rent a bicycle (and ask for a free map) opposite the **Ramkhamhaeng Museum**, a short walk from where *songthaews* drop passengers and just outside the entrance to the central zone. A copy of King Ramkhamhaeng's inscription and bell, an armoury and intriguing items such as gambling chips and bullets are on display in the museum.

Next to the museum, **Wat Trapang Thong** is a still functioning monastery on an island surrounded by lotus-filled ponds. Here monks weed the stone Ceylonese-style *chedi* trees which have words of wisdom attached to them. The *mondop* (a square-shaped spired construction) contains a 14th-century giant Buddha footprint.

> **RAMA THE STRONG**
> King Ramkhamhaeng (Rama the Strong) was the most important of the royal city's kings. He established a forerunner of modern Thai script, promoted Theravada Buddhism (the school taught by the Buddha, meaning "doctrine of the elders" and following the Hindu theory of reincarnation) and pushed the boundaries of the kingdom to almost the size of present-day Thailand. His much-quoted stone inscription of 1292 describes a bell in front of the palace gate that could be rung by any subject who wanted to air a grievance.

The ruins at Wat Mahathat have some 200 Khmer and Ceylonese brick *chedis*

Take the first left inside the entrance to the central zone to **Wat Mahathat**. The largest and most important temple in Sukhothai was at the heart of the kingdom both politically and spiritually. The complex, surrounded by a moat and brick wall, contains 200 (mostly ruined) brick *chedis* in the Ceylonese and Khmer style. Two blocks southwest is **Sri Sawai**, built as a Hindu shrine with three Khmer-style *prangs* (central towers). Due north is **Wat Trapang Ngoen**, which features a classic lotus-bud *chedi* and an ordination hall, and **Wat Sra Sri**, with its circular *chedi*.

Outside the Central Zone

Leaving the central zone via the Northern Gate, turn left into **Wat Phra Pai Luang**, which shows a variety of building styles. The *prangs* were built by the Khmers and the *viharn* (temple assembly hall) and *chedis* are later Buddhist additions. At its northeast corner is **Thuriang Kiln**. There is not much to see, but it is a reminder that ceramics were an important revenue for Thailand, exported to the Philippines and Japan.

Continue south and take the second road on the right to visit a string of temples in the western zone. First stop is **Wat Si Thon**, where a monk is said to have lived surrounded by mango fields. **Wat Saphan Hin** is the fourth temple, reached by a short, steep climb to a standing Buddha with an outstretched palm and views of the surrounding countryside.

TAKING A BREAK

The **café in the Ramkhamhaeng Museum** is a pleasant place for a cup of tea next to the water. The restaurant opposite is a good spot for lunch. In New Sukhothai, try the **Kru Lew** (► 85) for authentic Thai food.

✚ 196 B3

Sukhothai Historical Park
🕐 Daily 8:30–4:30, 7–9 💵 Separate entrance inexpensive; central entrance moderate

Ramkhamhaeng Museum
🕐 Daily 9–4 💵 Inexpensive

SUKHOTHAI: INSIDE INFO

Top tips The **single ticket**, which includes entry to all five zones, doesn't save you money, although it is valid for a month.

■ From the end of October to mid-November the festival of **Loi Krathong** gives thanks to the goddess of water. Lighted candles, incense and lotus buds are set sail in banana-leaf boats. The festival is celebrated all over Thailand but it is more of a spectacle here, with illuminations and fireworks.

■ The temples are lit by spotlights **at night** and very few visitors are about despite the beauty of the scene.

Hidden gem The north and west zones where **buffalo, cows and farm workers** dot the lush green landscape where once stood a mighty city.

At Your Leisure

Just one of Erawan Falls' seven tiers,
Kanchanaburi Province

9 Kanchanaburi Province

The spectacular waterfall in **Erawan National Park** in Kanchanaburi Province is something of a national symbol. Each of the seven tiers has its own clear water pool which invites swimming. The park's 2km (1.2-mile) trail leads to the triple cascade at the top and requires suitable footwear. This very attractive park, just 65km (40 miles) from Kanchanaburi Town, is popular with Thais, especially at weekends and holidays. It is worth avoiding these times if you want to enjoy the peace of the landscape.

Trekking trips in Kanchanaburi Province can include elephant safaris, visits to waterfalls and river-rafting, rather than hiking.

The two-hour train journey along the section of the Death Railway from Kanchanaburi to Nam Tok starts by crossing the bridge over the River Kwai (► 68). This highly scenic and very popular trip grimly illustrates the horror experienced in building the railway.

Hellfire Pass, 18km (11 miles) northwest of Nam Tok, is the highest of a series of mountain passes and was one of the most treacherous parts of the Death Railway. The prisoners of war who were forced to cut through the rock gave it the name "Hellfire" because of the nightmarish scene created by the fires, torches and lamps when they worked through the night. Three-quarters of those who worked on this stretch died, and they are sensitively remembered at the **Hellfire Pass Memorial Museum**, with accounts from survivors. A 90-minute memorial trail passes the site of the Pack of Cards Bridge, so called by the prisoners because it collapsed three times. A regular bus service between Kanchanaburi and Sangkhlaburi via Hellfire Pass stops at Nam Tok. The last bus back to Nam Tok and Kanchanaburi passes Hellfire Pass around 4pm.

Sai Yok National Park, 10km (6.2 miles) further up the road, lays claim to two large waterfalls, limestone caves, teak forests and natural springs. Wildlife here includes gibbons, barking deer and the world's smallest mammal – the hog-nosed (bumblebee) bat. It was, however, also the venue for disturbing scenes in the film *The Deerhunter*. It is possible to stay in the park (book through www.dnp.go.th) in bungalows but you will need to bring your own food provisions as there is no restaurant.

Phra Pathom Chedi, Nakhon Pathom, is one of the tallest Buddhist monuments

Erawan National Park
➕ 196 B2 🕐 Daily 8–4 💲 Expensive

Hellfire Pass Memorial Museum
➕ 196 B2 ✉ At the start of the memorial trail
☎ www.dva.gov.au 🕐 Daily 9–4 💲 Free
(donations gratefully accepted)

Sai Yok National Park
➕ 196 B2 🛈 TAT, Kanchanaburi ☎ 03 451
6163 🕐 Daily 8–4 💲 Expensive

⑥ Nakhon Pathom

Phra Pathom Chedi is the main attraction in Nakhon Pathom (56km/35 miles west of Bangkok), and is said to be the tallest Buddhist monument in the world. It dominates the skyline all around. A quick visit to the *chedi* is usually squeezed in to a tour from Bangkok on the way back from the Damnoen Saduak Floating Markets (► 70–71) and Kanchanaburi Town (► 68–69).

Although there is not much else here to see for visitors, Nakhon Pathom is thought to be Thailand's oldest town, and the place where Buddhism first entered the country. There are two museums in the town, both confusingly called **Phra Pathom Museum**. The newer one has 6th- to 11th-century local artefacts and the other, a small room, is crowded with amulets, Chinese ceramics, Thai musical instruments and gems.
➕ 198 C4

Phra Pathom Museums
➕ 198 C4 ✉ Phra Pathom Chedi compound
🕐 Wed–Sun 8–4 💲 Inexpensive

⑦ Lop Buri

The monkeys that have overrun Lop Buri, one of Thailand's oldest inhabited towns, are almost a tourist attraction in their own right. Lop Buri was a Khmer provincial capital in the 11th century and Thailand's second capital from the 17th to 19th centuries. The **Narai National Museum**, in a 17th-century palace complex, displays plenty of Buddhas. **Wat Phra Si Ratana Mahathat** has a 12th-century Khmer central *prang*. Both are worth a look and are within easy walking distance of the train station. A frequent bus service runs to Wat Phra Phutthabat, the Temple of the Buddha's Footprint, 17km (10.5 miles) southeast of town.
➕ 196 C2 🛈 TAT, Ropwat Phrathat Road
☎ 03 642 2768/9

Narai National Museum
🕐 Wed–Sun 9–4 ☎ 03 641 1458
💲 Inexpensive

Wat Phra Si Ratana Mahathat
🕐 Daily 8–6 💲 Inexpensive

SCENIC JOURNEYS

■ Walking trail to the waterfall in **Erawan National Park** (► 78).
■ Day-long rail route to **Three Pagodas Pass** from Kanchanaburi (► 81).
■ Three-day trek from **Umphang** (► 81), offered by guest houses, including trekking, rafting and an elephant ride.

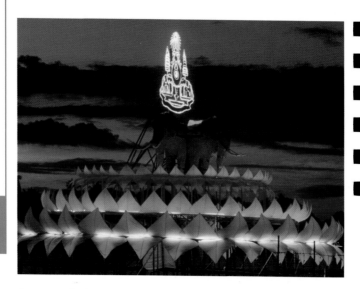

An enormous *krathong* (Songkran float) in the River Ping at Kamphaeng Phet

❽ Kamphaeng Phet Historical Park

In the 13th century this ancient riverside city was part of the Kingdom of Sukhothai and was an important centre in the Khmer Empire. Today it is a provincial town whose partly restored old buildings form a historical park and a World Heritage Site. The star attraction is Wat Phra Kaeo, with its weather-sculpted Buddha statues. The Emerald Buddha, Thailand's most important Buddha image, was once held here, but is now kept in Wat Phra Kaeo in Bangkok (➤ 45).

The monastery of Wat Phrathat and San Phra Isuan Shrine are also worth a look. The **National Museum** has archaeological finds from all over Thailand as well as from excavations in Kamphaeng Phet. Next door is the **Provincial Museum**, displaying collections introducing the history and traditions of Kamphaeng Phet province. A group of forest (*arunyik*) temples to the north of the walled city were built by meditating monks.
✚ 196 B3 ☎ TAT: 05 551 4341

Kamphaeng Phet Historical Park
☎ 05 571 1921 🕐 Daily 8–4:30
💷 Inexpensive

National Museum
☎ 05 571 1570 🕐 Wed–Sun 9–4
💷 Inexpensive

Provincial Museum
☎ 05 572 2341 🕐 Wed–Sun 9–4
💷 Inexpensive

BORDER COUNTRY
Around seven million Mon people live in Thailand and Burma. Originally thought to have hailed from India or Mongolia, they established a kingdom in south Burma before even the Burmese arrived. They have suffered oppression for centuries from the Burmese, who continue to oppress them. Use of the Mon language has been banned since the mid-18th century, but forced labour, rape and illnesses associated with underprivilege are more disturbing modern atrocities, and the reason for the large number of refugee camps in the area around Sangkhla Buri.

Children of the Karen hill tribe in the village of Umphang

🟨 Umphang

This riverside village surrounded by spectacular scenery doesn't get too many visitors. On the border with Burma and in the middle of nowhere, it is reached by a roller-coaster road or "Sky Highway" that zooms past pretty hill-tribe villages. This is trekking country, with trips to Mae Sot and the Tee Lor Su Waterfall as well as river-rafting expeditions. In and around the village, inhabited mostly by the Karen, you will see elephants working in the fields.

South of Umphang, on the road to Sangkhla Buri, a wildlife sanctuary is home to Thailand's largest waterfall.
🟥 196 B3

🔟 Three Pagodas Pass/Myanmar

Three Pagodas Pass (Phra Chedi Sam Ong) is an outpost on the Burma/Thailand border where there is really nothing much to see apart from the trio of pagodas from which it takes its name. It is said that they were built in the 18th century as a demonstration of peace between Thailand and Burma (modern Myanmar). Thailand traditionally prevented foreigners crossing into Burma from the Three Pagodas Pass as a precaution due to border fighting between the Burmese military and Mon and Karen rebels.

Things are generally peaceful now and if the border is open you can visit the Burmese village of Payathonzu for the day, although it's a good idea to check the current situation first.

The market in Payathonzu has exotic goods from neighbouring countries. On both sides of the border you can find hand-embroidered textiles from India, precious gems from Cambodia and intricate Indonesian woodcarvings. Hard bargaining is expected.
🟥 196 A2

🔟 Sangkhla Buri

Around 20km (12.4 miles) from the Three Pagodas Pass, Sangkhla Buri is a nicer place to stay the night if you are intending to visit the Pass.

Populated with mostly Mon and Karen people, it is more Burmese than Thai and very little English is spoken. Its focus is a reservoir that was created by the damming of the Khwae Noi River. You can still see parts of the drowned villages and trees. A daily morning market at Wat Wangwiwekaram sells crafts from Burma, China and India. There are canoeing trips on the Kheuan Khao Laem Reservoir and a long wooden bridge leads over the body of water to a welcoming Mon settlement.
🟥 196 A2

Where to... Stay

Prices

Expect to pay per double room per night:
£ under 2,000 baht   ££ 2,000–5,000 baht   £££ over 5,000 baht

KANCHANABURI

Felix River Kwai ££–£££

On the west bank of the River Kwai and in landscaped tropical gardens, the Felix is within walking distance of the famous bridge (▶ 68). This luxurious resort offers every facility including a fitness centre, tennis courts, two large swimming pools and a number of excellent restaurants. The Good Earth serves fine Chinese cuisine. Rooms are spacious with satellite TV and a personal safe.

✚ 198 B4 ⊠ 9/1 Moo 3 Thamakhan
☎ 03 451506l; www.felixriverkwai.co.th

Inchantree Resort £

The facilities at this resort are on a modest scale but the location is attractive, with a breakfast terrace right by the side of the river. All the rooms have air-conditioning.

✚ 198 B4 ⊠ 433 Mae Nam Khwae
☎ 03 462 4914

Kasem Island Resort £

This resort is in a wonderful location on its own island in the middle of the Mae Klong River, south of the main town. Pretty thatched cottages and houseboats sit peacefully away from the busy town. Rooms are clean and tastefully decorated. The resort offers river-rafting and fishing trips, as well as a pleasant bar. The free ferry from the Chukkadon Pier slightly to the north of the island stops operating after 10pm, so be careful not to be caught out too late on the wrong side of the river.

✚ 198 B4 ⊠ Kasem Island, Chukadon Pier,
River Kwai ☎ 03 451 3359;
www.ourweb.info/Kir

River Kwai Hotel ££

The River Kwai Hotel is an old favourite, centrally located and a little way from the river. The advantage of its position is that you miss the whine of longtail boats during the day, and the noisy disco boats on the river into the early hours of the morning. All rooms are air-conditioned. It is well situated for visiting the JEATH War Museum (▶ 69) and the Allied War Cemetery (▶ 69). There's a coffee shop, a disco and a swimming pool.

✚ 198 B4 ⊠ 284/3-16 Thanon Saengchuto
☎ 03 451 3348; www.riverkwai.co.th

Royal River Kwai Resort & Spa ££

More than 60 rooms nestle in a peaceful riverside location, but the resort is too far from town to walk so it helps a lot if you have your own transport. The garden is beautifully landscaped and the restaurant overlooks the river. All the rooms have a balcony with sweeping views of the River Kwai. The spa is not expensive when compared with Bangkok or Chiang Mai rates.

✚ 198 B4 ⊠ 88 Kanchanaburi-Saiyok Road
☎ 03 465 3342; www. royalriverkwai.com

AYUTTHAYA

Ayutthaya Grand £

The Ayutthaya Grand is one of only a handful of good hotels to be found in the main city area of Ayutthaya. A large, comfortable establishment, it's situated a little to the east of the main town, beyond the Pa Sak River. The well-appointed rooms offer a haven from the busy town centre and include all modern amenities. The Grand's nightclub is one of the most popular in town, with an attached coffee shop. There is also a large swimming pool.

∰ 196 C2 ⊠ 55/5 Thanon Rotchana ☎ 03 533 5483; www.ayutthayagrandhotel.com

Krungsri River ££

Situated at the eastern end of the Pridi Damrong Bridge and overlooking the busy Pa Sak River, this is considered to be the best hotel in Ayutthaya. The imposing foyer sets the tone for the rest of the hotel and the beautifully decorated rooms will not disappoint. All rooms have satellite TV and mini-bar. There is an attractive pool, fitness centre, sauna, bowling alley, snooker tables and pub. It also houses the excellent Gu Cheung Chinese restaurant.

∰ 196 C2 ⊠ 27/2 Moo 11, Thanon Rotchana ☎ 03 524 4333; www.krungsirivier.com

U-Thong Inn £

Don't confuse the U-Thong Inn to the east of Ayutthaya, beyond the Pa Sak River, with the more downmarket U-Thong Hotel. It is well positioned for all the main historical sights and regularly used for conferences, so it is often quite full. The new wing has proved to be the better value of the old and new wings. All rooms are clean and airy with satellite TV and mini-bar. Breakfast is included in the price of the room. Other facilities are a pool and sauna.

∰ 196 C2 ⊠ 210 Thanon Rotchana ☎ 03-521 2531; www.uthonginn.com

SUKHOTHAI

Lotus Village £

A French-Thai couple run this enchanting resort-style hotel near Sukhothai's central market. Accommodation is in cosy timber-built bungalows nestled in shady gardens near the Yom River. The main house, where breakfast is

served, is strewn with interesting antiques and bric-a-brac, collected by the owners during their extensive travels; they have an encyclopaedic knowledge of the area – "Tourist office?" responds Kun Daen, "We're it".

∰ 196 B3 ⊠ 170 Thanon Ratchathanee ☎ 05 562 1484; www.lotus-village.com

Tharaburi Resort £-£££

A true boutique hotel, the Tharaburi Resort has only five guestrooms and one Thai-style house, decked out in contemporary Asian styles. Prices vary a lot depending on the time of year and type of room, and good deals are sometimes available. There is a pleasant restaurant in a garden setting that serves authentic Thai food. The resort is in a good location, convenient for Sukhothai Historical Park (▶ 76).

∰ 196 B3 ⊠ 11/3 Srisomboon Road ☎ 05 569 7132; www.tharaburiresort.com

Sabaidee £

Well located, between the bus station and the town centre, Sabaidee is a very pleasant, elegantly furnished guest house, offering a choice of accommodation. You can stay in a bungalow, with an electric fan or air-conditioning, or in a room in the main house, which will mean sharing a bathroom. There is also a restaurant in the tropical gardens, laundry service, bicycle and motorbike rental, and internet access. The staff will be pleased to help with arranging local tours.

∰ 196 B3 ⊠ 81/7 M13 Charodwithithon Road ☎ 05 561 6303; www.sabaidee-guesthouse.com

PHITSANULOK

La Paloma £

La Paloma is one of a number of fine hotels offering remarkably good value considering the excellent facilities. It's geared towards Thai families, and the staff are very friendly. Comfortable air-conditioned rooms with satellite TV are very reasonable if the hotel is empty, although you will have to bargain for this rate. Expect to pay double the bargain rate in the high season. Other facilities include a swimming pool and a good restaurant serving traditional Thai food.

🕂 196 C3 ⊠ 103/8 Thanon Srithamatraipidok ☎ 05 521 7930/4; www.lapalomahotel.com

Phitsanulok Thani Hotel £

Situated a little way from the interesting riverfront, this large, quiet, comfortable hotel is well located for the Phitsanulok Folklore Museum and the Buranathai Buddha Casting Foundry on Thanon Wisut Kasat. The large, attractive foyer/lounge regularly has live music. As with some of the other good hotels in the town, it may be possible to receive discounts on rooms at certain times of the year. The large, pleasant rooms all have a fridge, mini-bar and cable TV.

🕂 196 C3 ⊠ 39 Thanon Sanam Bin ☎ 05 521 1065; www.phitsanulokthani.com

Sappraiwan Grand Hotel and Resort ££

Nestled in the hills 50km (31 miles) northeast of Phitsanulok, this is the perfect place to relax. There are mountains, waterfalls, rivers and jungle in the surrounding countryside. The Kaeng Sopha Waterfall is particularly beautiful and not far away. All rooms in the main building have either river or tropical garden views, satellite TV and elegant wooden furniture. Dotted around the 150ha (370-acre) site are private one- and two-bedroom chalets. There's also a fitness centre on site, a swimming pool and the excellent Wang Thong restaurant.

🕂 196 C3 ⊠ 79 Moo 2, Tambon Kaeng Sopha ☎ 05 529 3293; www.resort.co.th

decorated using a variety of Thai textiles and crafts. Each is dedicated to one of Thailand's 76 provinces. The facilities include a sauna and fitness centre and a large swimming pool. The hotel's Kongjien Chinese restaurant is very good.

🕂 196 C2 ⊠ 144 Thanon Phahonyothin (opposite Lopburi Inn Plaza) ☎ 03 642 0777; www.lopburiinnresort.com

MAE SOT

Central Mae Sot Hill Hotel ££

This is a good place to recover from the rigours of a trip to Umphang (▲ 81). It's a large, comfortable hotel with tennis courts, swimming pool and fitness centre, and well located for the Friendship Bridge marking the border between Thailand and Burma. The bridge crosses the Moei River and trips to the Burmese border town of Myawaddy are possible; ask at reception for the latest information.

🕂 196 B3 ⊠ 100 Asia Road ☎ 05 553 2601/8; www.centralhotelsresorts.com

Topland ££

A large, modern hotel, Topland is set in the heart of the city. There are beautifully appointed rooms and suites with all the facilities associated with a first-class hotel. The large marble bathrooms are the perfect place to relax after a day in the sun. The hotel is connected to the Topland Plaza Shopping Complex, which has a department store, several smaller shops and a number of good places to eat, in addition to Topland's restaurants.

🕂 196 C3 ⊠ 68/33 Thanon Ekathotsarot ☎ 05 524 7800; www.toplandhotel.com

LOP BURI

Lopburi Inn Resort £–££

Few visitors to the ancient town of Lop Buri take the time to stay the night, which is a pity as it's one of the most interesting places in central Thailand. The Lopburi Inn Resort, slightly out of the old town to the west, is the newest and best hotel. The rooms are all

Where to...
Eat and Drink

Prices

Expect to pay per person for a three-course meal, excluding drinks and service:

£ under 300 baht   ££ 300–600 baht   £££ over 600 baht

KANCHANABURI

Felix River Kwai ££

This hotel (▶ 82) is a reliable stop for breakfast, lunch or evening meal. The food is a broad mix of Asian and international dishes; the riverside setting is a bonus. Some people don't like walking home from the hotel at night because of stray dogs on the bridge.

🔒 198 B4 ⊠ Kanchanburi ☎ 03 451 5061 🕒 Daily 7am–9pm

Mae Nam ££

A number of floating restaurants vie for business south of the centrally located Rattanakarn Bridge. Mae Nam, one of the largest, offers freshwater fish and seafood. Particularly good is the *pla nung khing* (steamed fish with ginger, chilli and mushrooms). There are also meat and vegetarian dishes. In the evenings there is live music.

🔒 198 B4 ⊠ On the river at the end of Lak Muang Road ☎ 03 451 2811 🕒 Daily 8:30am–midnight

AYUTTHAYA

Chainam £

Chainam serves excellent Thai coffee accompanied by a good Western breakfast. For the rest of the day reasonable Thai and average Western dishes are available.

🔒 196 C2 ⊠ Thanon U-Thong, opposite Chan Kasem Palace ☎ 03 525 2013 🕒 Daily 8am–9pm

Phae Krung Kao ££

This attractive floating restaurant on the Pa Sak River is a great place to sit and relax and watch the activity on the rivers surrounding the town. The restaurant specializes in seafood and also offers a wide range of Thai chicken and pork dishes.

🔒 196 C2 ⊠ South of Pridi Damrong Bridge, Moo 2 Thanon U-Thong ☎ 03 524 1555 🕒 Daily 10am–9pm

SUKHOTHAI

The Dream Café £££

The most attractive-looking restaurant in Sukhothai, The Dream Café is filled with antique-style bric-a-brac and tables tucked into corners surrounded by wood-panelled walls. The food is a mixture of Thai and standard Western dishes.

🔒 196 B3 ⊠ 86/1 Thanon Singhawat ☎ 05 561 2081 🕒 10am–11pm

Kru Lew £

Come here for authentic *pad thai* (▶ 10), wrapped in a thin omelette, and *naim nueng* (rice paper rolls). The service is friendly.

🔒 196 B3 ⊠ Soi Mahasaranon 1 ☎ 05 561 2710 🕒 Daily 8am–10pm

PHITSANULOK

Rim Nan ££

Rim Nan is a floating restaurant with a superb house speciality, *neua yang* (barbecued beef). Moored by the west bank of the Nan River, the restaurant feels more like a brightly lit pleasure cruiser than a floating platform. The river catches the cool breezes during the hot season, so it's a great place to sit and relax any time during the day or night.

🔒 196 C3 ⊠ 63/2 Thanon Wang Chan 🕒 Daily noon–2:30, 7:30–10:30

Where to...
Shop

AYUTTHAYA

Bang Sai Royal Folk Arts and Crafts Centre (Tambon Chang Yai, Bang Sai, tel: 03 536 6252, moderate) trains local people in traditional arts and crafts, and has a well-stocked sales outlet. It's 24km (14.8 miles) southwest of Ayutthaya, but worth the journey. At the **Ayutthaya Park Complex** (126 Thanon Asia, Klong Suan Plu District), which is slightly out of the main town, there's an indoor floating market offering a range of interesting souvenirs.

SUKHOTHAI

Owing to the excellent clay found in the Si Satchanalai and Sawankhalok area north of Sukhothai, an ancient **ceramics** tradition still thrives and is sold in shops in Si Satchanalai and Sukhothai.

Kilns in Si Satchanalai and Sawankhalok have been producing **celadon** for centuries. Little finds its way to local shops, but you can buy from **Sawankhalok's principal factory**, opposite the PTP filling station on the Phitsanulok highway (open Mon–Fri, 9–6). Sukhothai gold and silver jewellery is highly prized for its flamboyant style and use of coloured enamel. The Sawankhalok road 3km (2 miles) north of Sukhothai has gold and silver merchants. **Lumchad Ancient Silver** (340/5 Sawankhalok Road) is recommended. The **Sathorn Gold and Textile Museum** and shop (Highway 101, Si Satchanalai) sells fine gold, silver and local textiles.

Where to...
Be Entertained

FESTIVALS

Big annual events to look out for include **Kanchanaburi's River Kwai Bridge Festival** (end November/beginning December, ▶ 25). The famous bridge (▶ 68) becomes the venue for a number of events that culminate each evening with a spectacular sound-and-light show.

The **Loi Krathong Festival** (full moon between late October and mid-November, ▶ 25) takes place within the Sukhothai Historical Park, with the ancient monuments lit up in dramatic fashion (▶ 75).

AYUTTHAYA

Ayutthaya Park Complex (126 Thanon Asia) has a bowling alley, cinemas and an artificial sea world.

OUTDOOR ENTERTAINMENT

Safarine (tel: 860 491662, www. safarine.com) offers customised jungle tours and river trips for all ages. **Good Times Travel** (63/1 Mae Nam Kwai Road, tel: 03 462 4441), offers a selection of one- and two-day tours.

NIGHTLIFE

Kanchanaburi has live music at the **Apache Saloon** (Thanon Saengchuto) and floating discos. **Phitsanulok Plaza** has a range of pubs and dance clubs. The **Tree House** restaurant (Airport Road, tel: 05 521 2587) and **Sukothai's Rajthanee Hotel** (229 Charodvitheetong Road) have live music nightly.

The North

Getting Your Bearings

Most visitors to Thailand make the pilgrimage to the scenic north to relax in the cool green mountains, to shop for some of the best crafts in the country and to trek to hill-tribe villages. The ancient and modern city of Chiang Mai is the capital of the area and, with its rich collection of temples, its moated old city, night market and night bazaar, is a place where people love to linger. This is the ideal part of the country to learn the art of Thai cooking, or even study the Thai language or Buddhist meditation.

The ancient kingdom of the north was known as Lanna, the "land of a million rice fields", a fertile region watered by chocolate-coloured rivers and plunging waterfalls. It is easy to spend a few weeks enjoying the unhurried pace of life and exploring the surrounding scattered villages in the lush mountains where the clean air is perhaps envied by the people who live in Bangkok.

The distinct region in the very north that borders Burma and Laos, known as Sam Liam Thong Kham (The Golden Triangle), was the legendary zone of drug smuggling in the 1960s and 1970s, and offers the chance to travel to these neighbouring countries. It's bordered by mountain ranges, including the highest peak in the country, Doi Inthanon (2,565m/8,413 feet), which is part of a national park of the same name and great for walking and trekking.

Pockets of mist sit between the mountain tops which surround Mae Hong Son

★ Don't Miss

0 — 100 km
0 — 50 miles

Mae Sai

Sam Liam Thong Kham
4

Chiang Khong

5
Chiang Saen

1708m
Doi Sam Sao Noi

Doi Mae Salong

2285m

Tha Ton

Fang

Chiang Rai **6**

Wiang Chai

Nong Ouk

Thoeng

Phan

Soppong

Pai

2 Trekking

Chiang Dao

2005m
Doi Mae Ya

3
Mae Hong Son

Wat Chan

Mae Khachan

Wang Nua

Phayao

Kwan Phayao

2031m
Doi Mae Tho

Khun Yuam

Chiang Mai
7
1

Bor Sang

San Kamphaeng

Chae Hom

Ngao

Chae Hom

Kiu Lom

2595m
Doi Inthanon

Lamphun
8

9 Doi Khun Tan

Mae Chang

Chom Thong

Mae Tha

Lampang

Mae La Noi

Hang Chat

Hot

Mae Sariang

At Your Leisure

Left: A monk entering a temple in Mae Hong Son

Page 87: An Akha tribeswoman at a market in Chiang Mai province

In Six Days

If you're not quite sure where to begin your travels, this itinerary recommends six practical and enjoyable days out exploring northern Thailand, taking in some of the best places to see using the Getting Your Bearings map on the previous page.

Day 1

Morning
The most comfortable way to get from Bangkok to ❶ Chiang Mai (left, ➤ 92–94) is to fly, or catch the overnight sleeper train. On arrival, spend a few hours exploring the old city with its moat and *wats* by bike or on foot. Take a *tuk-tuk* to the **Hill-Tribe Museum** (➤ 93–94) on the outskirts of town.

Lunch
Take a *songthaew* to have lunch at Galae (➤ 106) on the lower slopes of Doi Suthep (the mountain that overlooks Chiang Mai), and check out some of their central and northern Thai dishes.

Afternoon
Take another *songthaew* further up the mountain to visit the temple **Wat Doi Suthep** (opposite below, ➤ 92), the north's most important temple, and enjoy the spectacular views of the surrounding countryside.

Evening
Enjoy the spectacle that is **Chiang Mai's night bazaar** (➤ 93), shopping for crafts and souvenirs, or just wandering around the many stalls. Have dinner at the Brasserie (➤ 106). There is live music every night and cocktails are served until the early hours. It can get busy at weekends, so arrive early.

Days 2–4

Go on a **2 three-day trek from Chiang Mai** (➤ 95–97). Most involve several hours' walking every day. Elephant-riding and river-rafting are optional extras. Hill-tribe communities (below) are the main attraction and accommodation is in village huts. Return to Chiang Mai.

Days 5–6

Complete the jeep tour (➤ 177–180) of the villages on the road to **3 Mae Hong Son** (➤ 98–99) starting from Chiang Mai. If you are back in Chiang Mai in time, you can go to a traditional show with a northern-style dinner at the Old Chiang Mai Cultural Centre (➤ 107) between 7 and 10pm.

Chiang Mai

Chiang Mai, capital of the north and Thailand's second-largest city, has more than a hundred temples. With its cooler climate, visible expatriate community and sophisticated atmosphere, it's a relaxing place to spend a few days before setting off on a trek. The moat-enclosed, partly walled old town invites wandering, as does the biggest night market in the country, which is a treasure trove of crafts.

Wat Doi Suthep

The mountain-top temple of Wat Doi Suthep, 16km (10 miles) west of town, is easily reached by *songthaew*. It is said that the location was decided by a sacred white elephant who picked this spot by trumpeting and then circling here three times before lying down to die. Wat Doi Suthep is the north's most important temple, where candlelit processions are made on major religious occasions. It is also part of a national park, rich in birdlife.

Opposite: Monks at Wat Chedi Luang

A saffron-robed monk by the old city wall in Chiang Mai

Other Temples

It would take several days to visit all the temples in town, so start with the top three, which can be visited on a half-hour walking route.

Wat Phra Singh, at the western end of Thanon Ratchdam-noen, is an impressive complex with a 14th-century *chedi* containing the ashes of King Kam Fu. The carved wooden **Viharn Lai Kam** is a classic example of Lanna-style architecture. Inside is one of three **Phra Singh Buddha** images, a highly revered statue believed to have been magically created in the second century. This one is in bronze and is surrounded by exquisite 18th-century murals depicting life in this part of Thailand.

Wat Chedi Luang, on Phra Pok Klao Road (off Ratchdam-noen), has a giant 60m (197-foot) ruined brick *chedi* that once sheltered the Emerald Buddha, now in Wat Phra Kaeo in Bangkok (➤ 45) and still contains the city's *lak muang*, or spiritual pillar.

Wat Chiang Man, near Thanon Wiang Kaeo, is Chiang Mai's oldest temple. Enter the *viharn* on the right of the main entrance to see two important Buddha images made from stone and crystal.

Night Bazaar
The night bazaar is a shopping haven full of fake perfumes, designer copies and tourist junk, as well as lacquerware, woodcarvings, silverwork, antiques and spices. Watch out for labels saying "100 per cent silk" – very often the fabric is in fact viscose or even polyester. Stalls are set up along **Chang Khlan** between Thanon Tha Phae and Si Don Chai at around 6pm and are not taken down until around 11pm.

During the day, **Warorot Market** sells more local goods and produce.

Hill-Tribe Museum
Almost half of the 750,000 hill-tribe people of northern Thailand are **Karen**. The last 20 years have seen an influx of around a million refugees from Laos, Burma and Cambodia, three-quarters of whom are Karen from Burma, fleeing the

A HARD BARGAIN

Goods on sale in Chiang Mai's shops and markets are often sold at over-inflated prices. Knowing the system – which applies to shopping anywhere in Thailand – is essential. Buying where there are no fixed prices is a ritualised game, with figures punched out on a calculator. The seller will quote you a much higher price than they expect to get. It is up to you to work out how much higher and to bargain hard, but politely. The rule is to offer half the demanded price and to settle for something in-between.

military regime there. Some hundred or so of these are **long-necked women** (▶ 99) living in tourist villages, which charge an entrance fee and display the women, as if in a zoo, for tourists to gawk at.

The Hill-Tribe Museum has fascinating and well-presented displays about the hill tribes. Information is given about the various communities, each with their distinct beliefs, dress and farming practices.

Housed in a three-storey pavilion in the middle of a lake in Ratchamangkhala Park on the city's northern outskirts, it is worth visiting for its lovely location alone. The easy-to-miss **crafts centre** on the ground floor is also worth a visit.

Lights twinkle over the night bazaar

TAKING A BREAK

Try **Heuan Phen** (▶ 106) on Thanon Ratchamankha, for good northern Thai food, or **Khao Soi Islam**, a Muslim restaurant on Thanon Charoen Prathet Soi 1.

➕ 196 B4 🛈 TAT, 105 Thanon Chiang Mai–Lamphun, opposite Lek Bridge
☎ 05 324 8604 🕓 Daily 8:30–4:30

Hill-Tribe Museum
✉ Ratchamangkhala Park ☎ 05 321 0872 🕓 Mon–Fri 9–4 💳 Free

CHIANG MAI: INSIDE INFO

Top tips Rent a **bicycle** for in town, but avoid the Superhighway around the city.
■ **Nancy Chandler's Map of Chiang Mai** (available from newsagents and tourist souvenir shops) has detailed plans of the night bazaar and Warorot Market as well as sightseeing tips, out-of-town trips and practical information about getting around.
■ As it can get hot in the city from April to June, it is worth considering booking into a hotel with a **swimming pool** or seeking out one of the **public baths.**
■ Chiang Mai Land Sports Club (off Chang Klan Road) is open to visitors, and has a 30m (98.5-foot) pool, tennis courts and an airy restaurant.

Hidden gem Examples of the different **styles of house** built by the various **hill tribes** can be found in the Hill-Tribe Museum grounds next to the lake.

2 Trekking

Much of the lure of northern Thailand comes from its trekking opportunities. Just about everyone who makes it to this region jumps at the chance to journey on foot through jungle and mountains, visiting unique hill-tribe villages and staying in the headman's house for the night. These treks do not normally involve strenuous hiking.

An elephant trek through the jungle is popular with visitors

Most treks are **organized from Chiang Mai**, where around two hundred agencies offer treks covering nearly everywhere that can be trekked in the north. **Chiang Rai, Pai** and **Mae Hong Son** also have tour agencies, but these tend to offer more local treks. A tour from somewhere other than these

TRIBAL ETIQUETTE

■ **Ask before taking photographs.** Many villagers are uncomfortable about having their picture taken; this especially applies to pregnant women and babies.

■ Though it is tempting to **take gifts** with you for the tribes, they can have a negative impact. Showing family photographs or postcards of home is a better idea.

■ **Dress modestly** (shirt or T-shirt, long trousers or a skirt).

■ **Do not show public displays of affection.** These are offensive to villagers as well as to Thai people in general.

■ **Respect the villagers' beliefs.** Do not touch or sit beneath the entrance gate or giant swing in an Akha village (Akha are the poorest of the hill-tribes; the gates and swing at the entrance to their villages are sacred). Do not photograph or touch shrines in houses.

CHOOSING A TREK

There is an overwhelming number of agents trying to sell treks. The first step is to decide on your requirements.

- **How many days** do you want to go for? It could be anything from two to fourteen – although three-day trips are by far the most common and enough for most people.
- Are you willing to **pay extra** for transport costs to a more remote area? It is worth confirming whether private vehicles – rather than public buses, which can mean long waits – are used.
- Do you want extras such as **river-rafting** and **elephant-riding**? These can be fun and are very popular.
- Try to **speak to the guide**, rather than just the person selling you the trek, before you commit yourself. That way you can check out his/her level of English and general approach. Most guides should speak some English and know about how to behave with the hill tribes.
- **Ask other travellers** who have just returned from a trip or get the list of licensed companies from TAT.
- **Establish in writing** what exactly is included in the trek cost (for example, what kind of food and what kind of bedding might be provided if it turns cold).
- **Establish exact departure and return times.**
- If you go on a trek organized by the place where you are staying, **make sure that there will still be a room** for you when you return; sometimes rooms can be booked out to other parties while you are on your trek.
- **Check who else is going on the trip with you** (eight is the maximum total).
- Ask about the **level of fitness** required for your route. Although most routes are not as strenuous as trekking in some other countries, a certain standard might be required.
- Make sure that the trek has **two guides** – someone at the front and someone bringing up the rear.

Women of the Karen hill tribe carrying packs in Nai Soi village

Opposite: Akha hill-tribe village, Chiang Rai province

four will probably be cheaper, but more informally arranged and with less regulation. There is a constant search by both tour operators and tourists alike for the next new and exotic villages. Ten years ago Pai was billed as the "untouristed zone", although now it has plenty of visitors.

Hill Tribes

Although the 750,000 hill-tribe people are usually referred to collectively, these "mountain people" – a more accurate translation of the Thai term – form distinct communities (➤ 19–21). They originate from countries as diverse as Burma (Karen people), Tibet (Lisu, Lahu and Akha) and China (Mien and Hmong). Belief systems, dress and agricultural practices all vary from tribe to tribe.

To get the most out of a trek, first visit the **Hill-Tribe Museum** (➤ 93–94) in Chiang Mai to learn something about the various tribes.

Eco-friendly Tourism

A rising awareness about the impact of tourism on the environment and local communities in recent years has brought about an increased number of eco-friendly and ethically orientated tours in these areas.

TAKING A BREAK

Food is provided on any organized trek, but check what it is likely to be. Village food can be very basic and it usually pays to pack your own "survival kit". Include plenty of fruit.

Tours from Chiang Mai
➕ 196 B4 ✉ Wayfarers Travel: 20 Tapae Road, Soi 4, Chiang Mai 50100
☎ 05 320 8271; www.wayfarersthailand.com 💷 For two people: 1,400 baht for a two-day/one-night trek or 3,500 baht for three days/two nights; costs go down as the number in the group increases

Tours from Mae Hong Son
➕ 196 A5 ☎ Trekking Thailand: 05 320 8271; www.trekkingthailand.com
💷 Phone for prices

3 Mae Hong Son

Mae Hong Son, more poetically known as the "City of Three Mists", is in fact a town of just 6,000 people. It was isolated until a paved road was built in the 1960s, and despite the airport bringing in people from Chiang Mai every day, it still has a remote atmosphere. The lush paddy fields, scenic waterfalls and mountains, and dense forest that surrounds it are home to many Burmese and hill-tribe people.

The Town

Most people come to Mae Hong Son to explore the surrounding area on treks, and it has more than its fair share of backpacker guest houses. Visit **Wat Doi Kong Mu** to the west, with memorable views over the town and valley. From the summit you can also see the mountains in Burma to the west.

LONG-NECKED WOMEN

One of the most disturbing tourist attractions here is the "long-necked" women of the Paduang tribe who have left Myanmar (Burma) to escape its repressive regime. The women wear brass coils up to 30cm (12 inches) high on their necks, increasing them in number from a young age. The coils force the collarbone and ribs down rather than stretching the neck, which is the visual effect. These women are put on show to those who pay the entrance fee to the village – predominantly at Nai Soi, 35km (22 miles) northwest of Mae Hong Son. Many tourists have reported feeling sickened at the sight, and there is some argument that visitors encourage the continuation of a practice that is outlawed in Myanmar as barbaric and would otherwise die out.

The Loop

A 600km (372-mile) twisting and steep route, much of it built by the Japanese during World War II, forms a **scenic loop** (➤ 177–180) from Chiang Mai, and halfway round is Mae Hong Son. Starting in Mae Hong Son, **Highway 108** goes to Chiang Mai and **Route 1095** goes from Chiang Mai to Mae Hong Son. You can do the loop in either direction.

Highway 108 winds south from Mae Hong Son to the well-maintained and much-visited **Doi Inthanon National Park**, home to hundreds of species of birds. Paved roads lead to Doi

Queen Sirikit's chedi at Doi Inthanon National Park

Inthanon, the highest mountain in Thailand, although at only 2,565m (8,413 feet) it is rather disappointing.

Two royal *chedis*, built to honour the 60th birthdays of the king and queen of Thailand, are where Thais come to pay their respects to the much-loved royal couple (➤ 12–14). Nearby, the **Kew Mae Pan Trail** follows a two-hour circular walk through the forest.

The first main stop on Route 1095 is **Pai**, 100km (62 miles) east of Mae Hong Son. It has a laid-back atmosphere, hot springs and some tourist facilities, including internet cafés and international cuisine.

The friendly market town of **Soppong**, strung along the Pai River, has the most important cave in the area, **Tham Lot**.

TAKING A BREAK

The **Golden Teak** terrace restaurant at the **Imperial Tara Hotel** (➤ 107) overlooks a large garden, or try **Bai Fern** (➤ 107) for Chinese and Thai dishes.

➕ 196 A5

Doi Inthanon National Park
☎ 05 326 8550; www.dnp.go.th ⓖ Always open 💷 Expensive 🚌 From Chiang Mai or Mae Sariang to Chom Thong, bus to Mae Klang, then *songthaew*

MAE HONG SON: INSIDE INFO

Top tip The **ideal time** to visit the area is between November and March although nights can be cold. Between June and October heavy rains can make travel difficult.

One to miss Despite the coachloads of tourists that flood **Fish Cave**, north of Mae Hong Son, it is relatively uninteresting and worth avoiding.

At Your Leisure

Monks beside a mermaid statue at the Golden Triangle

❹ The Golden Triangle

The area of Sam Liam Thong Kham is where the borders of Thailand, Burma and Laos meet, and the Ruak and Mekhong rivers converge.

Coachloads of tourists stream in every day to the village of **Sop Ruak**, with its souvenir stalls and two large, chic hotels. Once a thriving centre of the opium trade, Sop Ruak has two excellent museums on the subject of narcotics: the **House of Opium Museum** is in the centre of the village; the grand **Hall of Opium** is just outside on the road to **Mae Sai**. If you're in a hurry, visit the Opium Museum, if you have the time the Hall of Opium is a must.

A climb to the hilltop temple of **Wat Phra That Phu Khao** above Sop Ruak is rewarded with panoramic views to Burmese mountains.

Take a **longtail boat trip** (a group of four can share the cost) on the Mekong River. You will get a look at Laos (and a chance to step briefly on its soil) as well as the mammoth casino and hotel on Burmese land, the Golden Triangle Paradise Resort, set up by Khun Sa, a drug warlord.
➕ **196 C5**

OPIUM

Illicit opium-growing and trading is firmly associated with The Golden Triangle in most people's imagination. Although it has been illegal to grow opium since 1959, it is only in recent years that there has been significant success in reducing crops with the help of government initiatives. However, rates of addiction still run high among the hill-tribes, opium is still grown in the north of Thailand and remaining production of heroin (a refined form of opium) has been pushed across the borders to Laos and Burma.

House of Opium Museum
✉ 30km marker, southeast edge of Sop Ruak
☎ www.houseofopium.com ⏱ Daily 7–7
💲 Inexpensive

Hall of Opium
✉ Sop Ruak ⏱ Tue–Sun 8:30–4 ☎ 05
378 4444/6; www.goldentrianglepark.org
💲 Expensive

The head of Buddha at the Chiang Saen National Museum

5 Chiang Saen

This ruined riverside settlement on the northern reaches of the country stands at an historic trading crossroads with Laos and China. The **Chiang Saen National Museum,** exhibiting finds from the Lanna period and displays of local arts and crafts, is not as grand as its title suggests. A short distance away, behind the museum, are the ruins of **Wat Chedi Luang** and there are a number of other *wats* in the vicinity. The one to try to see is **Wat Phakhaopan,** situated near the river, owing to its impressive *chedi* and walking Buddhas. It is easy to get around the area using motorbike taxis and *saamlaws*. There is activity along the Mekong River where boats from China, Laos and Myanmar call in. Possibly once the capital of an ancient kingdom, the town was founded in the 14th century, destroyed by the Burmese in 1804 and has existed in its present form for 100 years or so.
➕ 196 C5

National Museum
✉ Thanon Phahonyothin 🕐 Wed–Sun 8:30–4:30 💰 Inexpensive

6 Chiang Rai

Situated on the Kok River, Chiang Rai was once the capital of northern Thailand. It has grown quickly over recent years to become a commercial tourist centre, offering upmarket

FOR KIDS
- The **Elephant Conservation Centre,** 30km (18.5 miles) northwest of Lampang, has elephant rides. Call 05 424 7875 or check www.changthai.com for information.
- The **visitor centre at Doi Inthanon National Park** has interactive displays about the wildlife, aimed at younger visitors.
- **Boat trips** on the Pai River from Huai Deua, near Nai Soi near the Burmese border.
- **Chiang Mai Zoo,** on the outskirts of the city (8–6, last entry 5pm, inexpensive), has masses of Asian birds as well as Thai elephants and Chinese pandas.

Looking across the Mekong River to Laos on the opposite bank from Sop Ruak

accommodation and package tours. During the day you might want to take a look at **Wat Phra That Doi Tong**, with its wooden *lak muang* (the city pillar, home of the city's guardian spirit), and **Wat Phra Kaeo** where the Emerald Buddha (➤ 45) was first discovered. Craft shops, the **Hill-Tribe Museum** and the night bazaar are other diversions, but the town is mostly used as a base for treks.

➕ 196 B5 ℹ TAT, 448/16 Thanon Singhaklai ☎ 05 371 7433 🕐 Daily 8:30–4:30

Hill-Tribe Museum
✉ 620 Thanon Tanalai ☎ 05 371 9167 🕐 Daily 9–8 💷 Inexpensive

🟢 Chiang Mai Courses

Cookery courses are a popular pursuit in Chiang Mai. They can teach you how to find your way around a Thai market, the art of pineapple-cutting, and recipes using fresh coconut milk, fiery chillies and sweet basil. The **Chiang Mai Thai Cookery School** was the first of its

kind, and so popular that the city is now packed with similar operations offering courses from one to several days. If you are not interested in things culinary, **Thai language, traditional massage, and Vipassana, Hindu and Buddhist meditation courses** run for up to a month.

➕ 196 B4

Chiang Mai Thai Cookery School
✉ 47/2 Thanon Moon Muang ☎ 05 320 6388; www.thaicookeryschool.com 💷 Expensive

AUA Language School
✉ 73 Thanon Ratchdamnoen ☎ 05 327 8407; www.auathailand.org 💷 Expensive

Old Medicine Hospital (massage)
✉ Soi Siwaka Komarat, opposite Old Chiang Mai Cultural Centre ☎ 05 327 5085; www.thaimassageschool.ac.th 💷 Expensive

Northern Insight Meditation Centre
✉ Wat Ram Poeng, Thanon Canal ☎ 05 327 8620 🕐 Month-long Vipassana courses only 💷 Expensive

8 Lamphun

This quiet town, surrounded by rice fields on the banks of the Kuang River, is best seen as a day trip from Chiang Mai, 26km (16 miles) away. Lamphun was the capital of the Haripunchai principality between 750 and 1281. It has many ancient temples, which are still in use today.

Wat Phra That Haripunchai is a temple complex thought to have been founded in the 11th century. It features the 46m (151-foot), 15th-century *chedi* **Suwan**, with a pure gold, tiered umbrella.

The small **National Museum** has a collection of religious artefacts, including some Buddha images. **Wat Kukut** (or Wat Chama Thewi), on the other side of town, has possibly the two oldest *chedis* in the country.

➕ 196 B4

National Museum
✉ Thanon Inthayongyot 🕐 Daily 9–4
🎫 Inexpensive

9 Doi Khun Tan National Park

This 225sq km (88-square-mile) former hill station is made up of bamboo, tropical forests and pine trees. It lies at the 1,363m (4,470-foot) summit of Doi Khun Tan, famous for orchids and other wild flowers. It is possibly Thailand's least visited national park, yet easily reached from Chiang Mai, with trains from Chiang Mai to the park's station, 1.5km (1 mile) from the headquarters. The tunnel on the train journey – at 1,362m (4,467 feet), the longest tunnel in Thailand – cuts right though the mountain. Self-guided trails (easy) run through the park and to the summit of Doi Khun Tan. Bungalow and camping accommodation is available near the park headquarters. At weekends and holidays there tend to be a greater number of visitors.

➕ 196 B4 ☎ 05 351 8726 🎫 Expensive

Doi Khun Tan National Park is famous for its exotic orchids

MAE SAI TO BURMA

From Mae Sai in the far north of Thailand you can cross into Burma for a day's shopping in the Burmese border town of Tachilek. The local market there is packed with traders selling local gems and uncut stones. Prices are low, but be wary when offered "rubies" or "sapphires" at knock-down rates – not everything that sparkles in this market is genuine. The Burmese authorities levy a US$10 fee for spending a day in Tachilek, but it also covers a two-week visa allowing you to travel as far as the Chinese border at Kengtung. Local taxis will take you there for around US$25 return. Visiting Tachilek is also a useful way of extending your Thai tourist visa – many expatriates use this route regularly to stay legally in Thailand.

Where to...
Stay

Prices
Expect to pay per double room per night:
£ under 2,000 baht   ££ 2,000–5,000 baht   £££ over 5,000 baht

CHIANG MAI

Amari Rincome ££

One of the older hotels in town, the Amari Rincome is tastefully decorated throughout with beautiful local crafts and artefacts. It's a good place for families with children, and has one of the best swimming pools in Chiang Mai. The hotel is renowned in the area for its reasonably priced lunchtime buffets, while regular food fairs promote a wide range of international cuisines.

➕ 202 A3 ⊠ 1 Thanon Nimmanhaemin
☎ 05 322 1130; www.amari.com

The Chedi £££

Superbly designed, this hotel stands on the banks of the Mae Ping River in the city centre. The former British Consulate stood on this site; its main building has been integrated within the hotel as the restaurant. There is a pool and spa. Bedrooms have dark timber floors, and teak and rattan furniture. The service is highly regarded.

➕ 202 D2 ⊠ 123 Charoen Prathet Road
☎ 05 325 3333; www.ghmhotels.com

Four Seasons £££

This resort tucked away in the spectacular Mae Sa Valley, with 8ha (20 acres) of gardens, is one of the north's best-kept secrets. There are two small lakes and terraced rice fields with their own water buffalo in the grounds. Large pavilions and 13 palatial Residence Suites housed in three- or four-storey villas dot the landscape. Each of the pavilions is roomy and decorated with rich Thai fabrics. Each Residence Suite offers master, guest and children's rooms with private plunge pools or rooftop penthouse and a live-in housekeeper. Other attributes include world-class spa facilities.

➕ 196 B4 ⊠ Mae Rim-Samoeng Old Road
☎ 05 329 8181; www.fourseasons.com

Lai Thai Guesthouse £

If you're planning to visit Chiang Mai during the annual water-throwing festival in April (➤ 24), and you don't mind getting wet for three days, then this is the place to stay. Located by the moat surrounding Chiang Mai's old city, Lai Thai offers good-value, no-frills accommodation and a relaxing pool.

➕ 202 C2 ⊠ 111/4–5 Thanon Kotchasan
☎ 05 327 1725; www.laithai.com

River View Lodge £

Overlooking the River Ping, this large, almost Swiss-style, chalet is secluded and yet close to the heart of Chiang Mai. It offers comfortable rooms decorated with traditional northern Lanna furnishings (wall-hangings made from woven Lanna cloth, low rattan tables, wooden and paper lanterns). Try to get one of the rooms with a river balcony. You'll find the River View at the end of a quiet little lane, not too far from the famous night bazaar (➤ 93). Facilities include a swimming pool.

➕ 202 D2 ⊠ 25 Thanon Charoen Prathet, Soi 2 ☎ 05 327 1110;
www.riverviewlodgech.com

Tamarind Village £££

Tucked away in the centre of the old city, shielded from the traffic by thick shrubbery and towering bamboo, Tamarind Village is a tasteful oasis of calm. Whitewashed corridors, embracing a secluded pool area, give it an almost monastic atmosphere, but the rooms are comfortable, furnished in teak woods and featuring selected antiques. There is also a spa, offering a good range of treatments, and a cooking school.

➕ 202 C2 ⊠ 50–1 Ratchadamnoen Road
☎ 05 341 8898; www.tamarindvillage.com

MAE HONG SON

Imperial Tara ££

Set amid extensive private tropical gardens, this beautifully situated resort, slightly to the south of the main town, offers genuine peace and tranquility. Mae Hong Son is an easy-going town with a slow pace of life and the Imperial Tara mirrors this feeling perfectly. The rooms are designed in the northern Thai style, with a hint of Burmese influence and they blend perfectly with the surrounding teak forest. The terrace restaurant is well sited, overlooking the large garden and a small stream.

➕ 196 A5 ⊠ 149 Moo 8, Tambon Pang Moo
☎ 05 368 4444/6; www.imperialhotels.com

GOLDEN TRIANGLE/SOP RUAK

Anantara Golden Triangle £££

It's difficult to think of a more romantic location than this fabulous luxury resort combining classic northern Thai and contemporary design, overlooking the junction of two rivers (Mekong and Ruak) and three countries (Thailand, Laos and Myanmar-Burma). In the heart of the fabled Golden Triangle (▲ 100), the hotel is surrounded by 160ha (395 acres) of lush gardens and bamboo forests. All the rooms offer unparalleled views of either Laos or Myanmar. Facilities offered include mountain biking, elephant rides and longtail boat cruises on the Mekong River.

➕ 196 C5 ⊠ The Golden Triangle, Chiang Saen district, Chiang Rai province
☎ 05 378 4084; www.anantara.com

CHIANG RAI

Dusit Island Resort ££

Although a large and somewhat impersonal place, this is nevertheless the best of the hotels in Chiang Rai. The Dusit occupies its own island in the middle of the River Kok. All rooms have wonderful views of the surrounding valley and the hotel's beautiful gardens. There are a number of good restaurants within the hotel complex, but the pick of the crop is undoubtedly Chinatown, their excellent Chinese restaurant.

➕ 196 B5 ⊠ 1129 Thanon Kraisorasit
☎ 05 371 5777; www.dusit.com

Golden Triangle Inn £

Within easy walking distance of downtown Chiang Rai, this attractive low-rise hotel has cleverly blended the modern with the traditional. All rooms are large and air-conditioned and an American breakfast is included in the rate. The attractive landscaped grounds

have a painstakingly cultivated Japanese/Thai garden. At weekends the attached café showcases traditional Lanna music, a quiet and relaxing affair using string and xylophone-like instruments. Also on the same site are a helpful travel agency and a car-rental office.

➕ 196 B5 ⊠ 590 Thanon Phahonyothin
☎ 05 371 6996;
www.goldenchiangrai.com/inn.htm

The Legend Resort ££

The location is superb, on an island in the Mae Kok River, and yet within walking distance of the town centre. The accommodation and landscaped gardens are attractive, with lots of space and outdoor bathroom facilities. The Lanna-style design makes good use of local wood and bricks, and white plastered walls. The resort's use of colours complements the elegant furniture and decor.

➕ 196 B5 ⊠ 124/15 Thanon Kohloy
☎ 053 910 400;
www.thelegend-chiangrai.com

Where to...
Eat and Drink

Prices

Expect to pay per person for a three-course meal, excluding drinks and service:

£ under 300 baht   ££ 300–600 baht   £££ over 600 baht

CHIANG MAI

Beccofino Trattoria ££–£££

An off-shoot of Beccofino Trattoria in Bangkok and under Italian management, this branch has a wood-fired oven for pizzas. Charcoal grills and pasta dishes complete the menu. If you want a particular dish it is worth asking.

➕ **202 A3** 🖂 20/2 Soi 7, Nimmanhemin Road 🕾 05 322 6590 🕘 Daily 11–10:30

Brasserie ££

Perfectly situated on the east bank of the River Ping near the Nawarat Bridge, the Brasserie is perfect for

an evening meal. This stretch of the river has many good restaurants, but the extensive Thai and European menu coupled with the live music sets the Brasserie apart.

➕ **202 D2** 🖂 37 Thanon Charoen Rat 🕾 05 324 1665 🕘 Daily 4pm–1am

Galae ££

For atmosphere, especially in the early evening, Galae is hard to beat. Situated on the lower slopes of Doi Suthep (the mountain that overlooks Chiang Mai) and at the edge of a small lake, it offers great views of the city itself. The menu consists mainly of central and

northern Thai dishes. The house dishes include *kai galae* (roast chicken with herbs).

➕ **202 A2** 🖂 65 Thanon Suthep 🕾 05 327 8655 🕘 Daily 11–8

Heuan Phen £

Excellent northern Thai food is served in the main building during the day and in an old wooden house to the back of the main restaurant at night. Specialities include *nam phrik ong* (minced pork with tomatoes and chillies, almost like a Thai bolognese sauce), and *kaeng hang lay* (curried pork with fresh ginger and peanuts).

➕ **202 C2** 🖂 112 Thanon Ratchamankha 🕾 05 327 7103 🕘 Daily 8am–3, 5–10

Le Coq d'Or £££

There is a choice of an English country house-style dining room or a tropical glasshouse setting in this fine-dining restaurant. Established for more than 30 years, Le Coq d'Or serves fine French cuisine. The foie gras is expensive, but affordable

delicacies include truffle soup and superb soufflés. Live music is played nightly, except on Sundays.

➕ **202 off D1** 🖂 11 Soi 2, Koh Klang Road 🕾 05 314 1555; www.lecoqdorchiangmai.com 🕘 Daily 5–10

Lotus Restaurant ££

Off the beaten track a little – best take a taxi – but this is an opportunity to enjoy some Lebanese food. The set of five *mezze* dishes is recommended as is the *kafta* (spiced minced meat cakes grilled on skewers) or *shish taouk* (marinated chicken grilled on skewers). The best dessert is the *namoura* (semolina cake) with almonds and cream.

➕ **202 off C3** 🖂 Lotus Hotel, 2/25 Tanon Viengbua, off Chang Puak Road 🕾 05 321 5376; www.lotus-hotel.com 🕘 Daily 8am–10pm

Moxie ££

A hip restaurant in a very style-conscious hotel, Moxie serves some unusual cocktails, innovative dishes (though not vegetarian friendly) and irresistible desserts. The style of the food is international, with a flair for mixing in Thai touches so that, for example, a pasta dish comes with Chiang Mai sausage and chillies. It all works very well; a break from traditional Thai cuisine.

➕ 202 D1 ⊠ D2 Hotel, 100 Changklan Road
☎ 05 399 9999 ⊙ Daily 6:30am–10:30pm

Old Chiang Mai Cultural Centre ££

Traditional northern-style *khantoke* meals are accompanied by Thai classical dance and music, set in a series of old teak houses, and the meal is served on a low, tray-like table called a *khantoke*. Central dishes include *nam prik ong* (minced pork and tomatoes), *kaeng hang lay* (curried pork with fresh ginger and peanuts), *khaep mu* (crispy fried pork rinds), and *tam makhua* (an aubergine and garlic dip with hard-boiled eggs and fresh mint).

➕ 202 B1 ⊠ 185/3 Thanon Wualai
☎ 05 320 2993/5 ⊙ Daily 7pm–10pm

MAE HONG SON

Bai Fern ££

Thai and Chinese dishes are served in this attractive old restaurant. The friendly ambience is enhanced by local decorative items on the walls. One of the best places in town, with a candlelit terrace.

➕ 196 A5 ⊠ Thanon Khunlum Praphat
☎ 05 361 1374 ⊙ Daily 10–10

Golden Teak Restaurant ££

This is part of the Imperial Tara (▶ 105). Thai food is available, but if you crave good Western food – rarely available in Mae Hong Son – this is the place to come. The Western-style breakfasts, served from 7am, are particularly good.

➕ 196 A5 ⊠ 149 Moo 8, Tambon Pang Moo
☎ 05 384 4444 ⊙ Daily 7am–midnight

GOLDEN TRIANGLE/SOP RUAK

Border View ££

Thai and Chinese food are served on a beautiful terrace of the Imperial Hotel overlooking the Mekong River in the heart of The Golden Triangle. The steaks are tender and the cooks know how to produce a satisfying and tasty Western breakfast, as well as other Western dishes.

➕ 196 C5 ⊠ Imperial Golden Triangle Resort, Chiang Saen ☎ 05 378 4001
⊙ Daily 6am–11

CHIANG RAI

Aye's Restaurant ££

Located opposite the town's bustling night bazaar and equipped with outdoor seating, Aye's Restaurant is an atmospheric place to people-watch in the evening. It also offers a wide variety of Thai and Western dishes.

➕ 196 B5 ⊠ 879/4-5 Thanon Phahonyothin
☎ 05 375 2535 ⊙ Daily noon–11

Haw Naliga £

Located near the Chiang Rai clock tower, after which it is named, this restaurant is always popular, especially late into the night as it's one of the last places in town to close. Recommended dishes include *khao kaa moo* (pork with pickled cabbage and boiled eggs), which is very good and warming on a cold northern night.

➕ 196 B5 ⊠ 402/1-2 Thanon Banprakhan
☎ 05 371 3738 ⊙ Daily 10–10

LAMPANG

Riverside Bar/Restaurant ££

On the banks of the Yom River, this very popular establishment serves excellent Thai food. Much of the magical atmosphere derives from the proximity of the Yom River, with its houseboats and floating restaurants. The house speciality is fish, prawns and seafood, but the usual ubiquitous dishes are available too. The fried chicken and cashew nut is recommended. Musicians perform live Thai folk music most nights.

➕ 196 B4 ⊠ 328 Thanon Tipchang
☎ 05 422 1861 ⊙ 11am–midnight

Where to...
Shop

CHIANG MAI

The **night bazaar** (Thanon Chang Khlan, daily 6–11pm; ▶ 93) provides a shopping mecca.

Out-of-town shopping trips include **Baw Sang Village** and **Thanon Sankhampaeng**, where there are dozens of high-quality showrooms, workshops and export centres offering every sort of local product, including Baw Sangs famous umbrellas and parasols.

Just to the south of Chiang Mai on Route 108, **Hang Dong** is the main centre for woodcarvings and rattan furniture.

Warorot Market, in the centre of the city's busy commercial district, is the main local market. Here you can find every kind of northern Thai food, exotic fruits,

and imported clothing and other goods from nearby Burma, Laos and South China.

The **Hill Tribe Products Promotion Centre** (21/7 Thanon Suthep, Wat Suan Dok, tel: 05 327 7743), under the patronage of King Bhumibol, sells a wide variety of hill-tribe paraphernalia such as hats, bags, jackets, jewellery, blankets and baskets.

The best department stores in town are **Central Airport Plaza**, at the corner of Mahidol and Hang Dong Roads and **Central** (99/4 Moo 2, Thanon Huay Kaew, tel: 05 322 4999), both with a wide variety of goods at very reasonable prices. Directly opposite Central there is a branch of **Shinawarra** (tel: 05 322 264) selling silk by the metre as well as other fabrics.

Where to...
Be Entertained

CHIANG MAI NIGHTLIFE

The **Northgate Jazz Co-op** (Sri Phoom Road, www.jazzco-op. blogspot.com) is a popular hole-in-the-wall bar that is at its best on Tuesday nights when local talent takes to the stage. Another place to go for a lively atmosphere is the **Tha Chang Jazz Club** (25 Charoenrat, next to the Gallery Restaurant, tel: 05 324 8601) or **Sudsanan** (off Huay Kaew Road near the Kad Suan Kaew shopping centre, tel: 085 038 0764).

The Peak (Thanon Chang Khlan, tel: 05 382 0776) offers a man-made cliff giving the intrepid a go at rock climbing. Bars and restaurants surround the cliff.

If you enjoy a show, reserve tickets for the **Simon Cabaret**

(next to the Rim Ping supermarket, Chang Puak Road, tel: 05 341 0321/3), a Las Vegas-style spectacular with a cast of stunning transvestites; shows nightly at 7:30 and 9:30.

TREKKING

A **trek** to a hill-tribe village is one reason why people travel to the far north. Trekkers usually walk for three to five hours a day. Thanon Charoen Prathet, in Chiang Mai between the river and the night bazaar, has many companies offering trekking tours. Among the best are **Wild Planet Adventure Centre** (73 Thanon Charoen Prathet, tel 05 327 7178), and **Sergeant Kai's Tours** (www.chiangmaitours.com).

East Coast

Getting Your Bearings

This corner of the country juts out into the Gulf of Thailand and is flanked by Cambodia on its eastern side. Its charms are varied and idiosyncratic and the islands off the rugged coast are less developed than the more polished resorts of the south. But the region is within much easier reach of Bangkok if you are short of time, with blinding white beaches on the islands, limited traffic and an altogether much more peaceful atmosphere.

Choose from the rocky fishing island of Ko Si Chang and the thickly forested national park islands of Ko Chang and Ko Samet. The beaches on the mainland coast have little to recommend them, having been blighted by oil industry developments. If you are really short of time, you can take a train journey that hugs the coast, stopping off at Ko Si Chang and Pattaya.

The theme here is essentially relaxation, but for the energetic, there is also diving, rainforest trekking and water sports at the brash international resort of Pattaya. The interior features the gem capital of Chanthaburi, with a large Vietnamese population, and Khao Yai National Park, which links with two other national parks (Thap Lan and Pang Sida). The park has hiking trails that follow animal tracks.

Page 109: A tall rainforest tree

Left: Catamaran sailing and windsurfing take place at Jomtien Beach in Pattaya

Opposite: A flowering plant in Khao Yai National Park

★ **Don't Miss**
1 Ko Chang ➤ 114
2 Ko Samet ➤ 117

At Your Leisure
3 Chanthaburi ➤ 120
4 Pattaya ➤ 120
5 Ko Si Chang ➤ 121
6 Khao Yai National
   Park ➤ 121

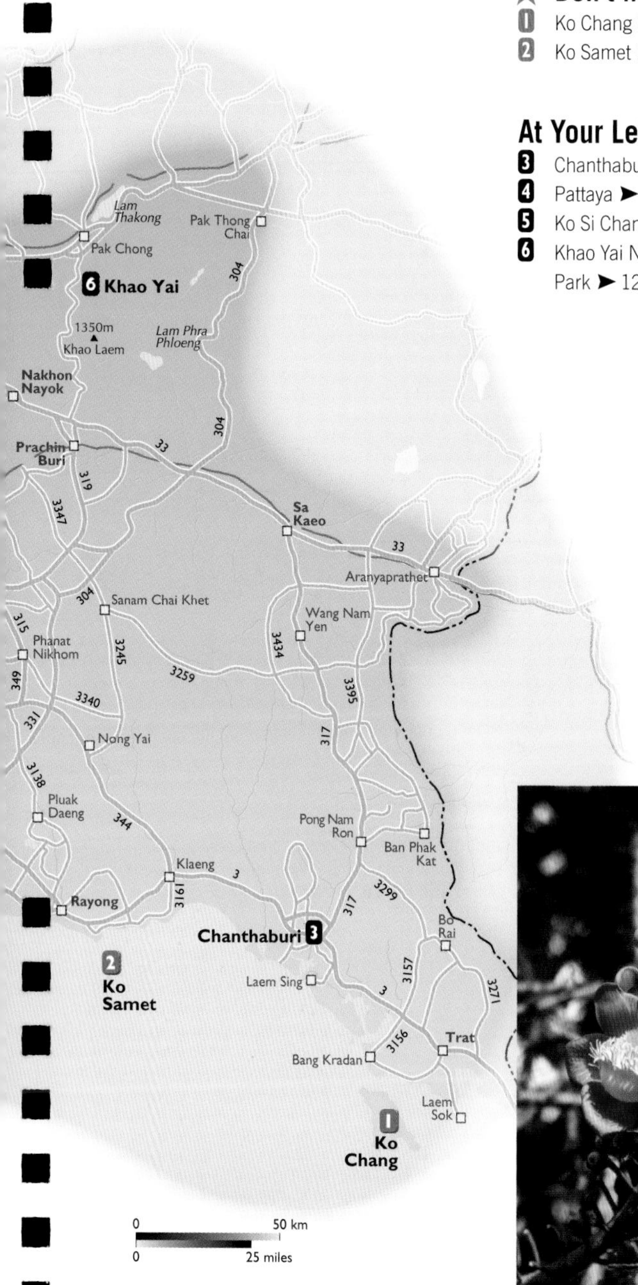

Lam Thakong
Pak Thong Chai
Pak Chong
6 Khao Yai
304
1350m ▲ Khao Laem
Lam Phra Phloeng
Nakhon Nayok
Prachin Buri
304
319
33
3347
Sa Kaeo
304
33
Aranyaprathet
Sanam Chai Khet
315
Phanat Nikhom
3245
3434
Wang Nam Yen
349
3340
3259
3395
331
Nong Yai
317
3138
Pluak Daeng
344
Pong Nam Ron
Ban Phak Kat
Klaeng
3
3299
Rayong
3161
317
Bo Rai
2 **Ko Samet**
Chanthaburi 3
3271
Laem Sing
3157
3156
Trat
Bang Kradan
Laem Sok
1 **Ko Chang**

0 ——— 50 km
0 ——— 25 miles

In Five Days

If you're not quite sure where to begin your travels, this itinerary recommends five practical and enjoyable days out exploring the East Coast, taking in some of the best places to see using the Getting Your Bearings map on the previous page. For more information see the main entries.

Day 1

Morning
Start on the island of ❶ **Ko Chang** (above, ➤ 114–116). Take a walk through dense rainforest to the **waterfall of Khlong Phu** from Hat Sai Kaew, making an early start to avoid the heat of the day. The clear pool of water is a great place for a scenic dip. Return to Hat Sai Kaew beach and tuck into a fresh crab salad at one of the many beachside restaurants.

Afternoon and Evening
Stroll along the white sands of **Hat Sai Kaew** (also called White Sand Beach) and through the freshwater streams. Then relax in a hammock on the beach or have a massage under the trees. Mac Resort on Hat Sai Kaew is a good place for a beach barbecue. Choose your fresh catch – maybe a barracuda or tiger prawns – from a bed of ice. Order the marinade of your choice and accompany it with a cocktail, perhaps a fresh banana daiquiri.

Day 2

Go on a guided jungle walk into the interior of **Ko Chang** (➤ 114–116). You can cross the island on foot in a day. Alternatively, take a snorkelling or diving trip to one of the many other islands in the archipelago.

Day 3

Morning
Catch the ferry to the mainland. From the pier it's a short *songthaew* ride to **3 Chanthaburi** (➤ 120). Take a look at the cathedral and the haggling sapphire and ruby dealers around Thanon Si Chan and Trok Kachang before a lunch of Chanthaburi noodles.

Afternoon
Catch a bus, then a ferrry to the island of **2 Ko Samet** (below, ➤ 117–119), a tiny island of white-sand beaches.

Day 4

Morning
Relax on one of Ko Samet's **beaches** along the east coast. Generally the further south you go, the quieter they are. The beach at Ao Nuan has a restaurant of the same name. It is less commercial than the other beaches and serves Thai and good vegetarian food.

Afternoon
Walk along the rocky coastline visiting a series of pretty beaches on the way. Cross over to the **west coast**, away from the crowds (the island is only a couple of kilometres wide) and watch the sun dip into the sea from a clifftop viewpoint. Take care here, as in most places it is not safe to go down to sea-level.

Day 5

Morning and Afternoon
Take a **fishing or snorkelling trip** (➤ 116) to the islands of Ko Mak, Ko Kham and Ko Kut. Have lunch on one of the islands' beaches.

Evening
Watch a film while eating dinner in one of the many restaurants on **Hat Sai Kaew** (➤ 117) that show videos.

◑ Ko Chang

Brightly painted fishing boats ferry passengers across the water from the mainland to Ko Chang, where wooden *song-thaews* chug up the steep winding road from the pier. This island of jungle-covered mountains has plunging waterfalls, trees filled with birds and rivers rushing down to the sea. Fishing hamlets and long, white-sand beaches fringe the coast and walking trails explore the untouched interior.

Ko Chang, named because it is thought to look like a sleeping elephant (*chang* is Thai for elephant), is the largest of 52 islands that make up the National Marine Park.

It measures 30km (19 miles) long and 8km (5 miles) wide. Despite being Thailand's second largest island after Ko Phuket (► 164–165), it remains relatively unspoiled. The island has only had a paved road (which runs all the way round it) and electricity for a few years but it is now developing rapidly. Much of the accommodation is low key and rustic and although some small resorts have sprung up in recent years, development is restricted to the west coast – where you'll find the best beaches.

Opposite: Prawns drying on a wooden jetty at Bang Bao

Below: The beautiful west coast of Ko Chang

Hat Sai Kaew

Hat Sai Kaew is a wide 5km (3-mile) stretch of fine white sand backed by trees and palms and cut through with rivers. This is the busiest and most attractive beach, where accommodation ranges from rustic shacks with hammocks slung on balconies to more upmarket places with

BEACH ACTIVITIES
- Succumb to a **Thai massage** on the sand.
- Enjoy a **candlelit dinner** on the beach with waves lapping at your feet.
- **Sip a cocktail** under a fairy-lit tree on a Moroccan rug.
- Swing in a **hammock** on the balcony of your beach bungalow.
- Take a **snorkelling** trip to one of the nearby islands.

HOW TO GET THERE
Boats run from Laem
Ngop, on the mainland,
to Ko Chang every hour
(every two hours in low
season). *Songthaews* are
timed in relation to boat
arrivals. At Hat Sai Kaew,
they pick up passengers
around 15 minutes after
the boat docks. There are
no particular stops, just flag
the *songthaew* down on the
main road.

swimming pools that cater to
package tourists. Although
there are pancake stalls,
cappuccinos on some menus
and internet cafés along the
road, the feel is essentially
local. Be careful when you are
swimming off the coast here,
the currents are strong.

You can take guided walks
though the jungle interior
from many of the resorts at
Hat Sai Kaew that include
routes past streams and
mangrove forests.

Other Sights
Hat Khlong Phrao is another
beach, 15 minutes south by
songthaew from Hat Sai Kaew.
There is less infrastructure
here, and it is nearly always
empty. There is not much
traffic, and thick vegetation
and rainforest borders the
route from Hat Sai Kaew.

Head inland to **Khlong
Phu waterfall**, about 2km
(1.2 miles) along the main
road. The clear pool is good
for swimming and you can
sunbathe on the rocks.

Continuing south for
2km (1.2 miles) is the beach
of **Hat Kai Bae**, with some
bungalow accommodation.
The beach here is narrow and
tends to disappear when the
tide is high.

The other islands that make up the archipelago include **Ko Mak**, **Ko Kham** and **Ko Kut**, each with limited accommodation. Few of these islands can be reached during the rainy season from May to October, but from November to April daily boats are available from Laem Ngop (ask at the ticket office near the pier for details). To go on snorkelling or diving trips to these islands contact Ploy Scuba Diving (tel: 01 451 1387, www.ployscuba.com); they have offices on almost every beach.

Bang Bao in southwest Ko Chang is a busy fishing village

TAKING A BREAK

Most of the **bungalows at Hat Sai Kaew** have restaurants offering European and Thai dishes. Many also offer evening beach barbecues. In the day there are restaurants and bars on the **beaches** around the island where you can fill up with seafood, pizzas, Thai food, cocktails, beer and soft drinks.

⊞ 199 D3

KO CHANG: INSIDE INFO

Top tips The island had a problem in the past with malaria-carrying mosquitoes, and flies are common so bring repellent.

■ Don't buy a **return boat ticket.** You won't save much money, and it means you are restricted to the return times of the same operator.

■ There are **banks and ATMs** at Hat Sai Kaew, but elsewhere travellers' cheques are cashed at very poor rates.

■ In **high season, at weekends and on public holidays** the island can get crowded and the more expensive accommodation gets booked up. Either avoid these times or make reservations well in advance.

② Ko Samet

White-sand beaches, low, forested hills and a wonderful dry
climate characterize Ko Samet. This tiny island is less than
6km (3.7 miles) long and its rugged west coast and beach-
fringed east coast are connected by rough walking tracks that
cross the jungle interior.

Although tourism has been established here for 20 years
and there is a ferry from Ban Phe on the mainland (30–40
minutes; every hour 8–5 from November to February, every
two hours rest of the year), there is still very little traffic. The
island was made a **national park** in 1981, but it is not as
protected as it could be and there are some unattractive areas.
A national park entrance fee (moderate) is payable at the
visitor information centre on arrival.

Hat Sai Kaew

The main beach, Hat Sai Kaew (Diamond Beach), on the
northeast of the island, is 30m (33 yards) wide and awash
with striped deckchairs, parasols, palm trees and bamboo
tables and chairs from the many restaurants. Development
is solid here and bungalows have been built back from the
beach on stilts in the trees. Food-sellers balance baskets of
fruit and other produce and hawkers lug boards of beaded
jewellery across the sand. Masseuses manipulate bodies on
cotton sheets in the shade. At night there are barbecues, fairy
lights and fire-eaters on the sand, and videos are shown in the
restaurants behind the beach.

**Sunrise over
the Gulf of
Siam, Koh
Samet island**

Other Beaches

The long bay of Hat Sai Kaew has a large rocky outcrop that separates it from the smaller and more attractive beach at **Ao Hin Kok** further south. Here you will find a statue of the *Prince and the Mermaid* – the subjects of an epic love poem by the country's most famous poet, Sunthorn Phu (1786–1856).

Butterflies abound in the trees of the east coast

Opposite: A small cove at Ao Phutsa

Several smaller and less crowded beaches nestle along the east coast south of Ao Hin Kok – all good places to relax and enjoy some excellent home-cooked Thai food.

The next main beach, in the horseshoe bay of **Ao Wong Duan**, tends to be a frenzy of hair-braiding, henna-tattooing and jet-skiing. Most of the holiday-makers here are keen to take in every experience.

The furthest beach to the south, with a feeling of real isolation and peace, is **Ao Kiu**. You will have to walk through forest to reach it.

The only beach on the west coast is **Ao Phrao**, also known as Paradise Bay (*ao* means "bay" in Thai). In fact the rest of the west coast is more or less inaccessible. With a handful of bungalows and restaurants, Ao Phrao doesn't get as many visitors as the east coast beaches, but is well worth a look.

From Top to Toe

From the northeastern tip of Hat Sai Kaew, where most people stay, take a walk along the coast. Clamber over craggy headlands, follow sandy paths through woodland and walk along white-sand beaches and quiet coves. It's around 3km (2 miles) from Hat Sai Kaew to **Ao Thian** (Candlelight Beach), with its spindly wooden pier. Secluded and quiet, it is a beautiful spot.

You can afford to explore, as it is difficult to get lost, and sooner or later you will reach the sea. If you take one of the tracks to the western side of the island from Ao Thian or Ao Wong Duan you will come across a windswept coast. Take the inland track back to the east coast for a change of scene, some shade and the chance to see dancing butterflies the size of small birds.

TAKING A BREAK

Seafood plays a big part in the menus of most of the restaurants. There are restaurants on all the **beaches** and the bungalows often have places to eat attached, providing good Thai food and Western dishes.

➕ 199 D3 ℹ️ TAT, Rayong ☎ 03 865 5420

KO SAMET: INSIDE INFO

Top tips Don't be tempted to buy a **return boat ticket** from the mainland. You won't save much money, and it means you are restricted to the return times of the same operator.

■ You can take **snorkelling and fishing trips** to the islands of Ko Kudi, Ko Mum and Ko Thalu, arranged through the various bungalow operations. Day trips include equipment.

■ When you arrive on the island, *songthaew* fares to the beaches are displayed on a board. Drivers will try everything, including ignoring you and taking other passengers, to get you to pay the charter rate. It is a good idea to gather a group together before approaching them.

■ In **high season, at weekends and on public holidays**, the island can get crowded and the more expensive accommodation gets booked up, so try to avoid these times or book in advance.

■ **Camping** is allowed on the beaches.

■ **Water** is brought in from the mainland, so use it sparingly.

At Your Leisure

▣ Chanthaburi

This pleasant town is the focus for a major gem-mining area. Since the 15th century, prospectors hopeful for plunder of sapphires and rubies have flocked in from Burma, Cambodia and China. But its main ethnic population is made up of Vietnamese Catholics who came here between the 18th century and the 1970s when trying to escape from various periods of persecution.

Chanthaburi has no obvious sights, but it is a pleasant place to wander around for a few hours. From the bus station, walk along Thanon Saritidet to the banks of the Chanthaburi River and turn right. Pass the wooden shop houses there until you reach the footbridge to the Catholic cathedral. The cathedral was built in 1880 by the French, who occupied the town during the latter part of the 19th century.

Back on the river's western bank is the gem-trading area. Just north of here is a market selling exotic fruits such as *durian* and *rambutan* which are grown in the surrounding orchards. Every year in May or June, the province (along with Trat and Rayong) hosts a fruit festival when there are a host of pageants, parades and competitions.

🞧 199 D3 🛈 TAT, Rayong ☎ 03 865 5420

A traditionally decorated tower in the Chinese temple at Chanthaburi

▢ Pattaya

It's hard to ignore this large, loud, international resort which welcomes visitors from every corner of the globe. Although many are here for the brash nightlife, you'll also see families and couples on package deals. Pattaya is Thailand's notorious centre for selling sex, a hangover from its days as an R&R destination for American troops during the Vietnam War. It has the largest gay scene in Thailand.

An international airport with good domestic connections serves world-class hotels, and water-sports facilities are excellent. Neon blazes along the palm-lined promenade of Pattaya Beach and down "Walking Street" next to shopping plazas, fast-food outlets and girlie bars. Jomtien Beach, further south, is nicer and a good spot for windsurfing.

🞧 198 C4 🛈 TAT, 382/1 Thanon Mu 10 Chaihat, Pattaya ☎ 03 842 7667

FOR KIDS

- **Hair-braiding** and **henna tattoos** at Ao Wong Duan Beach on Ko Samet.
- **Mini Siam** in Pattaya (north of the intersection of Thanon Pattaya and Thanon Sukhumvit) is a cultural theme park featuring buildings and monuments in miniature (www.minisiam.com).
- Hour-long **night safaris in Khao Yai National Park** (➤ 121), with sightings of deer and elephants.

5 Ko Si Chang

This rocky fishing island is two hours by bus and boat from Bangkok. Ferries go from Si Racha every hour from 6am to 8pm. The rugged coastline and the passing cargo ships mean it is not a lazy beach retreat (crowded at weekends and on public holidays), but it is a break away from more commercial resorts. Don't buy a return boat ticket as it's not much cheaper and you'll be restricted to the operator's return times.

Rama V's summer palace, built here in the 1890s, was moved in 1910 to create Bangkok's Vimanmek Teak Palace (➤ 53). The remaining buildings were left as ruins after occupation by the French in 1893, although they are being restored. Hat Sai Kaew has sand and is the best place to swim; most of the other beaches are too rocky. On the central western side of the island, the Buddhist temple of Tham Chakra-prong offers good views if you can make the steep climb to the top of the cliff it is perched upon. Nearby Hat Khao Khat is an obvious vantage point for watching the sun set.

🚹 198 C4

6 Khao Yai National Park

Thailand's first national park, about 120km (74 miles) from Bangkok, is its most highly esteemed and popular. Mountains and five types of forest make up the landscape. Hundreds of elephants, a few endangered tigers and some white-handed gibbons live here, along with many species of birds, while fast-flowing waterfalls and rivers are breeding grounds for kingfishers and orchids.

In order to get the most out of a visit it is best to spend a night or two in or near the park. You can camp and there is basic accommodation at the park headquarters, but you are more likely to stay at one of the private lodges situated along the road that runs from Pak Chong town to the park entrance. The lodges send transport to pick up guests in Pak Chong where the buses from Bangkok arrive. All the lodges run full-day tours, starting early in the morning to catch sight of the white-handed gibbons. Other highlights are a dusk visit to caves to see thousands of birds flying out on feeding trips, and a night safari using open trucks and flashlights to spot nocturnal wildlife. The park may be closed in the monsoon season (➤ 188).

🚹 197 D2 ☎ Information and accommodation at park headquarters: 037 319 002, 0860 926 529; www.dnp.go.th/parkreserve 🛈 TAT, 2102 Thanon Mitaphap, Khorat ☎ 04 421 3666

Khao Yai National Park forest

CAMBODIA

The crossing from Ban Hat Lek in Thailand to Cham Yeam (Koh Kong) in Cambodia may take some time but the process can be speeded up by obtaining a visa in advance, online from the Cambodian Ministry of Foreign Affairs (www.mfaic.gov.kh). If obtaining a visa at the border, you will need to provide a passport photo of yourself. There is a daily minibus service from Trat to the border crossing at Ban Hat Lek.

Where to...
Stay

Prices
Expect to pay per double room per night:
£ under 2,000 baht   ££ 2,000–5,000 baht   £££ over 5,000 baht

KO CHANG

Cookies Hotel and Bungalows ££

The rooms here have balconies and some have sea views. The rooms are air-conditioned and a there is a swimming pool (plus a children's pool). The hotel is close to the beach, and there's also a restaurant serving Thai and Western food.
➕ 199 D3 ✉ Hat Sai Kaew
☎ 081 861 4227

Klong Prao Resort ££–£££

With more than a hundred rooms, this is a good, family-friendly place to relax. There is a pool, sauna and two restaurants. The resort can arrange scuba-diving and snorkelling trips to the nearby coral reefs.
➕ 199 D3 ✉ Ao Khlong Phrao
☎ 03 955 1115; www.klongpraoresort.com

Mac Resort Hotel ££

The Mac Resort Hotel has bungalows, all with air-conditioning. There are verandas with sea views and a swimming pool. This is a good place to watch the sun set and moon rise over a fresh seafood beach barbecue.
➕ 199 D3 ✉ Hat Sai Kaew ☎ 03 955 1124

KO SAMET

Samet Ville Resort ££

All the bungalows at this resort overlook pretty Ao Wai beach and village. Both fan-cooled and air-conditioned bungalows are available, and there are quite a few options regarding types of rooms and bungalows.
➕ 199 D3 ✉ Ao Wai
☎ 03 865 1681; www.sametvilleresort.com

Vongdeuan Resort £

This hotel in beautiful Ao Wong Duan has air-conditioned bungalows with large balconies. There are also cheaper rooms available, with fans.
➕ 199 D3 ✉ Ao Wong Duan
☎ 03 865 1777; www.vongdeuan.com

PATTAYA

Grand Jomtien Palace ££

Most accommodation in Pattaya is big and brash, and the Grand Jomtien is large, but more friendly. It's in the middle of Jomtien Beach, some way from Pattaya's raunchy nightlife, so is a good choice for families. The Grand Jomtien Palace has some of the best restaurants the Jomtien area has to offer.
➕ 198 C4 ✉ 356/1 Thanon Jomtien Beach
☎ 03 823 1405;
www.grandjomtienpalacehotel.com

Royal Cliff Beach Resort £££

One of Pattaya's oldest and best hotels, the Royal Cliff Beach Resort is really four hotels. The 545-room Royal Cliff Beach Hotel caters mainly for package tourists, the low-rise Royal Cliff Terrace has a more personal atmosphere for independent travellers, the Royal Cliff Grand looks after the business market and the Royal Wing offers pure luxury. There are eight excellent restaurants in the complex, three swimming pools, six floodlit tennis courts and a wealth of other sports facilities.
➕ 198 C4 ✉ 353 Thanon Phra Tamnuk
☎ 03 825 0421; www.royalcliff.com

Where to...
Eat and Drink

Prices

Expect to pay per person for a three-course meal, excluding drinks and service:

£ under 300 baht   ££ 300–600 baht   £££ over 600 baht

KO CHANG

Oodie's Place £

One of the better places on the island for a meal and entertainment is sociable Oodie's Place. The food includes pizzas from a wood-fired oven and above-average Thai food. Oodie and his band play at night.

🚼 199 D3 🔀 Hat Sai Kaew 🕿 03 955 1193 🕒 Daily 11am–late

KO SAMET

Sea View Restaurant ££

Even if you are not staying at the Ao Prao Resort, it is worth a trip to the northern end of the relatively secluded beach to enjoy lunch or an evening meal in the congenial surroundings of the resort's restaurant. The food is not exceptional, but the superb views and the relaxing atmosphere are hard to beat.

🚼 199 D3 🔀 Ao Prao Resort, Ao Prao 🕿 03 864 4100; www.samedresorts.com 🕒 Daily 7am–midnight

PATTAYA

Lobster Pot £££

One of Pattaya's longest surviving seafood restaurants, Lobster Pot, sitting on a pier overlooking Pattaya Bay, serves the best seafood in town. There's a friendly atmosphere, and an extensive menu that includes a wonderful king lobster thermidor. If the delicious seafood can't tempt you there are tender steaks, baked potatoes and a range of Thai favourites, which are highly recommended.

🚼 198 C4 🔀 288 Walking Street, South Pattaya 🕿 03 842 6083 🕒 Daily noon–1am

PIC Kitchen ££

Located on a quiet street in central Pattaya, this establishment has become something of an institution over the years. Fine Thai cuisine is served in a series of elegant teak houses set amid lush tropical gardens. The food is served in traditional style at low wooden tables, but with the taste buds of foreign visitors very much in mind – if you ask for your meal *mai phet* ("not spicy"), then it won't be. There are more than 200 Thai and European dishes on the menu. The ambience at PIC Kitchen is sophisticated and relaxed, and there's a separate air-conditioned section for those who don't like to feel the heat.

🚼 198 C4 🔀 Soi 5, Pattaya Beach Road 🕿 03 842 8387 🕒 Daily 8am–midnight

Ruen Thai ££

Located in central-south Pattaya, this large restaurant is set in a series of wooden pavilions surrounded by water features – fountains, waterfalls and fishponds. Popular with visitors, Ruen Thai puts on nightly performances of classical Thai dancing (8–midnight) and serves high-quality Thai food, including everything from chicken with cashew nuts and dried peppers to *tom yam gung* (spicy prawn soup) and *tom kha gai* (chicken in coconut and ginger). The restaurant caters for families by means of its own children's facilities, including a fun playground.

🚼 198 C4 🔀 485/3 Thanon Pattaya 2nd 🕿 03 842 5911 🕒 Daily 11–11

Where to...
Shop

NORTH PATTAYA

Pattaya has a variety of shopping opportunities, but the best can be found in the large air-conditioned malls. **Central Festival Centre** (Pattaya 2 Road) has some attractive shops, and good craft outlets. The largest mall in Pattaya, **The Royal Garden Shopping Plaza** (adjoining Pattaya Marriott Hotel), has a Boots chemist and a branch of the American Ripley's Believe It Or Not! Museum (▶ this page). A dancing fountain is on the ground floor.

SOUTH PATTAYA

South Pattaya is the main shopping area, with many shops selling crafts, silk, jewellery and gems. One of the woodcarving outlets, **Luukmai**

Gallery (234/4 Walking Street, tel: 03 842 0334), sells exquisite carved panels and large wooden elephants.

Tom's Gems (239/2 South Pattaya, opp. Diamond Hotel, tel: 03 842 2811) has been in business since 1975 and makes fine jewellery to order. For excellent leather goods, try the **Pattaya Shoes Department Store** (109/19 M10 Thanon Phatumnak, tel: 03 842 3919), which sells much more than only well-made shoes. It has a "walking street" section stocked ceiling-high with everything from suitcases to leather belts.

Pattaya has a number of **portrait painters**. One of the better galleries is **NL Gallery** (593 South Pattaya Road, tel: 03 871 0975). Their reproductions from photographs are very good.

Where to...
Be Entertained

NIGHTLIFE

Ko Chang and **Ko Samet** nightlife is limited. **Pattaya**, with more than 400 beer bars, is the place to go. Once you look beyond the fact that it is a town selling sex, it does have other entertainment options.

MIXX Nightlife (upstairs in the Bali Hai Plaza) has the Crystal Palace for house and trance, and the more lounge-like Rouge Club for hip-hop. If you're a Hammond organ enthusiast, **The Blues Factory** (Soi Lucky Star, off Pattaya's Walking Street; www.thebluesfactorypattaya.com) has the best bands when it comes to blues and rock music. **Alcazar** (78/14 Pattaya 2 Road, tel: 03 842 8746; www.alcazarpattaya.com) is the ultimate transvestite cabaret club.

FAMILY ENTERTAINMENT

The **Pattaya Kart Speedway** (248/2 Thanon Thepprasit, tel: 03 842 2044) is a fun place with vehicles for adults and children.

The **Elephant Village** (east of Pattaya, off Thanon Sukhumvit, tel: 03 824 9818; www.elephant-village-pattaya.com) has daily shows including elephants log-rolling and football.

Ripley's Believe It Or Not! Museum (Pattaya 2 Road, tel: 03 871 0294) has some curious and mind-boggling displays.

Northeast of Pattaya, the **Si Racha Tiger Farm** (341 Moo 3, Nongkham, Si Racha, Chonburi Province, tel: 03 829 6556) has the world's largest collection of tigers, and plenty of other animals.

Gulf Coast

Getting Your Bearings

Weaving its way down the east side of Thailand's peninsula is the 750km (465-mile) Gulf coastline. Dip into its delights, or do as many visitors do and follow the train line that hugs the coast until Surat Thani, the jumping-off point for the Ko Samui archipelago. From here the train traces an inland and less well-trodden route all the way to Malaysia. A Muslim influence becomes noticeable in the mosques and curries as you approach Malaysia.

It is the beaches and islands that are the major magnets in this part of Thailand. Only a few hours from Bangkok is the royal resort of Hua Hin and King Bhumibol's chosen retreat.

The international hotels soon give way to a very different kind of hideaway: Khao Sam Roi Yot National Park. This sleepy backwater has subtle charms of bird life, marshlands, deserted sands and local rural life.

The idyllic islands of the Ko Samui archipelago attract both package tourists and budget travellers. While by no means undiscovered, these islands remain enchanting, with a reputation for excellent seafood and water sports. Many visitors arrive by plane; others board ferries from the mainland which spirit them across the turquoise waters to enjoy white-sand beaches fringed with towering palms.

For those who want something other than just glorious beach retreats, Phetchaburi offers an historic alternative in its temples, and the city of Nakhon Si Thammarat provides a cultural stop-off, with a host of Hindu shrines, Buddhist temples, mosques and churches.

Deserted beach on Ko Tao in the Ko Samui archipelago

Page 125: The golden Big Buddha statue, Ko Samui

★ Don't Miss
1 Hua Hin ► 130
2 Khao Sam Roi Yot
   National Park ► 132
3 Ko Samui
   Archipelago ► 134

At Your Leisure
4 Phetchaburi ► 138
5 Nakhon Si
   Thammarat ► 139
6 Thale Noi Waterbird
   Park ► 140
7 Songkhla ► 140

**Detail of the ornate carving of the
Hindu God Garuda, Phetchaburi**

| 0 | | 100 km |
| 0 | | 50 miles |

In Seven Days

If you're not quite sure where to begin your travels, this itinerary
recommends seven practical and enjoyable days out exploring
the Gulf Coast, taking in some of the best places to see using
the Getting Your Bearings map on the previous page. For more
information see the main entries.

Day 1

Morning
Take an early train or bus from Bangkok to **4 Phetchaburi** (➤ 138–139).
The journey takes two and half hours from the southern bus station, or
three hours by train from Hualamphong station.

Afternoon
Spend several hours exploring the temples on foot before taking a bus (an
hour-and-a-half journey) to **1 Hua Hin** (above, ➤ 130–131). Travelling by
rail is less practical as trains arrive in Hua Hin either in late evening or
early morning. Check into the beautifully restored 1920s, colonial-style
Sofitel Centara hotel, formerly the historic Railway Hotel (➤ 142).

Evening
Sip a cocktail in the Elephant Bar of the Sofitel Centara. Wander through
the gardens, with their giant animal topiary, maze and life-size chess
set, to the beach. Walk along the sand to the Seaside Restaurant (31–4
Thanon Naresdamri). This atmospheric, family-run place serves seafood –
try the king prawns or rock lobster – as well as international dishes.

Day 2

Morning/Afternoon
Hire a jeep early to increase the chance of seeing wildlife (it tends to appear at sunrise or sunset) and drive an hour south to **2 Khao Sam Roi Yot National Park** (➤ 132–133) and follow the tour (➤ 184–186).

Evening
Return to **Hua Hin**. Walk along the beach for a Singha beer in a deckchair at sunset and then wander around the **night market.** It is compact, with a good mix of merchandise and friendly traders. Even bargaining can be relaxing here. If you want something more substantial than a seafood snack at a food stall, there's the Brasserie de Paris (➤ 144), an excellent French restaurant on Thanon Naresdamri, or the Railway Restaurant (➤ 145) in the Sofitel Centara for Thai and international dishes.

Days 3–7

Take the train or fly from Bangkok to the **3 Ko Samui archipelago.** The overnight sleeper train arrives at Surat Thani, from where you need to take a short bus ride to catch the ferry. Flights take one hour and twenty minutes and there are lots of flights daily. Each of the three islands – **Ko Samui** (below, ➤ 134), **Ko Phangan** (➤ 134–136) and **Ko Tao** (➤ 136) – has a distinct personality, so choose one that suits you. If you have time, do an island hop. Spend the days relaxing on the lovely beaches and the nights enjoying the seafood for which the islands are famous. Or try some of the many water sports on offer. From Ko Samui, try to make time for a day trip to **Ang Thong National Marine Park** (➤ 135). Boats leave daily at 8:30am, returning at 5pm.

❶Hua Hin

At night the illuminations of the naval ships protecting the royal family and the neon green fishing lights in the bay blaze out the twin attributes of this town – a charming mix of ramshackle fishing village and a royal resort. It's Thailand's oldest beach resort – check out the pastel parasols, striped deckchairs and horse rides on the huge, open expanse of sand.

Hua Hin is a good place for a splurge – either as an introduction to the country or as a final fling before you leave. You will get much more for your money in an upmarket hotel here than in Bangkok, but try to avoid weekends when they can get busy.

Hua Hin became fashionable as a **beach resort** in the 1920s when the Bangkok–Malaysia rail line, the royal Klai Klangwon Palace (➤ panel opposite) and the Railway Hotel (now the Sofitel Centara, ➤ 142) were built.

The 5km (3 mile) beach is not as pretty as Ko Samui, Krabi and Ko Samet, but the shoreline, with a **traditional pier** and "**monkey island**", an outcrop covered with monkeys and

Opposite: Celebrating a local festival in Hua Hin

View of the grounds at the Royal Garden Resort (now the Marriot) in Hua Hin

THE ROYAL PALACE

In 1926 the Klai Klangwon Palace (not open to the public) was completed on the seafront 2km (1.2 miles) north of Hua Hin. This is where King Bhumibol and Queen Sirikit stay when they are in town. Locals know when the much-loved royal family are in residence by subtle changes in security and traffic regulations. The name Klai Klangwon means "far from worries". It could be considered a bit of a misnomer when you consider that in 1868 King Rama IV caught malaria on a visit to Khao Sam Roi Yot National Park near here and died almost as soon as he returned to Bangkok. It was also when staying here in 1932 that King Rama VII heard news of a *coup d'état* that resulted in the beginning of the constitutional monarchy.

topped with a temple, has an undeniable charm. The resort's more recent success as a weekend break destination for Bangkok residents has led to the construction of some high-rise hotels and a few girlie bars. There are also six golf courses in the area (➤ 148).

TAKING A BREAK

For really fresh seafood, go to **Saeng Thai** (➤ 145) on the seafront near the pier.

✚ 198 C3 ▐ TAT, corner of Thanon Damnoen Kasem and Thanon Phetkasem ☎ 03 253 1047 ③ Daily 8:30–4:30

HUA HIN: INSIDE INFO

Top tips Don't be tempted to order food from the **stalls on the beach** if you are not prepared to wait an hour or so. When it does come, it will invariably be delicious, but the stallholder has to order it by mobile phone from someone who cooks it at home and then delivers it!

■ In the early morning and evening **fishermen** unload their catches by the pier. Wander down to watch the scene, and locals bargaining for the latest catch.

2 Khao Sam Roi Yot National Park

This peaceful national park on the coast is a sleepy backwater of marshland, mangroves and mudflats and is a breeding ground for birds. There are empty beaches of golden sand backed by pine trees and communities of shrimp farmers and fishing families. Its name means "mountain of three hundred peaks", which refers to its dramatic limestone outcrops of up to 650m (2,132 feet).

There are several hundred species of birds here, including waterbirds such as purple herons and spotted eagles in winter, as well as animals such as dusky langurs (a type of monkey), long-tailed macaques, barking deer, mongooses and lizards. Take a pair of binoculars.

Only 60km (37 miles) south of Hua Hin (➤ 130–131), the park is an easy day trip. Don't take a taxi or public transport, because you will need transport to get around the park as the attractions are widely spread out. You can take an organized tour, but the best option is to hire a car and follow the circular guided tour of the park that starts from Hua Hin and links the park's highlights (➤ 184).

Hat Laem Sala is a small beach with a visitor's centre, bungalows and campsites. It can only be reached by boat from the sands east of the village of Bang Pu (to which there is no entry), or by following a 20-minute walk over the steep headland.

From Hat Laem Sala it is a half-hour walk to **Tham Phraya Nakhon**, a secluded royal pavilion built by Rama V (➤ 133).

To the south of the park is the **headquarters**,

Above:
Craggy karst outcrops form distinctive features

Right:
Mountains and marshland complement each other in this tranquil haven

Left: A leaf monkey surveys the scene in the park

which are not worth a visit unless you need to buy water. The displays and some short trails starting from here are all rather decrepit and the staff speak little English, but you will probably see lots of monkeys by the road.

You will be rewarded with great sweeping views if you climb up **Khao Daeng** – the access point is about 50m (164 feet) before you reach the park headquarters.

TAKING A BREAK

Have lunch at **Hat Sam Phraya**, in a pretty beachside spot set in pine trees. The restaurant serves mostly seafood dishes.

✚ 198 C3

KHAO SAM ROI YOT NATIONAL PARK: INSIDE INFO

Top tips At lunchtime you might be lucky enough to see the locals in their fishing boats lined up on shore near **Bang Pu**, disentangling their small fish catches from their nets.

- The best time for spotting **birds and wildlife** is early morning or early evening (see www.thaibirding.com).
- Although the leaflet you are given at the entrance checkpoint is in Thai, it has a useful, if basic, **map** in English.
- Although the chances of catching **malaria** are slight, it's worth taking insect repellent with you.

Hidden gem Tham Phraya Nakhon is a beautiful royal pavilion built in 1890 and named after two lords who were both called Nakon. Rama V visited in 1890 and signed his name in the cave. Rama VII continued the tradition in 1926 and Rama IX made the trip twice. Although it is popular with Thais, it is in a very remote location, reached by boat and a 30-minute walk.

❸ Ko Samui Archipelago

This 80-island archipelago includes a trio with global reputations – Ko Samui as an international resort, Ko Phangan for the biggest beach party in the world and Ko Tao for diving. Turquoise waters edged with dense palms and pristine beaches provide the ultimate image of a tropical paradise.

From the sea, the islands rise above the horizon like desert islands waiting to be discovered: palm trees border bays and beaches of gleaming white sand, backed by jungle-clad hills.

Ko Samui

The story goes that Ko Samui has more **coconuts** per square metre than anywhere else in the world. But it is world famous for its international **beach scene**.

The large, sweeping, scenic beaches of Chaweng and Lamai are justifiably the most popular. **Ban Chaweng**, patrolled by hawkers, has a cosmopolitan atmosphere, with Mexican restaurants, Irish pubs and large hotels. It is bigger, busier and altogether more urban than neighbouring **Hat Lamai**.

The 12m (40-foot) **Big Buddha** statue on the north coast is an immaculate golden surreal image which looks inland. The beach of the same name, dotted with ramshackle piers made of tree trunks, is where boats leave for the island of Ko Phangan.

Ko Phangan

Ko Samui's younger, wilder sibling has dirt roads, rustic accommodation and a lively nightlife. Young backpackers flock here throughout the year and during its world-famous **full-moon parties** it is overrun with people in a hedonistic party mood.

The pretty, tiny crescent of beach of **Hat Rin Nok**, known as Sunrise Beach, is the focus for the activity, but still manages

Opposite:
Decorated boat
on Ko Tao

Coconut palm
tree on
Ko Phangan

to be friendly and intimate. The eastern side of the little tail of land in the south of the island has crooked alleyways packed with tourist facilities and shops selling Nepalese goods. Paradise Bungalows provides a barbecue on the sand and is the prettiest spot on the beach. A selection of freshly caught seafood and a glass of wine makes an inexpensive meal, and a cocktail beach bar is attached to the restaurant. At night the beach fills up with eager party animals who sit on Moroccan cushions on the sand and dance to techno music in the bars and clubs.

On the less scenic, but quieter western side of the island, **Hat Rin Nai,** or Sunset Beach, acts as a kind of overflow, with cheaper and more basic accommodation. Predictably, it is a good sunset spot – Coral Bungalows is the place to go for cocktails as the sun disappears into the water.

If you want to find more upmarket accommodation, try **Ao Chaloaklam** on the north coast, which tends to be popular with Thai visitors.

It is possible to walk along the beach from Hat Rin to Ban Tai. At the village of **Ban Tai** – like others on the island

ANG THONG NATIONAL MARINE PARK

Day trips run from Ko Samui to Ang Thong National Marine Park, a group of 41 small islands which makes up half of the islands in the Ko Samui archipelago. There are limestone caves and coral reefs, and you may be lucky enough to see dolphins, wild pigs, lizards, dusky langurs and even leopard cats. **Ko Wua Talub** (Sleeping Cow) is the largest island and the site of the national park headquarters. A climb to its peak offers panoramic views. Ang Thong gets its name, which means "golden bowl", from a volcanic lake on the island of **Ko Mae Ko,** which features in the best-selling novel and Hollywood film *The Beach*.

– locals can be seen playing football, shooting pool and repairing motorbikes as if the first longtails bringing tourists had never arrived. You can continue all the way to the port of **Thong Sala** and the **Pang Waterfall National Park**, a few kilometres inland. You can climb the 250m (273-yard) trail to the top of the falls for an extensive view over the south and west of Ko Phangan.

Ko Tao

This tiny, turtle-shaped island (*tao* means "turtle" in Thai) offers some of the cheapest and best **diving** in the world and a peaceful alternative to the sophisticated delights of its sister islands.

The village of **Mae Hat** is the base for most of the dive operations, as well as tourist facilities. Accommodation north and south of here is reached in a 10-minute walk.

Hat Sai Ree to the north of Mae Hat is the longest stretch of sand and the centre for accommodation. **Ao Chaloke Ban Kao** on the south coast has become popular with several dive companies, but development is sadly out of keeping with the character of the rest of the island.

Most of the dive companies here are of a very high standard, with English-speaking instructors and well-organized trips. Big Blue and Buddha View are recommended. Although diving in the exceptionally clear waters around Ko Tao is possible all year round, visibility can be affected by heavy rain.

**Opposite:
Fishing vessels
at the port of
Thong Sala on
Ko Phangan**

**Ko Tao attracts
divers from all
over the world**

KO TAO'S TOP FIVE DIVE SITES
Of the 25 or so dive sites around Ko Tao, the following are the best:
- **White Rock** (Hin Khao) – amazing coral and plenty of fish.
- **Ko Nang Yuan** – good for beginners.
- **Shark Island** – coral, angelfish and parrotfish.
- **Sail Rock** – underwater chimney, colourful fish.
- **Southwest Pinnacle** – the top site for scenery, visibility and variety of fish.

On **Ko Samui**, Ban Chaweng offers Indian dishes at **Ali Baba** (➤ 145) and an innovative Mediterranean menu and good wines are available at **Ocean 11** (➤ 145). Further south you could try **Sala-Thai** (➤ 146) on Lamai Beach for Thai and international food and a lively atmosphere.

🔢 198 C2 🚹 TAT, Na Thon, Ko Samui ☎ 07 742 0504

Big Blue Company
✉ Big Blue Resort, 17/18 Moo 1, Ko Tao ☎ 07 745 6415;
www.bigbluediving.com 🛏 Accommodation to suit all budgets

Buddha View Dive Company
✉ Buddha View Dive Resort, 45/1 Moo 3, Ko Tao ☎ 07 745 6074;
www.buddhaview-diving.com

KO SAMUI ARCHIPELAGO: INSIDE INFO

Top tips Hat Rin Beach on Ko Phangan is the venue for the **full-moon parties,** which attract thousands of young revellers. If they don't appeal, stay away as the whole island gets completely taken over and the music and crowds can become overwhelming.

■ Post-parties, the island of **Ko Tao** receives a mass exodus from Ko Phangan when it can therefore be difficult to find accommodation and the atmosphere changes.

■ December to March is **peak season** for all of the islands. During this time prices shoot up and accommodation can be scarce.

■ June to October is the time of the **southwestern monsoon.**

■ **Car and motorbike rental** is not recommended on either Ko Samui or Ko Phangan. Vehicles race around Ko Samui's main road as if it were a motorway, resulting in around 20 tourist deaths a year. Ko Phangan's road is a hair-raising roller-coaster.

Hidden gem Visitors tend to ignore the **interiors** of all three islands, where there are deer, pigs, orchids and jungle treks.

At Your Leisure

Khmer-style *prangs* at Wat Mahathat, Phetchaburi's most important temple

❹ Phetchaburi

This compact town, dissected by the River Phet, is full of temples dating from several different periods. The town began life in the 11th century when the Khmers ruled the area, and it took off as a trading post in the 17th century. Rama IV had a palace built here in the mid-19th century and today it is a centre for sweet-making, using sugar from the sweet-sapped palms in the area.

You can see the sights in half a day. The best option is to visit on a trip from Hua Hin (➤ 130–131) or Bangkok (often combined with Damnoen Saduak Floating Markets, ➤ 70–71), or stop off going south.

Focus on the five most significant temples, which can be seen on a walk of a couple of hours. **Wat Yai Suwan-naram**, **Wat Borom** and **Wat Trailok** form a cluster on the northeastern edge of town. The restored, 17th-century **Wat Yai Suwannaram** has various Buddha images, a *bot* (main sanctuary) with interesting murals and a library built on stilts to prevent insects from nibbling at the books.

A short walk south is **Wat Kamphaeng Laeng**. Built in the 13th century in the Khmer style to house Hindu deities, it has since been adopted for Buddhist worship.

Due west and across the river is **Wat Mahathat**; though much

A monk makes shadow puppets in Nakhon Si Thammarat

destroyed by the Burmese, it's the most significant temple of all, with Buddhist relics donated by the king. If you have time you can take a tram up to Rama IV's palace, **Khao Wang**, on the western outskirts and visit the museum of **Phra Nakhon Khiri**, once the king's summer house.

There are also two cave *wats* on this side of town – **Khao Banda-it**, and **Khao Luang**, which has long been a favourite picnic spot for King Bhumibol and Queen Sirikit and their family.

➕ 198 C4   ℹ️ TAT, Cha-am   ☎ 03 247 1005

Phra Nakhon Khiri
🕐 Daily 9–4   💷 Inexpensive

Tram to Khao Wang
🕐 Daily 8–4   💷 Inexpensive

🖐 Nakhon Si Thammarat

Many people are so dazzled by the lure of Ko Samui and its islands that they fail to see this town altogether.

Strung out along the Khlong Na Wang River, this religious centre has a collection of Hindu shrines, Buddhist temples, mosques and churches that testify to its role as a major missionary centre.

Wat Mahathat – the most sacred and the largest shrine in the south – is a majestic and highly photogenic sight. The **National Museum** has

---

FOUR ROYAL RETREATS
- **Klai Klangwon Palace** in Hua Hin (▶ 131) is used by the present King Bhumibol.
- **Tham Phraya Nakon**, in Khao Sam Roi Yot National Park (▶ 133), is an elegant hidden royal pavilion built by Rama V.
- **Khao Wang** in Phetchaburi (▶ this page) was Rama IV's hilltop palace.
- **Khao Tung Kuan** in Songkhla (▶ 141) is a hilltop royal pavilion built by Rama V.

an unmissable ninth-century statue of Vishnu and two rare Vietnamese bronze drums.

Shadow puppets (*nang thalung*) are found throughout Southeast Asia, but life-size puppets, *nang yai*, are unique to Thailand and are used in the epic *Ramayana*. At the **Suchart House**, watch Suchart Subsin making the puppets from water buffalo or cowhide and then projecting them on to a giant screen. You can buy them as souvenirs. There are set characters such as a wizard and a furious man wielding a sword, but performances are limited to special occasions.

➕ 198 B1 ℹ️ TAT, Sanam Na Muang ☎ 07 534 6515/6

National Museum

✉️ Thanon Ratchadamnoen ☎ 07 532 4480 🕐 Wed–Sun 9–4 💲 Inexpensive

Suchart House

✉️ 110/18 Thanon Si Thammasok Soi 3 ☎ 07 534 6394 💲 Inexpensive

Wat Mahathat

✉️ Thanon Ratchadamnoen

⑥ Thale Noi Waterbird Park

The name *thale noi*, meaning "little sea", describes this area of marsh, lagoon and sea where hundreds of bird species breed. You may see white egret, purple heron and brown teal. The best variety of the mostly

---

KORLAE

Korlae are hand-crafted wooden fishing boats used by Muslim fishermen in the Gulf. They take four months to construct. You can watch craftsmen carve and paint intricate designs in Ban Pasey Yawo, 2km (1.2 miles) north of Saiburi, and in Pattani. The design is hundreds of years old and has changed little, although engines are now the practical replacement for the original sails of the ancient craft. Favourite animals to decorate the wooden hulls include lions, mythological birds and sea serpents.

FOR KIDS

- The **seaside attractions** of Hua Hin (► 130–131).
- The **gardens of the Sofitel Centara Hotel** in Hua Hin (► 142), with topiary dancing elephants, a life-size chess set and maze, have an Alice in Wonderland appeal.
- **Wading through the mud** to a boat bound for the royal pavilion of Tham Phraya Nakhon (► 133).
- Spotting **monkeys** and other wildlife in Khao Sam Roi Yot National Park (► 132–133).
- Ko Samui's **go-karting track** just west of the village of Bophut (Samui Kart Club, daily 9–9, moderate).

---

migratory birds are seen in March and April. Even if you are not much of a bird-lover, it's an atmospheric spot where you can take longtail boat trips (two hours from Phatthalung) that steer you through the surreal landscape of vines and reeds.

➕ 199 E2 ℹ️ TAT, Sanam Na Muang ☎ 07 534 6515/6

⑦ Songkhla

Perched on a tongue of land between the Gulf of Thailand and the Thalay Sap lagoon, Songkhla is known as the "big town of two seas". As capital of the province, it has a small fishing port and some historic buildings built during the Na Songkhla dynasty. A splendid Chinese mansion built in 1878 houses the **National Museum**, which has exhibits ranging from local agricultural implements to Chinese furniture. **Wat Matchimawat** temple is set in stately gardens and ornately decorated. **Khao Tung Kuan**, a hill on the northwest edge of town, has a royal pavilion and good views. To the south, **Khao Saen** has a lively fish market every afternoon except Friday.

➕ 199 E2 ℹ️ TAT, 1/1 Soi 2 Thanon Niphatuthit 3, Ampoe Hat Yai, Songkhla ☎ 07 424 3747

National Museum

✉️ Thanon Wichianchom 🕐 Wed–Sun 9–noon, 1–4 💲 Inexpensive

A beautifully decorated *wat* in Songkhla

TRAVELLING IN THE DEEP SOUTH
The most southerly provinces in Thailand (Yala, Pattani and Narathiwat; and Songkhla to a lesser degree) have experienced bouts of violence by separatist groups opposed to the Thai government. Tourists have not been attacked but targets have included places where civilians have been victims, and if you are thinking of travelling in these regions, especially the border crossing at Sungai Kolok, you should check the current situation and assure yourself that it is safe. Visit www.fco.gov.uk for current advice.

Where to... Stay

Prices

Expect to pay per double room per night:

£ under 2,000 baht   ££ 2,000–5,000 baht   £££ over 5,000 baht

HUA HIN

Anantara Resort and Spa £££

This resort is a virtual palace, blending traditional Thai architecture, landscaped gardens and modern conveniences. Special spa packages are available. All guest rooms have large private terraces which overlook lagoons and have stunning rattan and teak furniture. The Baan Thalia restaurant, in keeping with the healthy manifesto of the Anantara, provides a well-balanced, delicious menu. Facilities include a pitch-and-putt course.

➕ 198 C3 ⌑ 43/1 Phetkasem Beach Road
☎ 03 252 0250; www.anantara.com

Chiva-Som International Health Resort £££

The Chiva-Som, (which means "Haven of Life") is a health resort par excellence, with a range of some 120 treatments. Every conceivable type of pampering that a stressed body could need is available. The resort is set in 3ha (7.5 acres) of gardens next to the beach. Pleasant pools (both decorative and for swimming) and even waterfalls surround the 57 deluxe rooms and suites. Healthy activities include t'ai chi, canoeing, mountain biking and horse riding.

➕ 198 C3 ⌑ 73/4 Thanon Phetkasem
☎ 03 253 6536; www.chivasom.com

Pattana £

Pattana is a very neat guest house, in the centre of town but away from the hustle and bustle. The accommodation, with air-conditioning or electric fans in the rooms, is built of teak wood and there is a pleasant little courtyard area with a small bar. Well-run and friendly, though the bedrooms could be larger, this is a place where guests soon bump into one another and swap travel stories over evening cocktails. There is also a restaurant on site.

➕ 198 C3 ⌑ 52 Thanon Naresdamri
☎ 03 251 393

Sofitel Centara Grand Resort & Villas £££

This fine, old colonial-style hotel opened in 1923 and was originally known as the Railway Hotel. At the time it was the most luxurious hotel for miles around. The interior still evokes the 1920s, with high ceilings and wood panelling. It is next to the beach, with gardens that have a wonderful topiary section. The hotel played the part of the French Embassy in neighbouring Cambodia in Roland Joffe's powerful 1984 film *The Killing Fields*. Facilities include three swimming pools, a croquet lawn and tennis courts, and there are six golf courses within 20 minutes' drive of the hotel. It is also justly famous for its excellent restaurants, which include the Railway Restaurant (▶ 145).

➕ 198 C3 ⌑ 1 Thanon Damnoen Kasem
☎ 03 251 2021;
www.centarahotelsresorts.com

Veranda Lodge ££–£££

Veranda Lodge is a boutique-style hotel – a dozen rooms and six suites – with most of the amenities normally confined to luxury accommodation. Rooms are air-conditioned and stylishly furnished.

There is a good choice of places to eat, including a gourmet restaurant serving fresh seafood and authentic Thai cuisine, and a small swimming pool set in a fragrant tropical garden facing the beach. The lodge is within easy walking distance of downtown nightlife.

🚹 198 C3 ⊠ 113 Soi 67 ☎ 03 253 3678; www.verandalodge.com

KHAO SAM ROI YOT PARK

Dolphin Bay Resort ££

This is the closest comfortable accommodation to Khao Sam Roi Yot National Park. The resort is set in pretty Phu Noi Bay on the coast, about 35km (21.7 miles) south of Hua Hin. There are 24 bungalows, 22 balcony rooms and 6 villas. The management and staff are very friendly and there are two swimming pools and great sea views. All rooms are air-conditioned with satellite TV and mini-bar. The restaurants provide both Thai and European dishes.

🚹 198 C3 ⊠ 227 Moo 4, Phu Noi Beach ☎ 03 255 9333; www.dolphinbayresort.com

KO SAMUI ARCHIPELAGO

Coral Cove Chalets ££

In a cove between Chaweng and Lamai beaches on Ko Samui, Coral Cove is framed by coconut palms. The beach here is usually very quiet and private. If you are a snorkelling enthusiast, the cove is an excellent place to go exploring; there are a number of reefs offshore. The traditional Thai-style bungalows are comfortable and all offer superb ocean views.

🚹 198 C2 ⊠ 210 Coral Cove Beach, Lamai, Ko Samui ☎ 07 742 2242; www.coralcovechalet.com

Kamalaya £££

Kamalaya is the healthiest and one of the most attractive places in which to stay on Ko Samui. The resort is centred around a cave formerly used by Buddhist monks for meditation. Its Wellness Sanctuary and Holistic Spa, offering holistic medicine and healing therapies to tired minds and bodies, is at the core of Kamalaya. Consult the website to see just how much the sanctuary offers. Accommodation is set amid Balinese-style gardens with a way down to a beach, and there is a pleasant café for lunch and a restaurant for evening meals.

🚹 198 C2 ⊠ 102/9 Moo 3, Laem Set Road, Ko Samui ☎ 07 742 9800; www.kamalaya.com

Natural Wing Resort ££

Hotels and resorts on Ko Samui often ignore the environment, and very few take the time at the design and planning stage to consider their situation. This is not the case with the Natural Wing, at Bang Po Beach on the northwest of Ko Samui. The villas nestling unobtrusively into the hillside have satellite TV and internet access. Tree-house accommodation is also available. A good spa and a restaurant serving Thai, European, Vietnamese and Japanese dishes complete this excellent resort.

🚹 198 C2 ⊠ 11/5 Moo 6, Hat Bang Po, Ko Samui ☎ 07 742 0871; www.naturalwing.com

Sea Scene Resort £

Sea Scene, on Ko Phangan, is good value for money: the standard bungalows have electric fans and balcony with partial sea view; the higher-grade accommodation has air-conditioning and sea-facing balconies. There are also family bungalows that come with a fridge as well as air-conditioning. The location is wonderfully tranquil, with superb views from the restaurant, and the cocktails that are not over-priced are an added bonus.

🚹 198 C2 ⊠ Aow Plaay Leam, Ko Phangan ☎ 07 737 7516; www.seascene.com

The Sarann £££

In addition to relaxation and luxury, this beachfront villa resort offers a

Where to...
Eat and Drink

Prices
Expect to pay per person for a three-course meal, excluding drinks and service:
£ under 300 baht   ££ 300–600 baht   £££ over 600 baht

HUA HIN

Brasserie de Paris ££

This excellent French restaurant has a terrace overlooking the sea. Seafood specialities include crab Hua Hin, and the fresh scallop dish *coquille Saint-Jacques*. There are classic French main dishes, appetizers and desserts. French management keeps standards high. The terrace affords a lovely view of Hua Hin's brightly painted fishing fleet. There is also a good selection of French wine, and it's not too expensive.

➕ 198 C3 ⊠ 3 Thanon Naresdamri
☎ 03 253 0637 ⏰ Daily 12–10.30

Let's Sea ££–£££

Let's Sea is a chic alfresco resort facing the sea on a beautiful stretch of the Gulf Coast and its location is perfect for this informal beach-style restaurant serving a mix of Thai and international dishes. The decor is casual but sophisticated, with modernist touches that sets Let's Sea apart from most of Hua Hin's other restaurants. The food is not disappointing but neither is it spectacular; it is the setting that makes it special.

➕ 198 C3 ⊠ 83/155 Soi Talay, Thanon Takiab ☎ 03 253 6022; www.letussea.com
⏰ Daily 10–10

---

level of intimacy that counteracts the hustle and bustle of nearby Chaweng. Pampering sessions and holistic treatments are available at the resort's spa, and there is an infinity edge pool, a fitness room, and a library and internet room. Good Thai and contemporary Western cuisine is served at the Wild Ginger restaurant facing the sea and beach.

➕ 198 C2 ⊠ Moo 3, Chaweng Noi Beach, Ko Samui ☎ 07 741 4600;
www.thesarann.com

PHETCHABURI PROVINCE

Regent Cha-am £££

Not far south of Cha-am on the road to Hua Hin, this large, self-contained resort is ideal if you have limited time. About 185km (115 miles) south of Bangkok and set in 16ha (39.5 acres) of beautifully landscaped gardens, the Regent, with more than 700 rooms, is actually made up of three parts: The Regent Cha-Am, The Regency

Wing and The Regent Chalet. An unspoiled, quiet beach fronts the whole resort. All rooms overlook one of the three swimming pools, the well-kept garden or the ocean. Facilities include a gym and sauna, squash courts, tennis courts and an outdoor jacuzzi.

➕ 198 B4 ⊠ 849/21 Thanon Phetkasem, Cha-am ☎ 03 250 8140;
www.regent-chaam.com

Pineapple Garden Beach Hotel and Resort ££

Pineapples grow in the garden of this attractive and friendly little resort on Cha-am's beachfront. Accommodation is in large, modern bungalows with tiled-floors, and each has its own patio with views of the gardens and the sea. Young guests are particularly well catered for, with water-sports equipment, a playground and a games room; there is also a private beach.

➕ 198 B4 ⊠ 335/1 Tambon Cha-Am, Cha-am ☎ 02 231 3671;
www.pine-apple.net

Railway Restaurant £££

A few years ago the Railway Hotel (now Sofitel Centara, ► 142) was thoroughly renovated, and one splendid offshoot was the Railway Restaurant. It is decorated and furnished in the style of Hua Hin Railway Station during the 1920s, complete with old station clocks and other railway paraphernalia. Apart from the regular Thai dishes there are usually various speciality buffets including French, Italian and Chinese.

🔢 198 C3 ☒ Sofitel Centara Grand Resort, 1 Thanon Damnoen Kasem ☎ 03 251 2031 🕑 Daily 7am–10:30pm

Saeng Thai ££

Hua Hin's fishing fleet lands its daily catch just along the pier from this popular, old seafood restaurant, in fact the oldest restaurant in Hua Hin. Reliable fresh food accompanied by good service is the draw at this large, open-air spot on the seafront. The smell of the sea and the faint aroma from the fish market only add to the overall ambience and atmosphere.

🔢 198 C3 ☒ Thanon Naresdamri (near the pier) ☎ 03 251 2144 🕑 Daily 10am–10:30pm

KO SAMUI ARCHIPELAGO

Ali Baba ££

This restaurant serves Indian dishes, but also a few Thai and European standards. It's rightly regarded as the best Indian restaurant on Ko Samui, and with its real tandoori oven Ali Baba is able to produce some excellent tikka and tandoori dishes. It's also well known for delicious Indian-style seafood dishes. A large selection of fine coffees helps to round off any meal.

🔢 198 C2 ☒ Chaweng Beach Road (opposite the Samui Hot Club), Chaweng ☎ 07 723 0253 🕑 Daily 10am–11pm

Ban Thai Food Garden & Antique House ££

The largest lobsters you're ever likely to encounter are a specialty of this spectacular Thai restaurant that is only a short walk from Chaweng Beach. They're known as "Dragon lobsters" and are prepared to a European recipe that's a secret of the chef. Other seafood is laid out buffet-style on ice. Traditional Thai dancing is presented nightly.

🔢 198 C2 ☒ Chaweng Beach Road, 157 Moo 2, Bophut, Chaweng Beach ☎ 07 723 1322 🕑 Daily 5pm–midnight

Big John's Seafood Restaurant ££

Regarded as the finest seafood restaurant on Ko Samui, Big John's also serves the island's finest margaritas, best enjoyed at a waterfront table with a sunset view. The seafood platter with rice baked in pineapple is legendary.

🔢 198 C2 ☒ 95/4 Moo 2, Lipanoi ☎ 07 742 3025; www.bigjohnsamui.com 🕑 Daily 7am–11pm

Captain's Choice £££

This beach restaurant, part of the Imperial Boat House hotel complex, is one of Ko Samui's very best. Lunches tend to be light, with plenty of fresh salads and fish. Evening meals are grander affairs consisting mainly of seafood delicacies such as prawns, squid, crab, lobster and crayfish – all caught locally. If it's available then this is also a good place to enjoy shark. An extensive wine list complements the meal.

🔢 198 C2 ☒ Imperial Boat House, 83 Moo 5, Hat Choeng Mon ☎ 07 742 5041 🕑 Daily 11–10:30

Happy Elephant ££

The Happy Elephant is just like it sounds, offering a friendly, cosy atmosphere next to Bophut Beach on Ko Samui. There are some very good Thai specialities, such as grilled prawns and sweet tamarind sauce with prawn cakes grilled on fresh sugarcane sticks. The menu is mostly fresh seafood with a few international staples like pizza, pasta and burgers. For something to drink there is a wide variety of fruit shakes and an admirable selection of wines.

Jing £££

Samui's top Chinese restaurant has been compared by the critics with favoured dining destinations in Bangkok and even Hong Kong. Not surprising, since the menu – comprising 70 dishes – was prepared by the head of the Bangkok Culinary Circle, Peter Lei. Head chef Chan Liu Lam is a Hong Kong veteran who also worked for 14 years at the Bangkok Hilton and Shangri-La Hotels. His Cantonese dishes are wonderful and authentic, but he also brings to the table such rarities as Mongolian lamb. Chan Liu Lam and his sous-chefs work in full view of the diners, who are treated to a fantastic show of culinary dexterity.

➕ 198 C2 ✉ Soi Calibri, South Chaweng (opp Central Resort) ☎ 07 741 3462 🕒 Daily 12.30–10.30

Ocean 11 £££

For that special meal to cap your holiday memories, Ocean 11 is currently one of the most popular restaurants on Samui. A beachside setting on Big Buddha beach is complemented by innovative Mediterranean cuisine and a superior wine list.

➕ 198 C2 ✉ Bophut ☎ 07 724 5134; www.o11s.com 🕒 Daily 2–late

Pakarang ££

Pakarang is in a great location, away from the bustle of Chaweng Beach, in quiet, beautiful surroundings, with a choice of dining areas. Sit indoors surrounded by paintings of Ko Samui, or outside under a huge bougainvillaea trellis. The chef makes no attempt to tone down the spices and subtle flavours of Thai food, unless requested to do so. The menu revolves around traditional curries, most of which use coconut milk to enhance the creaminess. There's also an extensive cocktail list to accompany the delicious food.

➕ 198 C2 ✉ 9 Moo 2, Tambon Bophut ☎ 07 742 7238 🕒 Daily 7am–10pm

Poppies ££

Poppies gives a choice of dining locations. Try the lovely teak pavilion, set in a verdant tropical garden, or the beachside marquee. The food is mainly dishes from central Thailand and seafood, and standards are very high. There's a fine selection of wines and cocktails. Live musical entertainment is provided by a classical guitarist on Tuesday, Thursday and Friday. Saturday is Thai night, featuring traditional Thai dancing.

➕ 198 C2 ✉ South Chaweng Beach Road ☎ 07 742 2419 🕒 Daily 7am–11pm

Sala-Thai ££

Lamai Beach on Ko Samui does not have a particularly great choice of eating places, but Sala-Thai is one of the better ones. It's in a romantic setting dotted with charming small waterfalls and fountains. The menu

features a selection of Thai and international dishes. Specialities include *tom kha gai* (chicken cooked in coconut milk) and *kung pao* (grilled prawns).

➕ 198 C2 ✉ Lamai Beach Road (opposite the Full Moon Bar) ☎ 07 723 3180; www.sala-thai.com 🕒 Daily 2–midnight

Shades ££

For a romantic dining experience, try to reserve a table overlooking the bay at this stylish beachside restaurant on Bophut's main street. Service here is friendly, attentive and very knowledgeable. Recommendations include any of the fresh seafood dishes such as tartar or fresh tuna, prawns and avocado. There is also a wine bar serving a selection of fine wines.

➕ 198 C2 ✉ Bophut high street ☎ 07 724 5688 🕒 Daily 1–10

Vecchia Napoli ££

The pasta and breads served at this exceptional and authentic Neapolitan restaurant are

Where to... Shop

HUA HIN

The Gulf Coast is not known for its shopping opportunities. Hua Hin is especially bereft of anything decent to buy, and is overrun with tacky souvenirs. Hua Hin does have a lively **night market** and a good selection of **boutiques** can be found along Thanon Naret Damri.

KO SAMUI

Ko Samui has a slightly better selection of shops than Hua Hin, with a few **gem shops**, but you should exercise real caution, especially regarding the purchase of unmounted cut stones.

The main beach areas, **Chaweng** and **Lamai**, are dotted with a number of **supermarkets**.

---

home-made and delicious. Portions are more than generous – the pizzas alone are a record-setting 30cm (12 inches) in diameter. And customers eat in an atmospheric dining room that could have been transported straight from the centre of Naples itself.

🚩 198 C2 ⊠ Center Point, Chaweng ☎ 07 723 1229 ⑥ Daily 11am–1am

PHETCHABURI PROVINCE

Poom ££

Poom is regarded as the best restaurant in Cha-am for quality seafood and it is advisable to make a reservation in advance during high season. Succulent fresh fish, crab and squid are barbecued and served with mouth-watering dips. Poom's popularity makes it a sociable place to eat, so romantic diners seeking a quiet table may be disappointed when the place is busy.

🚩 198 B4 ⊠ Thanon Ruamchit, Cha-am ☎ 03 247 1036 ⑥ Daily 7:30am–10pm

Rabieng Rim Nam £

Centrally located in a lovely teak house by the Chomrut Bridge on the banks of the River Phet, this popular and attractive restaurant (there's also a guest house) has a Thai and English menu with a listing of more than a hundred dishes. Seafood is a speciality, as are spicy yam salads. A good choice to try is a local dish, *khanom jiin thawt man* (noodles with spicy fish cakes). The restaurant/guest house is a useful source of local information for travellers, and it has the added advantage of offering internet access.

🚩 198 C4 ⊠ 1 Thanon Chisa In, Phetchaburi ☎ 03 242 5707 ⑥ Daily 8am–midnight

NAKHON SI THAMMARAT

Bovorn Bazaar £

It is worth seeking out Bovorn Bazaar for its plethora of popular eateries ranging from simple cafés to restaurants serving well-cooked local dishes. One particularly

worthy of note is Khrua Nakhon. The bazaar is a great place to enjoy a tasty Thai breakfast or just a coffee (excellent from Hao Coffee) or a cold drink and a snack.

🚩 198 C1 ⊠ Bovorn Bazaar, Thanon Ratchadamnoen ☎ Khrua Nakhon: 07 531 7197 ⑥ Daily 8:30am–2pm

SONGKHLA

Naiwan £

Catch of the day at this outstanding fish restaurant on Samila beach includes lobster, squid, giant prawns and clams, all imaginatively prepared in southern Thai style. The *pla muek khai yat sai* (squid caviar in a lemon sauce) is a truly local speciality, but if it's not to your taste then try something more simple such as the sea bass or prawns straight from the grill, which are wonderfully fresh and delicious.

🚩 199 E2 ⊠ 8/13-16 Rachadamnoen Road, Muang Songkhla ☎ 07 431 1295 ⑥ Daily 10–10

Oriental Gallery Arts and Antiques (Chaweng Beach Road, tel: 07 742 2200) has a fine collection of teak furniture and crafts, and can arrange shipping to anywhere in the world.

If you need swimwear, try **Life's A Beach** (Chaweng Beach Road, tel: 07 742 2630), which advertises the latest Australian imports.

Joop! Tailors (Choeng Mon beach, tel: 07 742 7011 and Chaweng Beach, tel: 07 741 3237) is the best tailor on the island and can knock up a suit or dress within 24 hours.

Ko Samui has won an international reputation for the handmade shoes produced by local craftsman **Nimit Meefuang**. You'll find his creations in the boutiques of all the top luxury hotels: the Anantara, Poppies, Meridien and the Santibury.

There's an array of arts and crafts stalls and designer boutiques all under one roof at the **Central Shopping Arcade**, Chaweng Beach.

Where to...
Be Entertained

GOLF

Hua Hin is home to the 18-hole **Royal Hua Hin Golf Course** (tel: 03 251 2475), the oldest in Thailand. Established in 1924, it has been followed by top-quality rivals, making Hua Hin and nearby Cha-am major golfing destinations. Green fees are about US$25 weekdays and US$50 weekends. Caddies are required at most courses and cost about US$6 plus a US$4–8 tip, depending on their experience and help. Electric carts cost about US$25, which usually includes a caddy.

NIGHTLIFE

Most nightlife and entertainment along the Gulf Coast is on Ko Samui and Ko Phangan. **Hua Hin** has a strip of beer bars between Thanon Naretdamri and Thanon Phunsuk.

Ko Samui

One of Chaweng Beach's favourite venues, the **Green Mango Disco** (Soi Green Mango, north end of central Chaweng), rarely gets going until after midnight. Also on Chaweng Beach, the **Reggae Pub** continues to be popular, with a large open-air dance floor swinging to the latest sounds and reggae.

Coyote (202/7-8 Moo 2, Bophut, tel: 02 663 6200; www.coyotesamui.com) opens at 11am, with "happy hour" lasting the entire afternoon, but the music doesn't start until 9:30pm. With 75 varieties of margarita available, the chance is you will find a drink that you've not tried before; there are also an amazing 50 different blue agave tequilas.

Over on **Big Buddha Beach** is the **Secret Garden Festival** (22/1 Moo 4, Ban Bangrak) from December to April, Sunday 2–10pm. What began as an impromptu jam session among friends has become a major scene, attracting international stars on occasion. Even so, it retains a friendly feel.

The main nightlife venue on **Lamai Beach** is **Bauhaus**, a large entertainment complex with giant screens showing sporting fixtures from around the world, and a busy dance floor. There are also drag shows and Thai boxing exhibitions.

Ko Phangan

One of the biggest social events in Thailand happens every full moon on Ko Samui's smaller sister island, Ko Phangan. The **full-moon parties** (▲ 134) have become a world-famous rave venue.

Andaman Coast

Getting Your Bearings

Thailand's Andaman coast wriggles down the western side of its skinny peninsula, and features spectacular scenery all the way down from the famous island of Ko Phuket to the border with Malaysia. The area's delights include stunning white beaches, calm turquoise sea, vertical limestone islands, tumbling waterfalls and renowned seafood.

Island jewels off the Andaman coast are all around. Choose sophisticated Ko Phuket, with its international airport and good travel connections; idyllic and justly popular Ko Phi Phi; or the remote peace of Thale Ban National Park further south. Transport to the islands is by colourful wooden longtail boats, and sea gypsies dive for pearls in the traditional way. Beneath the surface, coral harbours exotic fish, providing excellent diving and snorkelling.

Ko Surin **5**

On the mainland the spectacle continues with the beautiful coastline at Krabi, exciting tours of Ao Phang Nga, coffee and cashew plantations, lush green rainforests and tropical mangroves.

The exotic varied plant and wildlife found here are protected in Khao Sok National Park, a wild and magical place and home of one of the largest flowers in the world, the *Rafflesia kerri meyer* (wild lotus).

5
Ko
Similan

The monsoon hits this coast more heavily than the Gulf side, and is most intense between May and October. More time is also needed to enjoy this part of the country, where the pace of life is unhurried.

Page 149: Fishing boats on the beach at Ko Tarutao

Mist hangs over the tropical rainforest in Khao Sok National Park

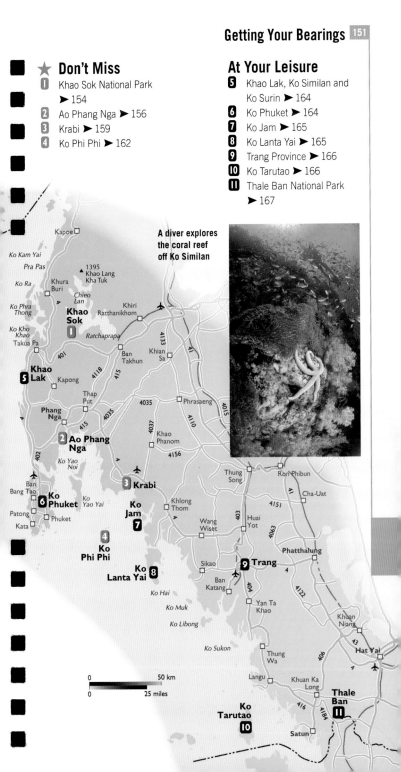

A diver explores the coral reef off Ko Similan

Kapoe
Ko Kam Yai
Pra Pas
Ko Ra
Khura Buri
1395 Khao Lang Kha Tuk
Chieo Lan
Ko Phra Thong
Khiri Ratthanikhom
Khao Sok 1
Ko Kho Khao
Takua Pa
Ratchaprapa
401
Ban Takhun
Khian Sa
4133
41
Khao Lak 5
Kapong
4118
415
Thap Put
4035
Phrasaeng
4015
Phang Nga
415
4035
4037
4110
Ao Phang Nga 2
Khao Phanom
4156
Ko Yao Noi
402
Thung Song
Ron Phibun
Ban Bang Tao
Ko Phuket 6
Ko Yao Yai
Krabi 3
4151
Cha-Uat
41
Patong
Phuket
Kata
Ko Jam 7
Khlong Thom
Wang Wiset
403
Huai Yot
4063
Ko Phi Phi 4
Phatthalung
Ko Lanta Yai 8
Sikao
Trang 9
Ban Katang
404
4122
Ko Hai
Yan Ta Khao
Ko Muk
Khuan Niang
Ko Libong
43
Hat Yai
Ko Sukon
Thung Wa
406
Langu
Khuan Ka Long
416
Thale Ban 11
Ko Tarutao 10
4184
Satun

0 ———— 50 km
0 ———— 25 miles

In Seven Days

If you're not quite sure where to begin your travels, this itinerary
recommends seven practical and enjoyable days out exploring the
Andaman Coast, taking in some of the best places to see using
the Getting Your Bearings map on the previous page. For more
information see the main entries.

Day 1

Morning
Take the 90-minute flight to **6 Ko Phuket** (➤ 164–165) from Bangkok
(avoid the long train and bus journeys). Flights are inexpensive (especially
from Pattaya, ➤ 120). Flights also go from Ko Samui, Chiang Mai, Hat
Yai and Surat Thani. Have lunch in Phuket – try Thai Naan (➤ 171).

Afternoon and Evening
Spend the rest of the day at **Ao Patong** (➤ 165), the most popular of Ko
Phuket's beaches, and the evening and night at one of the **luxury resorts**
(such as The Royal Phuket Yacht Club ➤ 170).

Day 2

Morning
Drive or take a bus to **1 Khao Sok National Park** (below, ➤ 154–155) via
Takua Pa. The trip should take about four hours.

Afternoon and Evening
Relax in a hammock hanging from a tree house and listen to the sounds
of the jungle. Take a night safari (➤ 155). When darkness falls, you have
a better chance of spotting the shyer inhabitants.

Day 3

Set off on a guided lake tour (➤ 155). This takes you deep into the Khao Sok National Park to explore the stunning **Chieo Lan Reservoir**, with its impressive limestone towers and river-fed caves. Stay in scenic raft accommodation at the lake.

Day 4

Morning
Drive or take the bus to **2 Ao Phang Nga** (below, ➤ 156–158), a spectacular bay studded with islets. Change at Takua Pa if you are going by bus. The journey will take about half a day.

Afternoon
From the bus station, take the tour of **Ao Phang Nga**. Sayan Tours have a trip leaving at 2pm that includes a seafood supper and overnight accommodation at a floating Muslim village (➤ 156).

Day 5

Morning
Drive or take an early bus to **3 Krabi** (➤ 159–161), a journey of about 90 minutes. Spend the rest of the day doing the road tour of **Krabi province** (➤ 181–183). Visit the forest temple of **Wat Tham Seua** (➤ 160) en route before skirting the scenic coast and having lunch at one of the beach restaurants (➤ 159–160).

Afternoon and Evening
If you have time, take a boat to one of the scenic beaches at **Laem Phra Nang** (➤ 159–160). Complete the loop by driving back to Krabi for dinner at the night market. Or treat yourself to an Italian meal at Viva (➤ 170).

Days 6–7

Catch a boat from the pier at Krabi to the island of **4 Ko Phi Phi** (➤ 162–163). Spend two days relaxing on the idyllic beaches or embark on a black shark boat trip (most of the agencies offer them). Sharks measuring 2m (6.5 feet) long can be found hanging around off the rocks and reef.

❶ Khao Sok National Park

This national park forms one of the oldest ecosystems on earth. Mist-shrouded limestone towers rise out of the pristine jungle fed by a network of freshwater rivers, which tumble into waterfalls. A Communist hideout in the 1970s, wild elephants, bears and even tigers now lurk in the dense trees. More visible are monkeys, lizards, wild pigs, barking deer and flashing fireflies. Gibbons call from the rainforest canopy and cicadas produce a daily cacophony.

The best way to enjoy the park is to immerse yourself in the unique environment. There are short walks to waterfalls from the visitor centre, which provides a free leaflet showing the trails. These take you past thick buttress roots, vine-tangled umbrella palms and towering bamboo. You may not come across some of the larger mammals, but you'll be able to see butterflies, huge dragonflies and exotic *rambutan* fruit trees.

The star attraction is the ***rafflesia***, one of the largest flowers in the world, measuring 1m (3.28 feet) across and weighing 7kg (15.4 pounds). It only blooms in January and February.

Much of the accommodation in the park is in simple but atmospheric wooden huts on stilts overlooking the rainforest

or river (see www.dnp.go.th for details). This is a good place to relax in a hammock in the day or by candlelight at night. All guest houses have guides offering **day and night safaris** – the guides usually speak good enough English to point things out along the way. Elephant rides, canoeing and "tubing" (floating down the river in a rubber ring – in the rainy season only) can all be arranged. Highly recommended is the overnight lake tour, which is usually combined with a spot of caving.

TAKING A BREAK

A panoramic view of one of the world's most ancient landscapes

All the private lodges have restaurants and you don't have to stay at one to call in for a meal or a drink.

🔹 198 A1 ✉ 40km east of Takua Pa ⏱ Visitor centre: Daily 8–4 ☎ 07 739 5025/5139; www.khaosok.com 💷 Expensive

---

KHAO SOK NATIONAL PARK: INSIDE INFO

Top tips Kilometre marker 109 is the stop for buses from Surat Thani to the park, but if you just ask for "Khao Sok", the driver will know where to stop. Here you will be met by touts waiting to take you to the various lodges.
■ The **wet season** (June to September) can be very wet. Trails are often slippery, and leeches can be a problem, but you may see more wildlife.
■ Along the road to the visitor centre, there are a number of privately run guest houses, all of which conduct **tours** into the park (▶ 168).
■ *Waterfalls and Gibbon Calls* by Thom Henley is on sale in the visitor centre. Its simple illustrations and accessible style provide a detailed background to the park and can act as a guide along the trails.

Hidden gem Chieo Lan Reservoir has limestone outcrops rising to 960m (3,148 feet) – three times higher than those in Ao Phang Nga (▶ 156–158). You need to take an overnight guided tour, which usually includes accommodation in one of the floating lodges on the shore (if not, it is easy to arrange your own accommodation, ask at the visitor centre). The lake is especially beautiful in the early morning when hornbills, eagles, gibbons and even elephants gather.

2 Ao Phang Nga

With more than a hundred spectacular vertical islets, this huge bay forms an extraordinary landscape. Buzzing longtail boats take you through tangled mangroves, and past limestone outcrops to hidden white-sand beaches, semi-submerged caves dripping with stalactites, a floating Muslim village and Ko Phing Kan, or James Bond Island, made famous by its appearance in *The Man with the Golden Gun.*

Longtail Boat Tours

Tours of the bay, which is a national park, start from the bus terminal of the nondescript town of Phang Nga. Sayan Tour, which have been established for nearly 20 years, provide a friendly and efficient service and are timed to miss the Phuket crowds. Half-day trips to the main islands and caves run in the morning and afternoon; full-day trips offer more islands and a chance to swim.

It is a short journey by road from Phang Nga to the pier where a brightly coloured longtail boat takes you across green waterways with high, mangrove-covered banks. Boats sail through the cave of **Tahm Lod**. You pass **Kao Marjoo** (Dog Island), so-named because of its shape, and **Kao Khien** (Writing Island) with rock drawings that date back at least 3,000 years. The final stop is Ko Phing Kan, or **James Bond Island**, which has souvenir shops on the small sandy beach.

*Opposite:
Ko Khao Tapu,
or Nail Island,
viewed from
James Bond
Island*

Ko Panyi

An overnight option combines the half-day itinerary with accommodation in the floating **Muslim village of Ko Panyi** and a seafood supper. This is the more leisurely, recommended option, if you don't mind basic accommodation. It gives you a glimpse of the community without the tourist crowds and there is not much reason to spend the night in Phang Nga town.

Established more than 200 years ago, Ko Panyi now has a population of 2,000, consisting of just four or five families. It's best seen in the evening when the seafood restaurants and souvenir shops wind down and the daytime tourists have left. Wander around the floating labyrinth of corrugated iron and wood, which is crowded with crab and lobster pots and fishing nets. Sit on the western side to watch the sun set over the water. Branches sticking out of the water become makeshift moorings for the weathered wooden longtail boats that serve as fishing boats for the traditional community. There is a call to prayer five times a day at the green and gold mosque.

*The charmingly
ramshackle
floating village
of Ko Panyi*

TAKING A BREAK

Tours include lunch at a seafood restaurant in a floating village and dinner in a private house if you are staying in the village overnight.

Traditional boats on a small beach, Phang Nga Bay

✚ 199 D2 ✉ Sayan Tour, 209 Phang Nga bus terminal, Phang Nga
☎ 07 643 0348; www.sayantour.com 🄳 Moderate

AO PHANG NGA: INSIDE INFO

Top tips Although you can go on a **tour round the bay** from Phuket, it is better to do it from Phang Nga as numbers will be smaller and it costs less.

■ In the Muslim village of Ko Panyi **respect the locals**, who dress conservatively and don't drink alcohol.

■ Pick up the **information leaflet** at Sayan Tour's office. It gives information about the route and points of interest. Guides speak little English, although Sayan's owner comes and chats after dinner and will answer any questions.

③ Krabi

When visitors talk of Krabi, they tend to mean the beautiful coast as much as the fishing town itself, which is a major jumping-off point for the area's fantastic beaches and emerald waters. Most of Krabi province's attractions are offshore. The snaking coastline shelters deep bays, many of which are only accessible by boat, circled by coral reefs. They are backed by sheer limestone cliffs which offer some of the best rock climbing in the world.

Krabi town is in a peaceful riverside setting with a tree-lined grass promenade and the charmingly named Ko Maew and Ko Nu, "**Cat and Mouse Islands**", on its eastern side. As well as being in some ways the capital of the Andaman coast, Krabi is also a culinary capital. At the lively **night market**, illuminated glass cabinets line a string of pavement tables where streetside chefs roll out dough for deep-fried pastry and toss just-caught sizzling seafood. An amazing range of international food, from Thai curry, pizza and Mexican food to American burgers and Greek salads, is served in the town's restaurants and cafés.

Lying under a limestone cliff is a 15m-long (50-foot) **Reclining Buddha**. In a kink in Route 404 it is easy to miss, but it is close to the 7km marker, which indicates its distance from Krabi. The image is part of **Wat Sai Thai**, although there are hardly any monks living in the temple here.

The Beaches

Some 18km (11 miles) northwest of Krabi, **Hat Noppharat Thara** is a beautiful, clean stretch of pine-fringed beach, part of a national park of the same name. Its name means "Beach of the Nine-Gem Stream" but it was previously called "Dry Canal Beach" because of the pretty canal which flows into the sea here. The tide retreats far into the bay, making swimming impossible at low tide, but it is a lovely, tranquil place for a stroll on the sand. There are picnic areas, and **boat and snorkelling trips** are available to islands such as Chicken and Poda, which stud the large scenic bay. No need to reserve, someone will probably offer you one at Hat Noppharat Thara.

Ao Nang is a developed stretch along a roadside beach that attracts package holidaymakers. Just south of here, the little headland of **Laem Phra Nang** is named after a local princess (*phra*

East Rai Lai is a popular centre for rock climbing

nang means "revered lady"). Although reached only by boat – longtails leave from near Krabi's pier – it is popular and famous for **rock climbing**, offering many world-class routes. Beginners are catered for as well, and it's a good spectator sport. Other activities on offer include kayaking through mangroves, and snorkelling and diving trips to nearby islands. The beach is packed with places offering activities.

There are three beaches: **Ao Phra Nang** at the centre and **East and West Rai Lai** on either side, separated by a few rows of bungalow accommodation. The east beach has rock-climbing shops and mangroves and mudflats rather than a real beach, but cheaper accommodation. At the main west beach, snorkelling, diving, kayaking and rock climbing are available.

Tiger Cave Temple

Most people pass by **Wat Tham Seua** (Tiger Cave Temple, free), on their way to the beaches. In a beautiful setting on the northeast of Krabi, it is one of southern Thailand's most important forest temples, where monks live in meditation huts in caves among the trees. In the first and main cave nuns make bracelets and Thais come to worship. Behind the altar, stairs lead to a smaller cave, featuring a **giant Buddha footprint**. If you walk through the temple grounds to the statue of the Goddess of Mercy, the first set of steps is a near-vertical route. It takes about an hour to get to the top, but there are views to the coast. The second series of steps leads to meditation huts and a temple with a **Big Buddha**. You can follow a path among ancient trees: one is said to be 1,000 years old. You can reach the temple by *songthaew* from Utrakit Road, but the best option is to rent a jeep or motorbike.

TAKING A BREAK

The night market on Thanon Khong Kha comes alive early in the evening when food stalls are set up and tables laid out to face the river. Most of the menus are in English, although it is a favourite eating place for locals, and the Thai food is excellent value. This is the place to enjoy authentic *tom yam kung* (shrimp soup with chilli and lemongrass).

Cliffs form a spectacular backdrop to Ao Phra Nang beach

➕ 199 D2 ℹ TAT, Utrakit Road ☎ 07 562 2163

KRABI: INSIDE INFO

Top tips Ao Nang is also sometimes called **Ao Phra Nang**, especially on road signs, which makes it easily confused with the beach on the cape.
- Some of the **accommodation** on Ao Nang is closed between May and October when the beach tends to be covered in debris brought in by the tide. At this time of year, the beaches around **Laem Phra Nang** are a much better bet.

One to miss Although all signs seem to point to the **Shell Cemetery of Su-San Hoi**, and trips are offered from Krabi, unless you are particularly interested in geology, you might feel you are just looking at slabs of concrete. The blocks are made up of 75-million-year-old mollusc shell fossils.

4 Ko Phi Phi

Phi Phi is actually two enchanting islands – Phi Phi Don and the smaller, virtually uninhabited Phi Phi Ley. Phi Phi Don is the tourist island, two upland tracts of jungle joined by the narrow strip of beach-lined land known as The Village. Two very pretty bays emanate from this strip, Loh Dalum Bay and the better known and more developed Tonsai Bay. Some of the hotels and resorts on these two bays can only be reached by boat, a very romantic way of starting a holiday.

The horrifying tsunami of 26 December 2004 hit the idyllic island of Phi Phi particularly badly, killing more than a thousand people, many of them tourists, and demolishing its double-sided seafront area. This strip of beach-fringed land, joining the higher north and south, was the heart of the island's holiday trade, with bars, budget hotels, restaurants and guest houses. Although virtually everything was destroyed, rebuilding has restored **The Village** to its former glory. Bars, restaurants, guest houses, resorts, diving and rock-climbing shops are as busy as they ever were. The only noticeable change is a drop in the range of budget accommodation and inexpensive places to eat.

The hotels and resorts on the higher ground in the north and south survived the tsunami untouched, and they are as welcoming as ever, their bays and beaches unscarred and beautifully maintained. On the coast, almost all of the top-end hotels and resorts are now back in business.

For a fine view of the island, climb the well-signposted path from The Village, which passes a tiny Thai settlement and leads after a mile or two to the deserted beaches of Ao Lanti and Ao Koh Bakao.

Opposite: The island's twin beaches from a verdant viewpoint

Boats moored at small and tranquil Ko Phi Phi Ley

TAKING A BREAK

The **Chao Koh Phi Phi Lodge** (53 Moo 7), under the same management as the popular **Carlito's Bar**, has an excellent restaurant overlooking central Tonsai Village beach. Early risers can breakfast there from a large a la carte menu, while evening diners can enjoy a cocktail or crisp Chardonnay watching the lights flick on along Tonsai Village beachfront.

You can escape the Tonsai Beach crowds by heading to the northeastern side of the island, to the **Phi Phi Island Village Beach Resort and Spa** (tel: 07 562 8900–3). At the resort's hillside **Wana Spa** you can enjoy a jacuzzi in a petal-strewn tub overlooking the ocean.

🕀 199 D2 🛈 TAT, The nearest office is at Krabi (▶ 160) or Phuket (▶ 165)

KO PHI PHI: INSIDE INFO

Top tips The website **www.phi-phi.com** carries the latest up-to-date information about Ko Phi Phi. Other tourist information is provided by the TAT offices in Phuket or Krabi.

■ Sunrise and sunset are magical times. Watch the sun rise over the Andaman Sea in front of the Beach Club at Tonsai Village, or sunset from the island's View Point.

At Your Leisure

Baby turtle on a beach in the Ko Surin archipelago

5 Khao Lak, Ko Similan and Ko Surin

The village of **Khao Lak** (part of the national park of the same name), has a laid-back atmosphere and is home to fishing families and thriving tourist-based concerns. Snorkelling, diving trips and jungle treks take you deeper into the spectacular scenery in the national park.

Khao Lak is a departure point for **Ko Similan** (a group of nine islands) and **Ko Surin** (five islands). These archipelagos offer some of the world's best diving among vast networks of coral teeming with exotic fish. Both groups of islands are remote, with only basic accommodation. Practically inaccessible during the monsoon season (between May and October), the islands are best visited as part of an organized tour during the rest of the year. Sea Dragon Dive Centre organizes a three-day tour in Khao Lak (tel: 07 648 5420; www. seadragondivecenter.com). The price includes boat trips, accommodation, food and equipment.
✚ 198 A1

6 Ko Phuket

The island once called "Junk Ceylon" was a resting place for sailors travelling between India and China.

Now called "Pearl of the Andaman", it is famed for its cuisine, yachting, fishing and world-class diving. Thailand's largest island, and its wealthiest province, everything is on a grand scale, with sweeping beaches, huge luxury resorts and high mountain roads. Commercial developments are centred on the

FOR KIDS
- **Elephant rides** and **bamboo rafting** on Khao Lak, **snorkelling** on Ko Phi Phi and many child-friendly activities are available through tour agencies on Phuket (see www.phuket.com).
- **Fantasea** in Phuket (near Hat Kamala, tel: 07 638 5000, www.phuket-fantasea.com, daily 5:30pm–11:30pm, expensive) is a spectacular night-time show combining modern light and sound technology, traditional Thai dance and a buffet.
- **Phuket Butterfly Garden and Aquarium** (Yaowarat Road, north of Phuket town, daily 9–5:30, expensive) has a wide variety of butterflies and reef fish.
- **Boat trip at Ao Phang Nga** (➤ 156).

west coast. Glitzy **Ao Patong** is the most built up and the centre for diving operations. Its seafront was badly hit by the December 2004 tsunami but swiftly reconstructed, and today is again Phuket's principal entertainment scene, a glittering strip of seafood restaurants, souvenir shops and bars. Neighbouring **Ao Karon** and **Ao Kata** are quieter. Upmarket hotels dominate the other beaches here, though at Kamala buffalo still come to the beach to cool down. Hat Mai Khao is a national park beach on the north coast. "Water-people" communities (➤ panel) are centred around the south and east coast, where the landscape has been destroyed by tin mining.

The centre of Phuket Town is pretty unexciting, although it does have traditional Sino-Portuguese mansions, antiques shops and a Chinese Taoist Temple, the **Shrine of the Serene Light** (free). There are Chinese and Portuguese influences, and around a third of Phuket's population is Muslim.

Phuket is expensive compared with the rest of the country. Because of the Sarasin Bridge linking it to the mainland, there are more cars here than on other islands. During the monsoon the water can be rough, so look for red flags when swimming. Phuket is too hedonistic for some travellers but its quality as a centre for water sports is undeniable, mainly owing to the top-class diving sites within easy reach of the island's shores. Dive shops are everywhere but most of them are just agents for actual diving companies and it is often better to seek out the operators themselves, many of which are to be found along Ao Patong. Courses for beginners are available and non-divers can often join trips to snorkel.

➕ 199 D2 🏛 TAT, 73–75 Phuket Road
☎ 07 621 2213 🕐 Daily 8:30–4:30

🔟 Ko Jam

This remote fishing island (also known as Ko Pu) has a wild, mangrove-lined shore, cashew-nut plantations and little else. A real get-away-from-it-all spot, and an antidote to Ko Phuket in nearly all respects, the northern section is almost impenetrable due to thick forest. Less than a handful of rustic bungalows operate here, sending out longtail boats to meet the Krabi and Ko Lanta ferries.

➕ 199 D2

🎱 Ko Lanta Yai

This remote island (www.lantayai.com) is wild and peaceful. It is the largest of a group of 52 islands known as Ko Lanta. If you do the Krabi tour (➤ 181–183), you could continue to Ko Lanta Yai by car (around 100km/62 miles). There are two very short ferry crossings from Krabi that take vehicles to the island, and a road bridge. Boats dock at a ramshackle village with

CULTURAL CONNECTIONS

The west side of Thailand which works its way down to Malaysia was once at the heart of trading routes with the countries that surround it – China, India and Malaysia. It's a history that can be seen everywhere; in the architecture of the minarets of Muslim mosques, in the traditional wooden Chinese shophouses and in the cuisine, with Chinese, Malay and Indian influences. Chinese merchants settled in the cities here, while Thais who are closely related to Malays live in the rural interior. In the far south, locals speak a dialect and a language close to both Malay and Indonesian. Muslim influences can be seen, too, in the fishing families of Chao Ley, or "water people", who dive for pearls, fish and shells with makeshift equipment. Different in appearance to other Thais, the Chao Ley, who often have dark skin and red hair, are thought to have originally come from Indonesia and speak their own language. Although many communities have been forced out by tourist development, they continue to fish the coast of the Andaman and live their unique lifestyle.

tourist facilities and wooden thatched restaurants on stilts over the water.

There are avenues of rubber trees, prawn farms and lush rice fields in the southern section, which has little tourist development, just the occasional roaming water buffalo.

During the monsoon season, Ko Lanta Yai is practically deserted. The wide, open beaches can be windswept and much of the

A sculptural tree growing on the edge of the rugged cliff face of Ko Lanta Yai

FIVE ISLAND RETREATS

Ko Jam (► 165)
Ko Similan (► 164)
Ko Surin (► 164)
Ko Lanta Yai (► 165)
Ko Tarutao (► right)

beach accommodation is either closed or heavily discounted.

⊞ 199 D2 🅸 TAT, Utrakit Road, Krabi
☎ 07 562 2163

🄰 Trang Province

The capital, Trang, once known as the "City of Waves", was a sea-trading and shipping centre. Today its wealth comes from rubber and the influence is mostly Chinese. It has a wealth of Chinese noodle restaurants, Muslim curry houses, traditional coffee shops and an annual Vegetarian Festival held every October.

The coast of Trang province is dotted with islands, long, wide sandy beaches and towering limestone mountains. **Hat Jao Mai** is a 5km (3-mile) stretch of sand that is part of the national park of the same name. Islands offshore – **Ko Hai**, **Ko Muk** and **Ko Kradan** – offer superb beaches and excellent snorkelling. **Hat Pak Meng** is another long stretch of beach which also has a long promenade pier and limestone caves.

⊞ 199 E2 🅸 TAT, Sanon Na Meuang city park, Nakhon Si Thammarat ☎ 07 534 6515

🄱 Ko Tarutao

The Tarutao National Marine Park is made up of 51 islands – most of which are uninhabited. There are idyllic beaches, limestone caves and mangrove-fringed shores to explore, along with more than a hundred species of birds, including sea eagles and reef egrets. Wild pigs, macaques and dusky langurs (a type of monkey) roam the rainforest, four species of turtles lay their eggs on the sands, and dolphins, whales and a variety of fish swim in the waters. Three of the islands, Ko Tarutao, Ko Adang and Ko Lipe, offer accommodation. The park is only accessible from November to April and is closed to visitors the rest of the year owing to the monsoon (check with the visitor centre for dates, which vary from year to year).

⊞ 199 E1 ✉ Ferries from Pak Bara

Visitor Centre
✉ Pak Bara ☎ 07 478 1285 💷 Inexpensive (donation to park)

Towering, rocky islands are dotted along the coast of Trang Province

🔟 Thale Ban National Park

Sitting on the border with Malaysia, this national rainforest park is home to rare birds such as booted eagles as well as honey bears and clouded leopards. There are guided trails (book at the park headquarters, expensive) through lush green valleys to a lily-covered lake; you can swim in tiered waterfalls and wonder at panoramic views from the limestone outcrops.

As the park receives heavy rainfall, it is best visited between December and March, to avoid the monsoon season.

➕ 199 E1 ✉ 40km (25 miles) northeast of Satun, 90km (56 miles) south of Hat Yai

Thale Ban National Park Headquarters
☎ 08353 31710

MALAYSIA

Many people who get to the southern end of Thailand's tail feel the pull of Malaysia, and even Singapore. It's a very well-connected route and a simple procedure to cross the border; plenty of visitors make this popular crossing just to renew their Thai visas. Probably the easiest way is to travel by rail across the border from Padang Besar (reserve a sleeper in advance if you're travelling at a weekend or on a public holiday). You will have to disembark with your luggage to clear immigration at the border before getting back on the train.

Where to...
Stay

Prices
Expect to pay per double room per night:
£ under 2,000 baht   ££ 2,000–5,000 baht   £££ over 5,000 baht

Khao Sok Rainforest Park £
Situated by the side of the Klong Sok River, this is perhaps the best of the lodges near Khao Sok National Park in terms of the organized eco- and fun-based tours available to guests. The accommodation is in bungalows and tree houses, all with electric fans, and there is the option of spending a night in a floating lodge and waking to the sound of gibbons in the trees.
198 A1 ⊠ On the approach road to the visitor centre ☎ 07 739 5006; www.krabidir.com/khaosokrainforest

Krabi City Seaview Hotel £
A short walk from the heart of the town and the pier, this modern hotel has a quiet location by the side of a river. There is a range of bedrooms and all are competitively priced. The breakfast room is on the top floor and there is a small garden with seating for guests. This hotel makes a good base for a short stay in Krabi and a variety of tours and activities can be booked at the hotel reception.
199 D2 ⊠ 77/1 Thanon Kong Kha ☎ 075 622 885; www.krabicityseaviewhotel.com

Maritime Park & Spa Resort ££
Beside the meandering Krabi River and set in tropical gardens, this resort has spectacular views of the limestone pinnacles. Its proximity to the natural environment sets it apart from the competition; you can take a trip into the mangrove forests on a longtail boat or to the coral reef for diving. All guest rooms overlook the lagoon and forest and have satellite TV, mini-bar and air conditioning. Other facilities include a swimming pool and spa, jogging and cycling track, and a lake with canoes.
199 D2 ⊠ 1 Tungfah Road, Muang Krabi ☎ 07 562 0028; www.maritimeparkandspa.com

Rayavadee £££
The surrounding limestone cliffs seals off the Rayavadee resort from the rest of the world; it's only accessible by boat or by foot along two tortuous footpaths. There are more than a hundred luxury pavilions and villas nestling amid an extensive lush coconut plantation. The resort is completely self-contained with its own video and CD library, a spa, spectacular swimming pool and very appealing choices when it comes to food: fine dining in the main restaurant, and three beachside eateries for authentic Thai, Mediterranean-style or barbecue snacks and cocktails.
199 D2 ⊠ 214 Moo 2, Tambon Ao Nang ☎ 07 562 0740; www.rayavadee.com

Tipa Resort ££
This extensive resort complex sits on a hillside site a short walk from Ao Nang beach. Choose between deluxe rooms furnished in dark woods, bamboo and rattan, and cheaper timber-built bungalows. It's an ideal holiday destination for families, with two pools, playground, bike and boat rental and even a "music corner" with Thai musical instruments.
199 D2 ⊠ 121/1 Moo 2, Ao Nang, Muang Krabi ☎ 07 563 7527/30; www.krabi-tiparesort.com

KO PHI PHI

Holiday Inn Resort £££

A boutique-style resort with 80 bungalows, the Holiday Inn group's Phi Phi Hotel is self-contained and away from the more hectic Ao Ton Sai area of the island. Bungalows cater for a maximum of three people, or there are family units comprising two bungalows with interconnecting doors. All have good views across to the adjoining islands of Ko Yung (Mosquito Island) and Ko Mai Phai (Bamboo Island). This is a great place to get away from the rest of the world and bask in the delights of an open-air spa bath, windsurfing, tennis courts, a spa offering traditional massage treatments, a sauna, and a swimming pool.
🚹 199 D2 🏠 Laem Tong Beach 🕾 07 562 1334; www.phiphi.holidayinn.com

Phi Phi Island Cabana £££

One of the first places you'll see on sailing into Ko Phi Phi's small harbour, this complex is beautifully situated between the island's two famous bays, Ao Ton Sai and Ao Lo Dalam. In an exotic jungle setting, the large, comfortable bungalows offer sea views and a tranquil place to retreat to. There is also a hotel with air-conditioned rooms. Facilities include a nightclub, snooker and swimming pool.
🚹 199 D2 🏠 Ton Sai Bay 🕾 07 561 1496; www.phiphi-cabana.com

KO PHUKET

Andatel ££

This is one of the best value-for-money places to stay in Patong. The rooms are not spectacular but they are comfortable and each has its own small balcony. There is an all-day restaurant and a pool, and free WiFi access.
🚹 199 D2 🏠 41/9 Rat-U-Thit, Patong 🕾 07 629 0480; www.andatelhotel.com

Diamond Cliff Resort £££

Situated on the hillside in extensive grounds at the quiet, northern end of Patong Beach, this resort and spa overlooks the clear waters of Ao Patong. All rooms have a sea view. There are two restaurants and a spa offering Thai, Swedish and sports' massages. Activities include Thai cooking lessons, fruit carving, free tennis lessons and miniature golf competitions.
🚹 199 D2 🏠 284 Prabaramee Road, Patong Beach 🕾 07 634 0501/6; www.diamondcliff.com

Dusit Thani Laguna Phuket £££

The Dusit Thani Laguna Phuket resort offers every amenity along with superb restaurants and health facilities. All 226 rooms, decorated with native woods, antique carvings and ceramics, have a private balcony that faces either the sea or the lagoons. The swimming pool has a water slide and there's a putting green, tennis courts and a health and fitness spa. You can also attend Thai cooking classes.
🚹 199 D2 🏠 390 Thanon Sri Sunthorn, Thalang 🕾 07 632 4324; www.dusit.com

Marina Phuket £££

The Marina Phuket is a collection of Thai-style cottages in a stunning natural environment, with coconut palms and a garden teeming with life. Fruit trees, ferns, palms and orchids provide a relaxing atmosphere. All rooms are attractively decorated with traditional Thai crafts and have either an ocean view or a jungle view. Enjoy the split-level swimming pool and Sala Thai, one of the better restaurants on the island. (▶ 171).
🚹 199 D2 🏠 47 Thanon Karon, Ao Karon 🕾 07 633 0625; www.marinaphuket.com

Ramada Resort £££

The 121-room Ramada Resort is a short stroll from Ao Karon's popular shopping and nightlife area. The rooms have satellite TV, mini-bar and in-house movie channels. The hotel is particularly popular with families as the children's facilities are very good. There's a children's swimming pool with slides and

Where to...
Eat and Drink

Prices
Expect to pay per person for a three-course meal, excluding drinks and service:
£ under 300 baht   **££** 300–600 baht   **£££** over 600 baht

KRABI

Reuan Mai £–££
This attractive, traditional-style Thai *suan ahaan* (garden restaurant) serves excellent southern and central Thai food in a garden setting. It's 1.5km (1 mile) north of the town, but worth the small effort. The seafood selection is extensive and excellent.
✚ 199 D2 **✉** Thanon Maharat
☎ 07 563 1796/7 **⏰** Daily 10.30–10

Tamarind Tree £
The Tamarind Tree restaurant is part of KR Mansion, a popular guest house and useful source of tourist and traveller information. It's enduringly good and offers Thai and Western dishes. The house specialities are healthy salads and macrobiotic dishes using organic produce. There's a rooftop bar offering fine evening views across the mountains.
✚ 199 D2 **✉** KR Mansion, Thanon Chao Fa
☎ 07 561 2761 **⏰** Daily 7am–10pm

Viva ££
Viva, run by Italians, serves wonderful home-made *ciabatta* bread, a fantastic choice of 40 kinds of real Sicilian pizza and fresh spinach pasta. To round off your meal, there are even imported Italian cheeses. It is well appointed with attractive bamboo furniture and seating inside and out.
✚ 199 D2 **✉** Thanon 29 Pruksa Uthit
☎ 07 563 0517 **⏰** Daily 10am–11pm

KO PHI PHI

Marlin Restaurant ££
The Phi Phi Island Village Beach Resort's restaurant is one of the finest on the island, an elegant, open-sided venue for dining on the terrace under the stars. The menu is an imaginative mix of Thai and international dishes.
✚ 199 D2 **✉** Phi Phi Island Village Resort and Spa **☎** 07 625 8185
⏰ Daily 6pm–11pm

Sunset Hilltop & Satay Bar £
Malaysian-style satays and sunsets make a great combination at this popular bistro-bar at the Holiday Inn Resort. It's only open for two hours every evening, coinciding

a supervised playground. Other facilities include a fitness centre and two pools. The View Point restaurant is recommended locally for its southern Thai cuisine.
✚ 199 D2 **✉** 4/8 Thanon Patak, Ao Karon
☎ 07 639 6666/75; www.ramadaphuket.com

The Royal Phuket Yacht Club
£££
Phuket's exclusive Yacht Club is situated at Ao Nai Harn, with good swimming and beautiful sunsets. It's a great place to be for the annual King's Cup Regatta in early December, when the bay is filled with yachts. This superb hotel overlooks the bay at its northern end and offers every luxury imaginable. All rooms have views of the bay, a CD system, mini-bar and in-house movies. Sports facilities include yachting, a fitness centre, tennis courts and The Royal Spa. The Regatta is a renowned restaurant (▶ 171).
✚ 199 D2 **✉** 23/3 Thanon Viset, Ao Nai Harn **☎** 07 638 0200, www.puravarna.com

with sunset, but the neighbouring Mong Talay bar continues until midnight and has live music.

➕ 199 D2 ☒ Holiday Inn Resort ☎ 07 562 1334 ◷ Daily 5pm–7pm; Mong Talay Bar 10am–midnight

KO PHUKET

Ka Jok See ££

Located in a 19th-century Sino-Portuguese shophouse in the heart of Phuket Town, this most popular of eating establishments serves traditional Phuket cuisine. Numerous antiques scattered about give the interior an agreeable atmosphere. Specialities include the delightful *haw mok thaleh* (seafood mousse) and green mango salad.

➕ 199 D2 ☒ 26 Thanon Takua Pa, Phuket Town ☎ 07 6217903 ◷ Tue–Sun 6pm–midnight; closed Mon

Mom Tri's Boathouse £££

Romantic views of Ao Kata from the terrace make this one of Phuket's most famous restaurants, with Thai

and European food. Renowned for its choice of quality wines, the cellar has more than 350 different labels. Live music makes for a pleasant atmosphere right on the beach.

➕ 199 D2 ☒ Boathouse Inn, 2/2 Patak Road, Ao Kata ☎ 07 633 0015 ◷ Daily 6:30am–11pm

Old Siam ££

Old Siam offers a choice of either the beautiful old teak house or the rooftop terrace overlooking the ocean. Sunsets can be a delight from here. Dishes tend towards central Thai cooking and if you like things more spicy you may need to tell the staff to pop in an extra chilli. Entertainment includes Thai dancing every Wednesday and Sunday, and nightly Thai music.

➕ 199 D2 ☒ Karon Beach Road at the Thavorn Palm Beach Hotel ☎ 07 639 6090 ◷ Daily 6:30pm–10:30pm

The Regatta £££

This is a fine Italian restaurant found in the exclusive Royal Phuket

Yacht Club (▲170). Dishes tend towards simple Italian home cooking, with lots of great pasta dishes and seafood. The resident European chef makes regular changes to the menu. The Regatta is a great place to sit and watch the sun set over Ao Nai Harn and sip one of the many delicious cocktails on offer.

➕ 199 D2 ☒ Royal Phuket Yacht Club, Ao Nai Harn ☎ 07 638 0200 ◷ Daily 7pm–11pm

Sala Thai £££

The Marina Phuket complex (▲169) has two excellent restaurants. Sala Thai or "Thai Room", with its remarkable adaptation of traditional Thai architecture and splendid views of the jungle and swimming pool, is one of Ko Phuket's most famous restaurants. At night, diners enjoy fine Thai cuisine to the accompaniment of traditional Thai music and dance in airy, open spaces defined by beautiful

woods, tiles and carved panels. The second restaurant, On the Rock, is famous for its seafood and southern Thai dishes and presents some of Ko Phuket's finest cuisine with sweeping views of the sea at Ao Karon.

➕ 199 D2 ☒ 47 Thanon Karon, Ao Karon ☎ 07 633 0625; www.marinaphuket.com

Thai Naan ££

Reputed to be the largest traditional teak restaurant in southern Thailand, Thai Naan serves a spectacular lunchtime buffet with numerous Thai dishes and more than twenty types of *dim sum*. Royal Thai cuisine (prepared so that the food does not need to be cut by the diner!) and Phuket favourites are presented in the special Srivichai set dinner. There is also a sophisticated cultural show each evening.

➕ 199 D2 ☒ 16 Thanon Vichitsongkhram, Phuket Town ☎ 07 622 6164/7; www.thainaanrestaurant.com ◷ Daily 11–2, 5:30–11

Where to...
Shop

ANTIQUES AND CRAFTS

Most of the antiques and craft shops are clustered around the Yaowarat, Thalang and Ratsada roads area in the old Sino-Portuguese part of Phuket town. **Ban Boran Textiles** (51 Thanon Yaowarat, tel: 07 621 1563) showcases gorgeous fabrics from six countries in the Southeast Asia region. The fabrics can be made into clothes.

The **Jim Thompson Silk Company** has six outlets in Phuket, five of them in luxury hotels and one in the centre of Phuket town (The Courtyard, tel: 07 626 4468).

For art and antiques, visit **Soul of Asia** (39 Ratsada Road, tel: 07 621 1122; www.soulofasia.com) or **Chan's Antique House** (99/42 Moo 5, Chalermprakiat Road, tel: 07 626 1416; www.chans-antique. com). Out of Phuket town **Touch Wood Antique Furniture** (Chao Fa Nok Road, tel: 07 626 3117) sells colonial-style antique items from Myanmar and Thailand. **Baanboonpitak** (30 Thanon Prachanukroh, Patong Beach, tel: 07 634 1789) has traditional Thai and Burmese furniture. At **Siam Arts** (382/5 Thanon Srisoonthorn, Cherngtalay, Thalang, tel: 07 632 5207) you'll find teak furniture, woodcarvings and antiques.

PEARLS

Phuket is a good source of fine-quality pearls and the **Pearl Centre** (83 Thanon Ranong, Soi Phutorm, Phuket Town, tel: 07 621 1707) has some good bargains.

Where to...
Be Entertained

NIGHTLIFE

Ko Phuket
The Star Club Entertainment Discotheque (198/4 Thanon Ratuthit, Patong Beach, tel: 07 634 6187) is the island's largest disco. **Banana Discotheque** (96 Thanon Thawiwong, Patong Beach, tel: 07 634 0301) has a pub attached and live music.

Simon Cabaret (8 Sirirach Road, Patong Beach, tel: 07 634 2011; www.phuket-simoncabaret.com) stages one of the most entertaining transvestite cabaret shows in Thailand and has live shows at 7:30 and 9:30 every night.

Ko Phi Phi
Carlito's Bar and nightclub, on the beach at Ton Sai Bay, has also become a kind of unofficial tourist information centre for the island.

OUTDOOR PURSUITS

The beautiful limestone cliffs of the Krabi coast offer world-class **rock climbs** of various degrees of difficulty. Professional instructors are on hand.

The area around Ao Phang Nga is ideal for **kayaking**. Canoes manoeuvre through narrow crevices, sometimes passing beneath overhangs so low that the canoeist has to lie flat.

Ko Phuket is famous for **big-game fishing** and you can charter a fully equipped fishing vessel or hire a small boat. Fish for marlin, sea bass, barracuda, king mackerel and yellowfin tuna.

Walks and Tours

1 BANGKOK'S CHINATOWN

Walk

This walk guides you around the tiny alleyways of Chinatown, which is situated between Thanon Charoen Krung (New Road) and the river. The area takes in exotic produce, hidden temples, shops selling gold and wood-lined apothecaries. Be warned: the crowds, smells and sights here are not for the squeamish. Try to set off mid-afternoon, stopping for cocktails at dusk at the revolving restaurant of the Grand Chinese Princess Hotel to see the lights of the city and ending with a taste of Little India. Avoid doing this walk at the weekend when many of the stalls are closed, and bear in mind that River Express boats do not run in the evening.

DISTANCE 2.5km/1.5 miles (one way)
TIME 2–3 hours depending on whether you stop for reflexology, cocktails or dinner
START/END POINT River Express Stop, Tha Ratchawong/Thanon Chakraphet ➕ 200 C2

1–2

Take the River Express boat to the Tha Ratchawong pier and walk up the road of the same name for about 300m (327 yards), past the gangs of motorcycle couriers and taxis. Turn right at the cluster of food stalls where

Food vendors in the bustling Chinatown market

a blue sign announces **Soi Wanit 1**. This tiny alley, also known as **Sampeng Lane**, is at the heart of Chinatown. Although barely wide enough for two people, load-bearing carts and motorbikes weave their way hazardously down here. Once the highlight for opium dens and gambling houses, now it has tourist commercialism at its heart and is a good place to buy Chinese silk and computer games.

TAKING A BREAK

On the 25th floor of the **Grand Chinese Princess Hotel** (215 Thanon Yaowarat, tel: 02 224 997; www.grandchina.com) is a **revolving restaurant** (5pm–1am, expensive) and "club lounge" with a bird's-eye view of the city. Order a cocktail and gaze at the floodlit riverside *wats* and illuminated high-rises of Siam Square. A full revolution takes three hours, so if you want to see the whole lot without walking around, consider having dinner here – they serve Thai, sushi and some international dishes.

PLACES TO VISIT

Wat Mangkon Kamalawat
➕ 200 C3 ⊠ Thanon Charoen Krung 🎟 Free

Sikh temple
➕ 200 B3 ⊠ Off Thanon Chakraphet 🎟 Free

2–3

Walk for two blocks past the 100-year-old **Tang To Kang gold shop** before turning left down **Soi 16**. This alley is lined with giant sacks of rice crackers, tea and dried mushrooms, and stalls selling local delicacies such as dried fish, plucked ducks, pigs' heads and sea horses.

Cross the main road of Thanon Yaowarat and turn left along Thanon Charoen Krung (New Road). Half-way down this block on the right is the bustling temple of **Wat Mangkon Kamalawat** (Dragon Flower Temple).

Combining elements of Buddhism, Confucianism and Taoism, the temple features both Chinese characters and Buddhist images. It's normally a busy place, filled with praying devotees clutching huge bunches of

SAFETY IN NUMBERS

Crossing the road in Chinatown can be difficult and hazardous. Cars, buses, motorbikes and *tuk-tuks* seem unwilling to stop even at pedestrian crossings. Do what the locals do, be mindful and wait until at least two other people are ready to stride out at the same time.

incense or clipping notes as offerings to a brightly coloured money tree, while monks sell amulets or dispense medicine from the temple apothecary.

3–4

Turn right as you come out of the temple and take the first left down the side street of Thanon Mangkon.

On the corner of its junction with Thanon Yaowarat, the **Old Market** is actually a modern complex of shopping stalls. Take the escalator upstairs for a highly professional reflexology or head and neck massage, lasting as long or as short as you like.

LOCAL TREASURES

This area is full of specialities not found in the rest of the city. Look for shops featuring candlelit Chinese shrines and selling green or jasmine tea in decorative containers. Sample some *dim sum*, Chinese ice cream or lychee juice and wander around traditional wood-lined apothecaries crammed with fascinating ancient remedies.

4–5

Turn right on to the main street of Thanon Yaowarat. Walk straight down this road past shops selling electrical goods and sunglasses. After five blocks, **Nakhon Kasen** (Thieves' Market) on your right on the corner with Thanon Boriphat sounds much more exciting than it actually is. Antiques have replaced the stolen goods that were traditionally sold here. On the left is the subterranean **Saphan Han market**. Dark, cramped and next to a festering canal, the market has a kind of Dickensian

appeal. You can cut through here if you are interested. Otherwise, cross over the bridge and turn left at the major road junction on to Thanon Chakraphet.

5–6

Now you are in **Little India**. Follow the green sign to the **Sikh temple** (said to be the largest outside India) via a small tangle of market stalls. Then return to **Thanon Chakraphet**, lined with many Indian restaurants and confectionery shops.

Buddhist monks at Wat Mangkon Kamalawat

2 MAE HONG SON LOOP
Tour

This neat loop makes a highly scenic drive through the beautiful mountainous region known as the "Roof of Thailand". The circuit takes in hill-tribe villages, a city of "three mists" and the country's highest mountain, but the journey itself is the inspiration. The route avoids spots that get swamped by tour buses and as few tourists make this trip independently, you will have the roads to yourself.

DISTANCE 600km (372 miles)
TIME 3 days
START/END POINT Chiang Mai ⊞ 196 B4

1–2
Leave Chiang Mai on the 107 following the signs to **Mae Rim**. At Mae Rim, route 1096 leads to a tourist trail of commercial elephant camps, butterfly parks and orchid farms. Mobbed by tour groups, they are not worth a special detour, unlike the **Queen Sirikit Botanic Garden**, 12km (7.5 miles) along this road. Built with the help of staff of London's Royal Botanic Gardens at Kew, at a cost of £1 million, highlights include a magnificent Tropical Rainforest House.

2–3
Continue north on the 107 and turn left on to the 1095, which wriggles all the way to Pai. If you feel like a hot bath, call in at the clearly signposted **Pong Ron Hot Springs** about 10km (6 miles) before the village.

Pai, once a remote village and now a comfortable traveller centre, with international cuisine and even jazz bars, is a good place to spend the night (Pai River Corner, Moo 3, Vientgai; tel: 05 369 9049, www.pairivercorner.com, has a delightful riverside setting and stylish bedrooms with private balconies, ££). For a more authentic village experience, consider staying in **Soppong** village, a couple of hours further on (Soppong River Inn, tel: 05 361 7107, www.soppong.com, has some lovely rooms).

3–4
From Pai, continue on the 1095 for one of the most picturesque stretches of the journey.

After around 20km (12.5 miles) the marked "scenic area" gives spectacular views over the valley. Just before Soppong, look for the sign to **Tam Lod**, a series of caves with stalactites and stalagmites and a river running through it. The landscape is particularly scenic here, with agricultural terracing. Drive through a

EMPLOYING A DRIVER
There is no need for a guide to do this tour, but if you don't feel like doing all the driving yourself (around four hours a day), a driver can be employed for about the same daily rate as a car – ideally a 4WD. You could also do half the loop from Chiang Mai to Mae Hong Son in either direction if you had the car collected and flew back to Chiang Mai. Before you set off, get hold of the Mae Hong Son Loop map (with the red cover) from a Chiang Mai newsagent.

tribal Lahu village and over the river and take the right fork at the Karen village of **Ban Tham**, with its houses on stilts. At the car park for Tam Lod (which is in Ban Tham) there's an information board telling how to get a guide, and providing some history and a map of the caves. A guide with a lantern (moderate) is necessary unless you have a powerful torch. Continue northwest to join the 1095, as long as rain hasn't made the road impassable. If it has, return the way you came (8km/5 miles).

4–5
Once you're back on the 1095 turn right. Around 15km (9.3 miles) after Soppong turn right on to the 1226 to **Mae Lana Cave,** with its interesting rock formations. With a 12km (7.5 mile) river running through it, it is said to be the longest cave in Asia. Before the Black Lahu (hill-tribe) village of Jabo, look to the right for beautiful views.

Take the right fork to Mae Lana village in the pretty valley below. Drive through the village to its lovely temple where figures from Burma act as protectors. The Mai Lun people who live here are half-Burmese and half-Thai. The village is close to the border with Burma, although there is no crossing for tourists.

If you want to see another cave, return to where you took the right fork and turn right to **Pa Puek Cave (rock formations)** behind the village of the same name.

5–6
Return to the 1095 and turn right. After 40 km (25 miles), you reach the mysterious **Fish Cave**, which attracts masses of mountain carp for no apparent reason. Continue on the 1095 all the way to **Mae Hong Son**. Turn right at the town's only traffic lights on the outskirts and bear right to **Wat Doi Kong Mou,** the hill-top temple. It's the view rather than the temple itself that is special, but note the Burmese-style Buddhas with their red lips and white faces. The temples by **Jong Kham Lake** in the centre of town are much prettier. At their entrance, the twisted trunk of a sacred

PLACES TO VISIT

Queen Sirikit Botanic Garden
196 B4 Mae Rim, Chiang Mai
05 384 1000; www.qsbg.org
Daily 8:30–4:30 Inexpensive

Bodhi tree shelters ageing spirit houses which cannot be destroyed because they are a sacred object to Buddhists. The Bodhi tree is deemed sacred because it is believed that the Buddha gained enlightenment under one.

6–7
After spending the night in Mae Hong Son (▶ 105), continue south along the 108 through Mae Surin. On the edge of the village of **Khun Yuam**, a ramshackle, dusty and low-key **war museum** commemorates the Japanese troops who poured into the area in September 1945 on their retreat from Allied forces in Burma. If you don't want to take a look here, turn left along the 1263 before the village.

7–8
The road passes valleys of bright green rice fields, winding its way to the next major settlement of **Mae Chaem.**

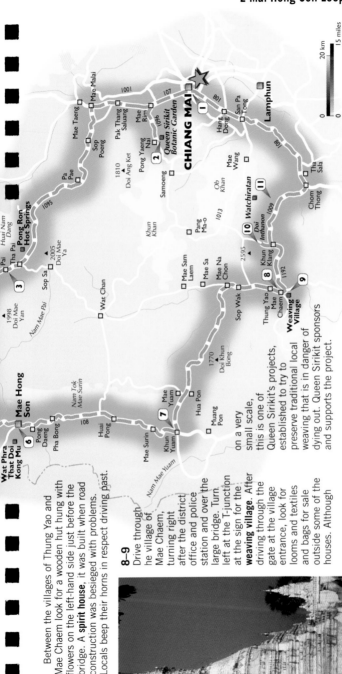

Between the villages of Thung Yao and Mae Chaem look for a wooden hut hung with flowers on the left-hand side just before the bridge. A **spirit house**, it was built when road construction was besieged with problems. Locals beep their horns in respect driving past.

8–9

Drive through the village of Mae Chaem, turning right after the district office and police station and over the large bridge. Turn left at the T-junction at the sign for the **weaving village**. After driving through the gate at the village entrance, look for looms and textiles and bags for sale outside some of the houses. Although on a very small scale, this is one of Queen Sirikit's projects, established to try to preserve traditional local weaving that is in danger of dying out. Queen Sirikit sponsors and supports the project.

Mae Hong Son's stunning hill-top temple of Wat Doi Kong Mou

9–10

Return to Mae Chaem and turn left at the sign for Chiang Mai on to the 1192. You may spot water buffalo or wild mushrooms in the wet season by the roadside. After 22km (13.6 miles), at the T-junction turn left at the sign to **Doi Inthanon National Park** (▲ 99).

At the end of the road you can walk up to the summit of Doi Inthanon, Thailand's highest mountain. Just below the summit are two **royal** *chedis* built to honour the present king and queen (▲ 99), a small information centre and a short circular walking trail.

10–11

Return to the 1192 and turn left. Around 20km (12.4 miles) along this road, the **Vatchirathan waterfall** makes a pretty stop close to the road before returning to **Chiang Mai**.

Vatchirathan waterfall at Doi Inthanon National Park

TAKING A BREAK

Eat fresh mountain trout at the restaurant of the royal project gardens next to the national park headquarters, and then stroll to the foot of the nearby Siriphum waterfall.

DISTANCE 80km (49.6 miles)
TIME Half a day
START/END POINT Krabi Town ✚ 199 D2

3 KRABI
Tour

Some of Krabi province's most interesting sights are difficult to see by public transport. This gentle tour makes a convenient loop from the popular riverside town of Krabi. It passes through dramatic limestone scenery to the remote forest temple of Wat Tham Seua (Tiger Cave) and a Buddha reclining at the roadside, calling in on the way at beautiful beaches, with boat trips as additional extras.

1–2

Leave **Krabi** town following Highway 411 north along the river. After about 4.5km (3 miles) turn right following the signs to Trang. After a few kilometres you will see a big outcrop on the right-hand side of the road.

Turn left here and follow the signs to the **Wat Tham Seua** (Tiger Cave Temple, ▲ 160). Figures of dancing elephants adorn the lamp posts down the centre of this road and on

Wat Tham Seua's community of monks and nuns

a clear day you can see a temple building perched on top of a mountain ahead of you.

Take time to explore this temple. Start with the main cave and follow the stairs up to the cave behind, with its giant Buddha footprint, and then wander through the temple grounds.

If you are feeling energetic you can make the hour-long climb up the hillside for spectacular views. Otherwise take a look at the meditation huts and walk through the ancient forest.

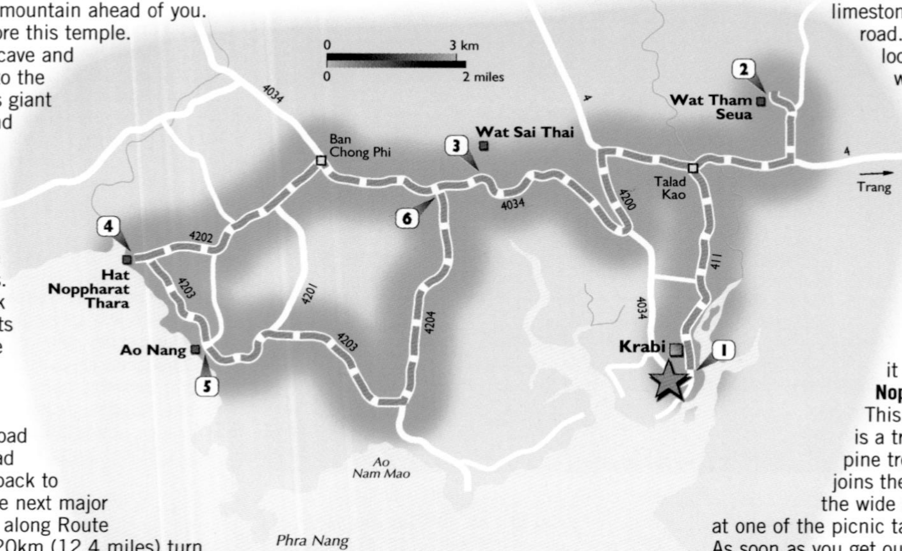

2–3

Return to the main road and turn right. Instead of turning left to go back to Krabi, continue to the next major junction, turning left along Route 4200. After around 20km (12.4 miles) turn right at the traffic lights at the sign for Hat Noppharat. Follow the wriggling route from where it is easy to miss the roadside **Reclining Buddha** at Wat Sai Thai, nestled into a limestone outcrop in a kink in the road. There is not too much to look at here, but you might want to stretch your legs.

3–4

Follow the signs to Hat Noppharat, turning left down the 4202 at the Muslim village of **Ban Chong Phi**. You may see women selling coconuts at the side of the road here and a green turreted mosque.

Follow the road until it stops at the sea at **Hat Noppharat Thara** (➤ 159).

This 2.5km (1.5 mile) beach is a tranquil spot backed by pine trees, where a pretty canal joins the sea. Take a walk along the wide stretch of sand or relax at one of the picnic tables under the trees.

As soon as you get out of your car here, a boatman will probably appear to offer you a snorkelling trip (moderate) to Chicken or Poda islands, sitting out in the bay.

4–5

The road vaguely hugs the coast to **Ao Nang** – a developed and not particularly attractive stretch of beach packed with shops and restaurants. Here the road swings inland. There's no road access to the headland of Phra Nang – if you want to visit its pretty **beaches** (▶ 160), you need to walk or take a boat trip.

The little headland of **Laem Phra Nang** is named after a local princess (*phra nang* means "revered lady"). Although reached only by boat – longtails leave from near Krabi's pier – it is very popular and something of a rock-climbing mecca, with hundreds of world-class routes. Beginners are catered for as well, and if you are not participating, it's a good spectator sport.

Other activities on offer include kayaking through the mangroves, and snorkelling and diving trips to nearby islands.

An alabaster image of the Reclining Buddha rests by the roadside at Wat Sai Thai

5–6

You can return to Krabi by following the 4203, then the 4204 and then turning right on to the 4034.

Ko Poda, south of Ao Nang, is surrounded by coral reef

4 KHAO SAM ROI YOT NATIONAL PARK

Tour

DISTANCE 150km/93 miles (one way)
TIME One day
START/END POINT Hua Hin ⊞ 198 C3

This leisurely tour explores peaceful coastal marshland and deserted golden beaches fringed by pine trees where there are hidden caves, scenic boat trips and forest trails. Shrimp farmers and fishermen eke out a living in this isolated, atmospheric backwater and thousands of birds from around the world come to breed. Known as "the mountain with 300 peaks", the park's forested interior provides challenging climbs with excellent views.

HOW TO VISIT

Although you can take organized tours of the park, by far the most enjoyable way to see it is to rent a car. Part of the park's charm is its isolation and taking a taxi or public transport isn't feasible because you need to be able to get around the park once you arrive. Try to catch either sunset or sunrise for the best chances of seeing birdlife. If you are very lucky you may also see a monkey-like, long-tailed macaque or a dusky langur which usually only appear at night.

1–2

Leave **Hua Hin** following Highway 4 south as far as Pran Buri (around 20km/12.4 miles). Turn left at the main intersection at Pran Buri, from where it is around another 20km (12.4 miles) to the park checkpoint. A fee is payable here (moderate) which includes a leaflet with a

useful, if rather basic map. Signs within the park giving the distances to Sam Roi Yot National Park confusingly refer only to the park headquarters.

2–3

Turn left at the signs to Hat Laem Sala past the entrance to **Tham Kaew Cave** and land

GETTING THERE

By Air The best way to get to Thailand is to **fly direct to Bangkok**. For the **cheapest flights**, compare fares from online travel agents with those available from airlines direct. You can save money if you are willing to make stopovers.

The following **airlines** all fly to Bangkok and other major cities in Thailand:

Thai Airways International
www.thaiair.com
UK: 0870 606 0911
USA: 800/426-5204

British Airways
www.britishairways.com
UK: 0844 493 0787
USA: 800/247-9297

Ethihad Airways
www.ethihadairways.com
Australia: 1800 998 995
UK: 020 8735 6700
USA: 888/8 ETHIDAD
USA: 800/552-9264

Singapore Airlines
www.singaporeair.com
Australia: 13 1011
New Zealand: 09 379 3209
UK: 0844 800 2380
USA: 800/742-3333

Malaysia Airlines
www.malaysiaairlines.com
Australia: 13 2627
UK: 0871 423 9090

TIME

There is only one time zone throughout the country. Local time is seven hours ahead of GMT and 12 hours ahead of New York (Eastern Standard Time).

CURRENCY AND FOREIGN EXCHANGE

Currency The monetary unit in Thailand is the **baht** (B) and **satang** (100 satang = 1 baht).

Notes come in 20 (green), 50 (blue), 100 (red), 500 (purple) and 1,000 (beige) denominations; the bigger the value, the larger the note.
Coins come in denominations of 25 and 50 satangs (rarely used because of their low value; most prices are rounded up to the nearest baht) and 1, 2, 5 and 10 baht.

All major **credit cards** are widely accepted and can be used for cash advances in certain branches of major banks. However, many restaurants, guest houses and businesses on the islands and in mainland towns accept only cash.

Exchange rates tend to fluctuate, so it is worth keeping your eye on them. Sterling or dollar **travellers' cheques** are widely accepted (commission rates vary). This is a safe means of carrying money, but keep details of cheque numbers, the original receipt and contact details of the issuer in case of loss or theft. **Cash withdrawals** can conveniently be made at 24-hour ATMs (cash dispenser machines) throughout the country. Make sure you have your pin number with you and check with your bank at home to ensure your card is cleared for cash withdrawals abroad. A 1.5 per cent handling fee is normally charged and 150 baht is charged through the Thai bank's ATM.

In the USA (Los Angeles)
TAT
611 North Larchmont
Boulevard, 1st Floor,
Los Angeles, CA 90004
☎ 323/461-9814

In Australia
TAT
Level 20
56 Pit Street
Sydney, NSW 2000
☎ (02) 9247 7549

WHEN YOU ARE THERE

NATIONAL HOLIDAYS

1 Jan	New Year's Day		enlightenment
Feb	(full moon) Maha Puja		and death)
	(the Buddha preaches	Jul	Asanha Puja (the
	to 1,250 monks)		Buddha's first sermon)
6 Apr	Chakri Day	Jul	Start of Buddhist
Apr	Songkran		"lent"
	(Thai New Year)	12 Aug	Queen's birthday
5 May	Coronation Day	5 Dec	King's birthday
May	Royal Ploughing	10 Dec	Constitution Day
	Ceremony		*Shops, tourist offices and*
May	Visakha Puja (the		*tourist services remain open*
	Buddha's birth,		*on these days.*

ELECTRICITY

The power supply is 220 volts, 50 cycles. Two pole pins are the usual plug sockets with some additionally taking two flat-blade pins. You'll find that adaptors and voltage converters are available in most electrical shops.

OPENING HOURS

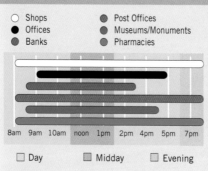

- ○ Shops
- ● Offices
- ● Banks
- ● Post Offices
- ● Museums/Monuments
- ● Pharmacies

8am 9am 10am noon 1pm 2pm 4pm 5pm 7pm

☐ Day ☐ Midday ☐ Evening

Shops Daily 8–8, although in tourist areas they may remain open until late at night and all weekend. Department stores usually open 10–9.
Banks Mon–Fri 8:30–3:30.
Post offices Main branches Mon–Fri 8–8, Sat–Sun 8–1.
National museums 8:30–4:30. Close lunchtime, Mon, Tue and public holidays.
Pharmacies 8am–9pm; later in Kao San Road and Sukhumuir Road in Bangkok.

TIPS/GRATUITIES

Some hotels and restaurants add a service charge. Simple Thai restaurants don't expect a tip but it's usual to round the bill up to the next 10 baht or so. In other restaurants, leave 10 per cent or more if the service is good. It's also customary to tip tour guides, porters, masseurs and masseuses, hairdressers, hotel concierges and taxi drivers with a 20 baht note. Self-service petrol stations are unknown in Thailand, so it's usual to tip the attendant 5 or 10 baht. In hotels and guest houses with daily room service, a 20 baht note for each night stayed is appreciated.

SCAMS

Avoid taxi touts at Bangkok's airport and don't be misled by their polite manner. At major visitor attractions, especially around the Grand Palace, touts also operate, giving false information and offering sightseeing tours. Beware of offers involving the purchase of gems or invitations to card games.

TIME DIFFERENCES

GMT
12 noon

Bangkok
7pm

USA (New York)
7am

USA (Los Angeles) 4am

Australia
10pm

New Zealand
11pm

STAYING IN TOUCH

Post Stamps are available from post offices, and from some shops and hotels, although hotels will usually charge you a bit extra. Major hotels will often post letters and packages for you. Post takes around seven days to Europe or the USA.

Public telephones International calls can be made from black and yellow public call boxes, but calls abroad can be made from most internet outlets for very low rates, where you don't have to feed coins into a call box. National calls from any call box cost as little as 5 baht. To make an international call from a public phone, feed in a 10 baht coin and have a lot ready to use if you make your connection. Drop the zero from a Thai phone number when calling from abroad, but include it when calling within the country. Phone cards are sold by stationers and some convenience stores. **Directory enquiries**: Dial 1133. English-speaking operators are available.

Thailand's international dialing code is 66.

International Dialling Codes
Dial 00 followed by

UK	44
USA/Canada	1
Ireland	353
Australia	61
Germany	49

Mobile phone providers and services Your mobile phone will work in Thailand if your provider has an arrangement with one or more Thai service providers; you can check this with your own service provider before leaving home. You should also know the charges for making and receiving international calls on your mobile phone while in Thailand. Consider buying a prepaid SIM card in Thailand to temporarily replace the one in your phone.

WiFi and internet Most large towns will have more than one shop or café offering internet access, and broadband is common. Charges are usually reasonable, depending on the speed available, though beware of the high rates often levied by hotels. Wireless zones are increasingly common in hotels, cafés and in shopping malls, especially in Bangkok.

PERSONAL SAFETY

Violent crime is rare, but take the following precautions:
- Lock your hotel room doors and windows at night.
- Don't accept food and drink from strangers on trains and buses as there have been cases of passengers being drugged and robbed.
- The Bangkok headquarters of the **Tourism Authority of Thailand**, TAT (tel: 02 694 1222) or the Tourist Police (tel: 1155) will contact the relevant emergency service as well as deal with complaints about services and products. The operators speak English.
- Be mindful about swimming in the sea, especially from the beaches on the west coast of Phuket, and look out for any red flags warning of dangerous conditions for swimmers.
- Visitors are killed every year on hired motorcycles because they drive carelessly on the small, winding roads. Be mindful and always wear a helmet.

POLICE: 1155
POLICE: Chiang Mai 05 327 6040
POLICE: Ko Phuket 07 621 9878
POLICE: Ko Samui 07 742 1282

AMBULANCE: 191

FIRE: 199

HEALTH

 Insurance Comprehensive health insurance is recommended, which may be included in your travel insurance policy. In the case of severe health problems, contact your embassy and insurance company.

 Dental services Dental treatment is best carried out in Bangkok. Ask at your hotel for names and qualifications of dentists in your area. Alternatively, your health insurance company should be able to supply details of dentists.

 Weather Avoid the sun during the middle of the day. Excessive exposure can cause heat rash, severe dehydration and diarrhoea. It is best to wear a sunhat and cover up whenever possible. Drink plenty of water.

 Drugs Both prescription and non-prescription drugs, international and local brands, are available from chemists or pharmacies, and are normally much cheaper than in countries outside Thailand. Most pharmacies (whatever size the town) have highly trained, English-speaking pharmacists.

 Safe water Never drink tap water, it may carry diseases such as hepatitis or typhoid. Always drink bottled water (the still variety), which is inexpensive and widely available throughout the country.

CONCESSIONS

Students/youths Discounted entrance to tourist attractions is rare, but it may still be worth carrying your international student identity card with you. Some organizations offer discounts to children.

There are several useful websites with information on budget travelling. Try the Internet Travel Information Service on www.itisnet.com, a useful resource with up-to-date information on current budget tips. The Open Directory Project, www.dmoz.org/Recreation/ Travel, has essential backpacker information and message boards; and www.wikitravel.org has useful information on Thailand especially directed at first-time visitors.

TRAVELLING WITH A DISABILITY

There is little provision for travellers with disabilities, but Thai people are helpful. Contact the following organizations: in the UK, RADAR, the Royal Association for Disability and Rehabilitation, tel: 020 7250 3222; in the US, The Society for the Advancement of Travel for the Handicapped, tel: 212/447-7284, or from the US, Access-Able Travel Source, www.access-able.com.

CHILDREN

Your children will, quite literally, be welcomed with open arms everywhere you go, and there are practically no restrictions on where you can take them.

TOILETS

Western-style flush toilets and toilet paper are in most hotels. Restaurants and tourist facilities may have squat toilets and no toilet paper. Always dispose of paper in the bin provided as Thai toilets are not equipped for dealing with paper waste.

CUSTOMS

The import of wildlife souvenirs sourced from rare or endangered species may be illegal or require a special permit. Check your home country's customs regulations.

EMBASSIES AND HIGH COMMISSIONS

UK
02 305 8333

USA
02 205 4000
02 287 2680

Australia
02 287 2680

Canada
02 636 0540

Netherlands
02 309 5200

USEFUL PHRASES AND GLOSSARY

Thai is a complex language written in an elaborate script containing more than 80 letters. It has five tones, or pitches (mid, high, low, rising and falling) which help determine the meaning of words. Although Thai is a difficult language to master, learning a few simple words will usually endear you greatly to the locals and can be very useful when bargaining for goods. However, English is widely used in tourist areas and many Thais know enough to communicate on a basic level. In polite speech, or to show particular respect, men add the word *krup* to the end of sentences; women add *ka*. Note that the words below are transliterated to give as clear a guide to pronunciation as possible. Spellings may vary on different signs, maps and menus.

GREETINGS AND COMMON PHRASES

Yes **Chai or krup/ka**
No **Mai**
Thank you **Korb-koon (krup/ka)**
Hello/Goodbye **Sawat dee (krup/ka)/ laa gorn**
How are you? **Sabai dee ru?**
Fine, thank you **Sabai dee (krup/ka)**
Excuse me/sorry **Kor tort (krup/ka)**
What is your name? **Khun chu arai?**
My name is… **Pom chu… (male), chun chu… (female)**
Do you speak English? **Koon poot pah sah Angrit?**
I don't understand **Pom (chun) mai kowjai**
I speak a little Thai **Pom (chun) puut pasa Thai nitnoy**
See you later **Pop gan mai**

EMERGENCY!

Help! **Chuay dooay!**
Fire! **Fai mai!**
Call the police! **Reeuk dtum roout hai noy!**
Call an ambulance! **Reeuk rot payah-bahn hai noy!**
I need a doctor **Tong haa mor**
I need a dentist **Tong haa mor fun**
Hospital **Rong payabarn**

DIRECTIONS

Where are you going? **Pai nai?**
I'm going to… **Jai pai…**
Where is…? **…yu thii nai?**
We want to go to…? **…rao yahk bpai**
How do I get to…? **Bpai…yung ngai?**
How long does it take? **Chai way-lah tao-rai?**
Please drive slowly **Prot put cha cha**
Turn right **Lieo khwa**; Turn left **Lieo sai**
Straight on **Trong pai**
Stop here **Jop tinni**

TRANSPORT AND PLACES

Air-conditioned bus **Rot tooa**
Ordinary bus **Rot tammada**
Bus station **Sattani rot may**
Minibus **Rot dtoo**
Car **Rot keng**
Ticket **Tua**
Timetable **Talang waylar**
Railway station **Sattani rot fai**
Train **Rot fai**
Express **Duan**
Sleeper **Rot nawn**
Seat **Tee nung**
Airport **Sanam bin**
Aeroplane **Krueng bin**
Boat **Rua**
Longtail boat **Rua harng yao**
Ferry **Rua doy sarn**
Ferry pier **Tha**
Taxi **Teksi**
Bicycle **Rot jakrayan**
Motorcycle **Rot motorsai**
Bank **Tanakaan**
Beach **Hat**
Embassy **Sa-tantoot**
Island **Ko**
Market **Talaht**
Museum **Pipitapun**
Police station **Satanee tamruat**
Post office **Prai-sanee**
Street **Thanon**
Town **Meung**
Village **Ban**

HOTELS AND RESTAURANTS

Do you have a vacant room? **Mee horng wahng mai?**
Air-conditioned room **Horng air**
Guest house **Guest how**
Hotel **Rong raem**
Key **Goon jair**
Shower **Fuk boo-a**
Swimming pool **Sa wai nahm**
Toilet/bathroom **Hong nahm**

A table for two please **Kor dto sum-rup sorng kon**
Please bring me the menu **Kor doo menu**
May I have…? **Kor…?**
The food is delicious **Ahan arroi**
The bill, please **Kor check bin**
Restaurant **Raan aahaan**
Café **Raan garfay**
Breakfast **Ahan chow**
Hot (spicy) **Pet**
Mild **Mai pet**
I can't eat... **Kin...mai dai**
I'm vegetarian **Kin jeh**
Water **Nam**
A glass of water **Nam plao**
Bottled water **Nam deum kuat**
Tea **Chaa**
Coffee **Cafee**
Beef **Neua**
Chicken **Gai**
Duck **Phet**
Fish **Pla**
Pork **Moo**

SHOPPING

How much is this? **Nee taorai?**
Do you have...? **Mee...mai?**
Cheap **Tuk**
Very good/No good **Dee mak/Mai dee**
Too expensive **Paeng pai**
Too big **Yai pair**
Too small **Lek pai**
A little **Nid noi**
Night market **Talaat toh rung**

TIME AND DAYS

Today **Wan nee**
Tomorrow **Proong nee**
Yesterday **Meua wan nee**
Now **Diao nee**
Later **Tee lang**
This week **Atit ni**
Next week **Atit na**
Minute **Na tee**
Hour **Chua mong**

Monday **Wan jun**
Tuesday **Wan ungkahn**
Wednesday **Wan poot**
Thursday **Wan pryhart**
Friday **Wan sook**
Saturday **Wan sao**
Sunday **Wan aathit**

GLOSSARY

Ao **Bay**
Ban **Village or house**
Bot **Main sanctuary of a Buddhist temple**
Celadon **Porcelain with a greyish green glaze**
Changwat **Province**
Chedi **Tower for relics in a Buddhist temple**
Doi **Mountain**
Farang **Foreigner**
Garuda **Half-man, half-bird mythical Hindu creature**
Hang yoa **Longtail boat**
Hat **Beach**
Hin **Stone**
Khao **Hill or mountain**
Khlong **Canal**
Ko **Island**
Laem **Headland**
Mahathat **A *chedi* (see above) containing relics of the Buddha**
Mondop **A square temple containing religious texts or small artefacts**
Nielloware **Metalwork engraved with design**
Prang **A central tower in a Khmer temple**
Soi **Lane**
Songthaew **Pickup taxi**
Thanon **Road**
That **Another word for *chedi* (see above)**
Viharn **Assembly hall in the temple, usually with the main Buddha image**
Wang **Palace**
Wat **Temple**

NUMBERS

0 **soon**	8 **bpairt**	16 **sip-hok**	50 **hah-sip**
1 **neeung**	9 **gao**	17 **sip-jet**	60 **hok-sip**
2 **sorng**	10 **sip**	18 **sip-bpairt**	70 **jet-sip**
3 **sahm**	11 **sip-et**	19 **sip-gao**	80 **bpairt-sip**
4 **see**	12 **sip-sorng**	20 **yee-sip**	90 **gao-sip**
5 **hah**	13 **sip-sahm**	21 **yee-sip-et**	100 **neung roy**
6 **hok**	14 **sip-see**	30 **sahm-sip**	101 **roy-et**
7 **jet**	15 **sip-hah**	40 **see-sip**	500 **hah roy**

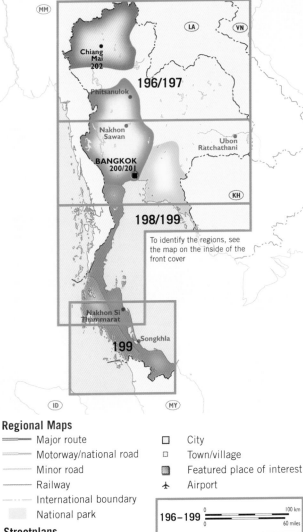

MM

LA

VN

Chiang
Mai
202

196/197

Phitsanulok

Nakhon
Sawan

Ubon
Ratchathani

BANGKOK
200/201

KH

198/199

To identify the regions, see
the map on the inside of the
front cover

Nakhon Si
Thammarat

199

Songkhla

ID

MY

Regional Maps

═══	Major route	☐	City
═══	Motorway/national road	▫	Town/village
───	Minor road	▣	Featured place of interest
───	Railway	✈	Airport
─·─·─	International boundary		
	National park		

196–199   0 ——— 100 km
           0 ——— 60 miles

Streetplans

▨	Important building	●●	Skytrain
	Park	●	Subway
▣	Featured place of interest	⛩	Temple
[i]	Tourist information	✝	Church

200/201   0 ——— 1 km
          0 ——— ½ mile

202   0 ——— 1 km
      0 ——— ½ mile

Atlas

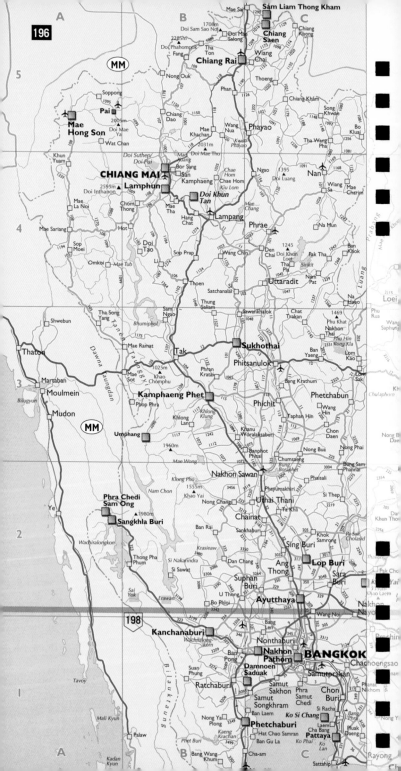

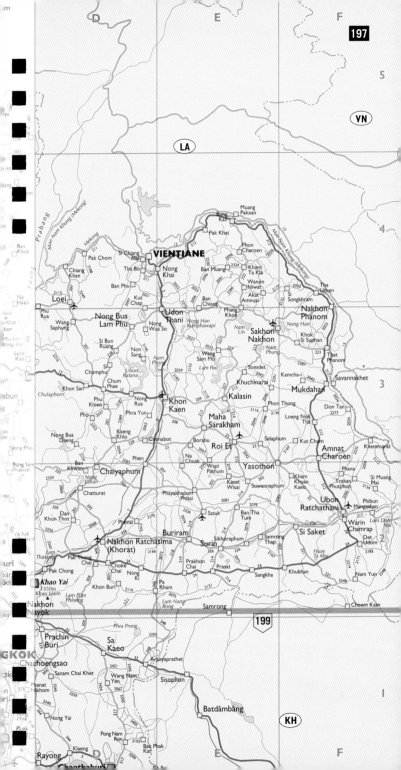

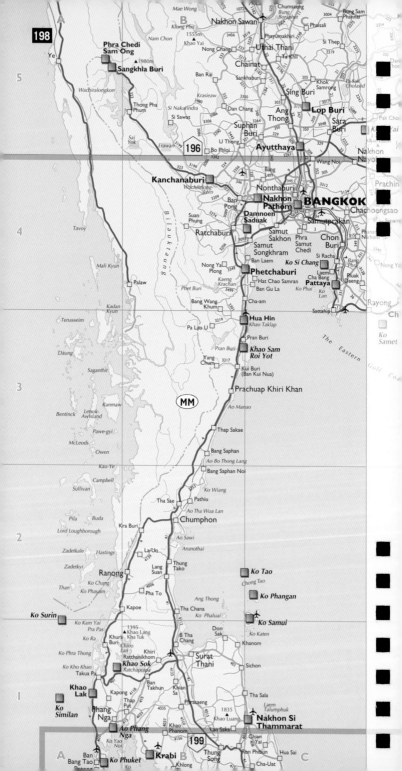

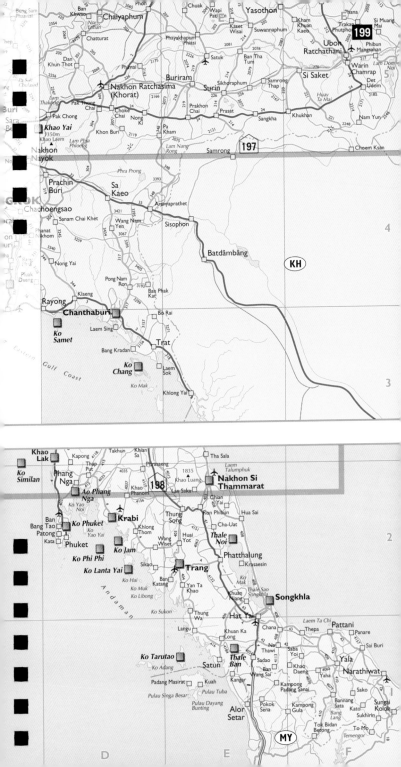

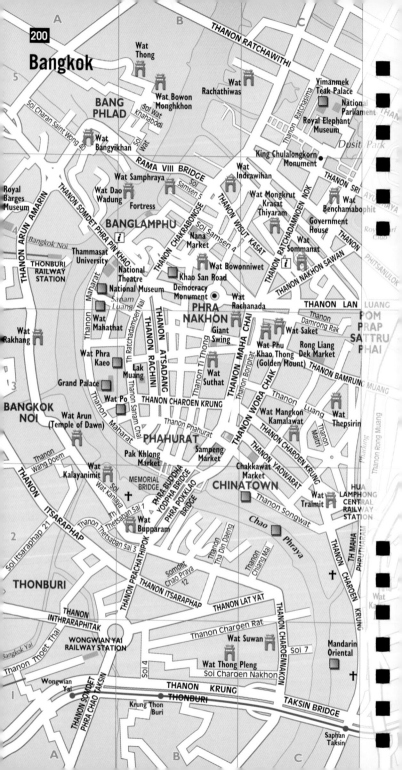

Bangkok

THANON RATCHAWITHI

Wat Thong

Wat Rachathiwas

Vimanmek Teak Palace

National Parliament

BANG PHLAD

Wat Bowon Monghkhon

Royal Elephant Museum

Dusit Park

Sol Wat Khahabodi

King Chulalongkorn Monument

Wat Bangyikhan

RAMA VIII BRIDGE

Wat Indrawihan

THANON SRI

THANON SOMDET PHRA PIN KHAO

Wat Samphraya

Wat Mongkrut Krasat Thiyaram

Wat Benchamabophit

Royal Barges Museum

Wat Dao Wadung

Fortress

BANGLAMPHU

Government House

THANON ARUN AMARIN

Bangkok Noi

THONBURI RAILWAY STATION

Thammasat University

Nana Market

Wat Sommanat

THANON PHITSANULOK

National Theatre

National Museum

Khao San Road

Wat Bowonniwet

THANON NAKHON SAWAN

THANON RATCHADAMNOEN NOK

Democracy Monument

Sanam Luang

PHRA NAKHON

Wat Rachanada

THANON LAN

LUANG

Wat Mahathat

Giant Swing

Wat Saket

Thanon Damrong Rak

POM PRAP SATTRU PHAI

Wat Rakhang

Wat Phra Kaeo

Lak Muang

Wat Suthat

Wat Phu Khao Thong (Golden Mount)

Rong Liang Dek Market

THANON BAMRUNG MUANG

BANGKOK NOI

Grand Palace

Wat Po

THANON CHAROEN KRUNG

Wat Mangkon Kamalawat

Wat Thepsirin

Wat Arun (Temple of Dawn)

Thanon Phahurat

PHAHURAT

THANON WORA CHAK

THANON MAHA CHAI

Thanon Luang

Thanon Rong Muang

Thanon Wang Doem

Pak Khlong Market

Sampeng Market

THANON YAOWARAT

THANON ITSARAPHAP

Wat Kalayanimit

MEMORIAL BRIDGE

Chakkawat Market

CHINATOWN

Wat Traimit

HUA LAMPHONG CENTRAL RAILWAY STATION

PHRA BUDDHA YODFA BRIDGE

PHRA POKKLAO BRIDGE

Thanon Songwat

Wat Bupparam

Chao Phraya

THONBURI

Somdet Chao Praya 12

THANON ITSARAPHAP

THANON LAT YAT

THANON PRACHATHIPOK

THANON CHAROENNAKON

THANON CHAROEN KRUNG

THANON INTHRARAPHITAK

Thanon Charoen Rat

Wat Suwan

Mandarin Oriental

WONGWIAN YAI RAILWAY STATION

Wat Thong Pleng

Soi Charoen Nakhon

Bangkok Yai

THANON THOET THAI

Wongwian Yai

THANON SOMDET PHRA CHAO TAKSIN

THANON KRUNG THONBURI

Krung Thon Buri

TAKSIN BRIDGE

Saphan Taksin

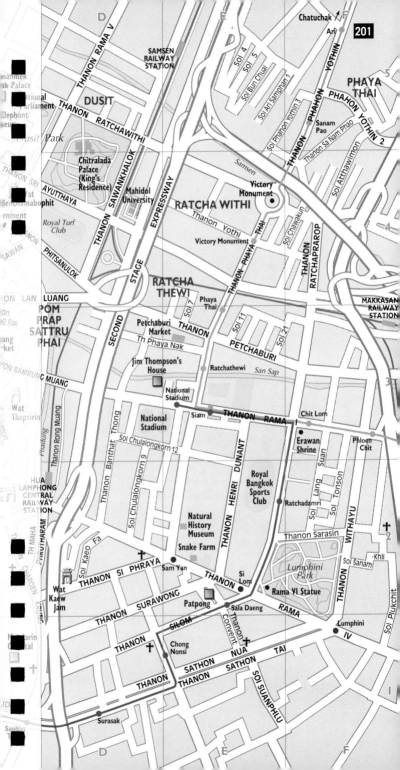

Acknowledgements

The Automobile Association wishes to thank the following photographers and organizations for their assistance in the preparation of this book.

Abbreviations for the picture credits are as follows – (t) top; (b) bottom; (l) left; (r) right; (c) centre; (dps) double page spread; (AA) AA World Travel Library

2t AA/D Henley; **2tc** AA/J Holmes; **2c** AA/D Henley; **2bc** AA/D Henley; **2b** AA/D Henley; **3t** AA/D Henley; **3tc** AA/D Henley; **3bc** AA/D Henley; **3b** AA/J Holmes; **5l** AA/D Henley; **5c** AA/J Holmes; **5r** AA/J Holmes; **6** Photolibrary; **7** © Jeremy Horner/Alamy; **8** AA/D Henley; **9t** AA/J Holmes; **9b** AA/R Strange; **9r** Photolibrary; **10/11** AA/D Henley; **11** AA/D Henley; **13** Picture Post/Stringer/Hulton Archive/Getty Images; **14l** AA/D Henley; **14r** AA/D Henley; **15** AA/D Henley; **16** AA/J Holmes; **17** Photolibrary; **18** AA/D Henley; **19t** James Strachan/Robert Harding; **19b** Neil Emmerson/Robert Harding; **20** AA/R Strange; **21** Photolibrary; **22/3** AA/J Holmes; **24/5** © Rungroj Yongrit/epa/Corbis; **26** AA/J Holmes; **26/7** AA/J Holmes; **27** AA/J Holmes; **28l** AA/J Holmes; **28r** AA/D Henley; **29l** AA/J Holmes; **29c** AA/J Holmes; **29r** AA/J Holmes; **39l** AA/D Henley; **39c** AA/J Holmes; **39r** AA/D Henley; **40** AA/D Henley; **42** AA/D Henley; **43t** AA/J Holmes; **43b** AA/J Holmes; **44/5** AA/D Henley; **45** AA/D Henley; **46** AA/R Strange; **47** AA/D Henley; **48** AA/R Strange; **49** AA/J Holmes; **50** AA/D Henley; **51** AA/D Henley; **52** AA/J Holmes; **53** AA/D Henley; **54** AA/J Holmes; **55** AA/J Holmes; **63l** AA/D Henley; **63c** AA/J Holmes; **63r** AA/D Henley; **64** Photolibrary; **65** AA/J Holmes; **66** Photolibrary; **67** AA/R Strange; **68** AA/R Strange; **69** AA/D Henley; **70** Photolibrary; **71** Robert Harding; **72/3** AA/D Henley; **73** AA/D Henley; **74** AA/D Henley; **75** AA/D Henley; **76** AA/J Holmes; **78** AA/D Henley; **79** AA/D Henley; **80** AA/D Henley; **81** AA/D Henley; **87l** AA/D Henley; **87c** AA/D Henley; **87r** AA/R Strange; **88** AA/R Strange; **89** AA/D Henley; **90t** AA/D Henley; **90b** Photolibrary; **91** Photolibrary; **92** AA/J Holmes; **93** AA/D Henley; **94** AA/D Henley; **95** AA/B Davies; **96** Photolibrary; **97** Photolibrary; **98** AA/D Henley; **100** AA/J Holmes; **101** AA/J Holmes; **102** AA/D Henley; **103** AA/D Henley; **109l** AA/D Henley; **109c** Nicholas Pitt/Photodisc/Getty Images; **109r** AA/D Henley; **110** AA/D Henley; **111** AA/D Henley; **112** AA/D Henley; **113** AA/D Henley; **114** AA/D Henley; **115** AA/D Henley; **116** AA/D Henley; **117** © World Pictures/Photoshot; **118** AA/D Henley; **119** AA/D Henley; **120** AA/D Henley; **121** AA/D Henley; **125l** AA/D Henley; **125c** AA/Neil Setchfield; **125r** AA/James A Tims; **126** AA/J Holmes; **127** AA/D Henley; **128** AA/J Holmes; **129** AA/D Henley; **130** AA/J Holmes; **131** AA/J Holmes; **132** AA/D Henley; **133b** AA/D Henley; **134** AA/D Henley; **135** AA/J Holmes; **136** AA/J Holmes; **137** AA/D Henley; **138** AA/D Henley; **139** AA/D Henley; **141** AA/D Henley; **149l** AA/D Henley; **149c** AA/D Henley; **149r** Photolibrary; **150** © David Noton Photography/Alamy; **151** Photolibrary; **152** AA/D Henley; **153** AA/R Strange; **154/5** AA/D Henley; **156** © Jon Arnold Images Ltd /Alamy; **157** AA/D Henley; **158** AA/R Strange; **159** AA/D Henley; **161** Photolibrary; **162** Photolibrary; **163** © imagebroker/Alamy; **164** Photolibrary; **166** AA/J Holmes; **167** AA/D Henley; **173l** AA/J Holmes; **173c** AA/J Holmes; **173r** Photolibrary; **174** AA/J Holmes; **176** AA/J Holmes; **179** AA/D Henley; **180** AA/J Holmes; **181** AA/D Henley; **183l** Photolibrary; **183r** © Simon Jonathan Webb/Alamy; **186** AA/D Henley; **187l** AA/J Holmes; **187c** AA/J Holmes; **187r** AA/J Holmes; **191t** AA/D Henley; **191c** AA/D Henley; **191b** AA/D Henley.

Every effort has been made to trace the copyright holders, and we apologize in advance for any unintentional omissions or errors. We would be pleased to apply any corrections in any following edition of this publication.

SPIRALGUIDE
Questionnaire

Dear Traveller

Your comments, opinions and recommendations are very important
to us. Please help us to improve our travel guides by taking a few
minutes to complete this simple questionnaire.

You do not need a stamp (unless posted outside the UK). If you do not want
to remove this page from your guide, then photocopy it or write your answers
on a plain sheet of paper.

Send to: The Editor, Spiral Guides, AA World Travel Guides,
FREEPOST SCE 4598, Basingstoke RG21 4GY.

Your recommendations...

We always encourage readers' recommendations for restaurants, night-life or shopping
– if your recommendation is used in the next edition of the guide, we will send you
a FREE AA Spiral Guide of your choice. Please state below the establishment name,
location and your reasons for recommending it.

_____

_____

_____

_____

_____

Please send me AA Spiral _____
(see list of titles inside the back cover)

About this guide...

Which title did you buy?

_____ **AA Spiral**

Where did you buy it? _____

When? m m / y y

Why did you choose an AA Spiral Guide? _____

_____

_____

_____

_____

Did this guide meet your expectations?

Exceeded ☐   Met all ☐   Met most ☐   Fell below ☐

Please give your reasons _____

_____

_____

_____

_____

continued on next page...

Were there any aspects of this guide that you particularly liked?

_____
_____
_____
_____
_____

Is there anything we could have done better?

_____
_____
_____
_____

About you...

Name (Mr/Mrs/Ms) _____

Address _____

_____

_____ **Postcode** _____

Daytime tel no _____ **email** _____

Please *only* give us your email address and mobile phone number if you wish to hear from us about other products and services from the AA and partners by email or text or mms.

Which age group are you in?

Under 25 ☐   25–34 ☐   35–44 ☐   45–54 ☐   55–64 ☐   65+ ☐

How many trips do you make a year?

Less than one ☐   One ☐   Two ☐   Three or more ☐

Are you an AA member? Yes ☐   **No** ☐

About your trip...

When did you book? m m / y y   **When did you travel?** m m / y y

How long did you stay? _____

Was it for business or leisure? _____

Did you buy any other travel guides for your trip? ☐ Yes ☐ No

If yes, which ones? _____

_____

Thank you for taking the time to complete this questionnaire. Please send it to us as soon as possible, and remember, you do not need a stamp (unless posted outside the UK).